David Jones, Henry T. Edwards

Wales and the Welsh Church

David Jones, Henry T. Edwards

Wales and the Welsh Church

ISBN/EAN: 9783337162115

Printed in Europe, USA, Canada, Australia, Japan

Cover: Foto ©Lupo / pixelio.de

More available books at **www.hansebooks.com**

WALES

AND

THE WELSH CHURCH

PAPERS

BY

HENRY T. EDWARDS, M.A.

LATE DEAN OF BANGOR

WITH A

BIOGRAPHICAL SKETCH OF

THE AUTHOR

"Sunt lacrimae rerum, et mentem mortalia tangunt"

RIVINGTONS
WATERLOO PLACE, LONDON
MDCCCLXXXIX

> We pass ; the path that each man trod
>   Is dim, or will be dim, with weeds :
>   What fame is left for human deeds
> In endless age ?   It rests with God.
>
> *In Memoriam.*

ADVERTISEMENT

WHEN it was decided to publish a selection of the writings of my brother-in-law, it was thought advisable to preface it by a short biographical sketch, which has been kindly written by the Rev. David Jones, Rector of Menai Bridge. It is, perhaps, necessary to add that the Speech on Temperance has been inserted in this volume by request.

M. K. J.

TREANNA, ANGLESEY,
October 12, 1888.

CONTENTS

	PAGE
INTRODUCTORY	1
BIOGRAPHICAL SKETCH	6
THE CHURCH OF THE CYMRY	94
WALES AND THE WELSH CHURCH	180
WHY ARE THE WELSH PEOPLE ALIENATED FROM THE CHURCH?	288
THE PAST AND PRESENT POSITION OF THE CHURCH IN WALES	337
THE CALLING AND EDUCATION OF THE CLERGY FOR THE CHURCH IN WALES	360
HOME REUNION	387
"STRIKE FOR THE KING!"	398

INTRODUCTORY

In response to inquiries from some of the friends of the late Dean Edwards, it has been decided to issue the present volume, containing a selection of essays and addresses from his published and unpublished writings. In making the present selection, we were principally guided by the wish to put together in a convenient and permanent form what appeared to us to embody his maturest thoughts on some of the favourite subjects over which he pondered deeply and patiently. It is unnecessary here to enter into a detailed and critical description of the various papers which are presented in this collection. They are, perhaps, the best biography that could be given of the author. The views propounded on the various topics, as well as the peculiarities of style, the masculine intellect, the bold utterance and the strength of conviction with which those views are expressed, summon before those who knew him, a personality which it is impossible for them not to recognize. Nor are they valuable merely as a record of the opinions of, in some respects, the most remarkable Welshman of the present century; they will also be welcomed as contributions of substantial merit, to the solution of problems which bear immediate and important relation to the highest interests of the Principality of Wales.

The Dean's ministerial life synchronized with an intense activity, both within and without the Church which he loved, and in the devoted service of which he spent his short day. He witnessed an educational and political crisis in the national life, a development of spiritual and material resources in the Church, and he promptly recognized their existence and significance. Such lives as his are public property—a legacy of examples bequeathed to posterity for guidance and instruction. Of the stirring events which agitated the public mind in Wales during the last twenty years of his life he could rightly say, "*Quorum pars magna fui.*" His history touches on all points the vital controversies of that period.

In the present partial and fragmentary biographical sketch, our endeavour has been to present the Dean, to the best of our abilities, as he really was; to place on record, from our too scanty resources, a few thoughts and quotations derived from some of the few private letters that have come to our hands, and from the personal reminiscences of those who intimately knew him, in order to enable our readers the better to understand the man who speaks and lives in the addresses and papers that follow. Our materials, as we have intimated, are by no means abundant. The Dean was not in the habit of keeping a private diary; he did not record his views and impressions of men and movements, further than in occasional and hurriedly written letters. Nor is this, perhaps, to be altogether regretted, as an eminent writer of the present day has said, that "we know a man truly when we know him at his greatest and his best; we realize his significance, for ourselves and for the world, when we see him in the noblest activity of his career, on the loftiest summit, or in the fullest glory of his life."

We cannot pretend to disguise that we are keenly conscious of the delicacy and difficulty of the task we have undertaken. The Dean was no ordinary man, nor did he live in ordinary days. Being the most prominent figure of his time in the Principality, he was exposed to the closest scrutiny and the most unsparing criticism. And though all would probably admit his striking individuality, his intellectual strength, his power as a controversialist, and his undoubted qualifications as a leader of thought and action, there are, nevertheless, many standpoints from which different observers would form different estimates of his life and character. We may, doubtless, stand in too close proximity to an object to obtain an accurate view of its just proportions. The burning controversies in which the Dean was engaged, have not yet subsided; the public questions which he discussed with comprehensive sweep and acknowledged ability, have not yet been settled; his name is still too closely identified with the theological and political disputes that emphasize the rival factions of our national life, to enable the world to do full and impartial justice to the soundness of his opinions or the consistency of his conduct. His intense yearning to discover a sound and broad basis for the ultimate restoration of national and religious unity amongst his countrymen, exposed him sometimes to the charge of self-contradiction; the impulsive frankness with which he would express his opinions, brought upon him the imputation of harshness; his uncompromising attitude of antagonism to the ruinous policy which he conceived to have been mainly responsible for the alienation of the masses from the Welsh Church during the last two centuries, made him occasionally the object of uncharitable and unjust insinuations of ambitious egotism.

It is true, indeed, that his life was always exposed to the public gaze; his character was singularly transparent; and he was, at all times, ready to communicate to the press, unreservedly, his thoughts on the events and controversies of the hour. But he also lived a private life, full of charming simplicity, conversational brilliancy, of unreserved communicativeness, of thoughtful and affectionate tenderness—a life broken into fragments by sad and sudden vicissitudes, in which were revealed, to their utmost depths, the sentiments and the sympathies, the strength and the weakness, of his impressible and impulsive nature.

While we do not affect to conceal our profound admiration of his many sterling qualities, and our no less profound gratitude for the noble services he was permitted to render to the Church and nation, we will endeavour to utilize our opportunity, and the materials that are at our disposal, to make the life of the Dean, like those of all other men who have consecrated their talents to the promotion of religion and the welfare of humanity, to sound its notes of warning as well as of encouragement.

BIOGRAPHICAL SKETCH

THE life of the subject of this memoir was an eventful one. Though short and rapid in its course, it enriched and fertilized the plain of human thought and life in its progress. It left behind conspicuous examples of Churchmanship and patriotism. We do not assert that the Dean conceived or carried out those examples to an ideal perfection; but no one who has studied his career with impartiality will deny that the great effort of his life was the realization of a position where the true patriot and the consistent Churchman could be reconciled. The Anglicizing policy, which has wrought such disasters for the Church, has too often looked with suspicion on our national movements and time-honoured social institutions, and has, not seldom, surrendered them into the hands of sectarianism; whereas the better and juster policy would have been, to enter into the true spirit of our national history and traditions, and, through the instrumentality of a cultured ministry, thoroughly imbued with the national spirit, and in full sympathy with the ineradicable peculiarities of the Celtic temperament, seek to employ the sacred ministrations of the Church in directing, purifying, and consolidating the national life and character. The Church, it must be confessed, has forfeited incalculable advantages. It is the oldest institution in the country, and is almost coeval with the growth of the nation. If the sources of our information were confined to the modern voice of Wales, we should almost conclude that true religion and national emancipation were born in the Principality less than a century and a half ago, and that the Church is an intruder. But the life of the Church and nation were practically identical for many centuries before the sound of the modern voice was heard. In close union did they resist both national and ecclesiastical encroachments. This is an historical fact of immense value, and is fraught with lessons, which it behoves us to ponder over, in the present state of national strife and confusion. After a period of fifteen hundred years of a close and almost undisturbed wedded life between the Church and nation, during which time they had sympathized and co-operated in the struggle for liberty and independence, great indeed must have been the causes which could have resulted in a divorce at the end of last century, and great have been the consequent calamities of that divorce. The Church became an alien, not indeed in her polity, or her doctrines, but in her chief shepherds, whose voice the people knew not. Dean Edwards saw all this; and, as a Church dignitary, did what he could to atone for the past. In taking a survey of his public career and the services he rendered to the Church, his chief claims to our gratitude rest, not so much upon the ability and thoroughness with which he contributed towards the solution of questions that absorbed his interest and consumed his energies, as upon his courage and candour in exposing what lies at the root of all our national dissensions, namely, the attempt to Anglicize the nation through the Church, and the persevering efforts with which he used the influence of his position and talents for the discouragement and discontinuance of that policy. The great aim of his life was the reconciliation of the Welsh Church and nation. He had satisfied himself as to the main cause of their estrangement; he never ceased to deplore it, or warn our rulers against its perpetuation; he pleaded vehemently and unceasingly for the prompt and complete reversal of the policy that created the separation, and for a renewal of that which alone can lead to the return of the Cymry to their Church. The central idea of his public utterances was the religious reunion of his countrymen, and the last word of his last paper is "unity." There is a melancholy interest connected with this paper, that, when engaged in its composition, the Dean was haunted by the foreboding that the work of his life had been accomplished.

Henry Thomas Edwards was born on September 6, 1837, and was the third son of the Rev. William Edwards, then Vicar of Llanymawddwy, in the diocese of St. Asaph. Four brothers, who are all in the ministry, and two sisters, complete the family circle. His mother still survives, and in her advanced years, takes as keen an interest as ever in her numerous family, with whom, especially with her grandchildren, she delights to carry on a regular correspondence. Her maiden name was Wood. She is descended from a Gloucestershire family of that name, to which family belonged also the late Lord Chancellor Hatherley, as well as some other names of literary celebrity. His father had received his education for the ministry at Ystradmeurig Grammar School, in his native county of Cardiganshire, and had two brothers in the ministry—the late Rev. John Edwards, Vicar of Llanfihangel-ar-Arth; and the late Rev. Ebenezer Edwards, the sweet evangelist of Mallwyd, and afterwards of Llanfechell. Mr. George Borrow, in his "Wild Wales," makes the following observations on the occasion of his visit to the vicarage of Llangollen, of which parish the Rev. William Edwards was then incumbent. "During tea, Mr. Edwards and I had a great deal of discourse. I found him to be a first-rate Greek and Latin scholar, and also a proficient in the literature of his own country. In the course of discourse, he repeated some noble lines of Evan Evans, the unfortunate and eccentric *Prydydd Hir*, or 'tall poet,' the friend and correspondent of Gray, for whom he made literal translations from the Welsh, which the great English genius afterwards wrote into immortal verse."

From his father Henry received his training in the rudiments of the classical languages, as well as in the elements of mathematics. In the remote vicarage of Llanymawddwy he also received his first lessons of life, its pleasures and its possibilities; surrounded by a varied scenery of mountains, cataracts, and gorges, he received his first impressions of external nature ; and if we are to credit the theories of life's development propounded by poets and professional delineators of human character, his early associations must have contributed to stimulate his youthful imagination, and to give definiteness and direction to his genius.

In the year 1849, when Henry was twelve years of age, his father was promoted to the living of Llangollen, where he continued for some time to superintend the education of his younger boys, in conjunction with a few other outside pupils. Two years later, it was decided that Henry should compete for an exhibition at Westminster School, and his success at the examination led to his entering that school. His progress there was rapid, and he soon convinced his masters that he possessed abilities of no ordinary merit. But his stay at Westminster was cut short, as, owing to *res angusta domi*, he was recalled at the age of sixteen, and was thus inevitably deprived of the manifest advantages which the thorough and systematic training of a public school would have secured him. Shortly after this, he was placed under the care of the Rev. F. E. Gretton, for whom he ever after entertained the profoundest respect, and to whom he was proud to acknowledge his indebtedness for having given impulse and direction to his mind. Mr. Gretton says of him, "When I had him in hand, I very soon discovered that he was full of talent, and a great amount of nervous excitability. I had a very strong affection for him.

We got on together without a hitch; as master and pupil, we enjoyed our work; as host and inmate, all went towardly. He left me for Oxford with my sure foreboding that he must achieve something. I had a strong conviction of his manifest abilities." Shortly after his return from Westminster, Henry turned his mind to the army, to which he seems to have had a strong inclination; but an effort to obtain for him a cadetship having proved unsuccessful, cut short his hopes. But as was said of another, whose early natural bias was similarly thwarted, so it may of him, "We trace the music of war and chivalry in all his utterances; and though he adorned a peaceful profession, there is discernible his old passion for the discipline and devotion of a soldier; 'we smell the battle afar off, and hear the shouting of the captains.'"

This disappointment led to a temporary unsettlement of his mind for reading. But a determination to enter the lists for the Powis examination caused him to renew his studies with zest and earnestness. The contest between him and Mr. Nicholas, subsequently Fellow of St. John's College, Cambridge, was unusually close, and the examiners, the late Dr. Rowland Williams and the present Bishop of St. David's, not being able to agree, resolved on a re-examination. The decision ultimately resulted in favour of Mr. Nicholas, who, it seemed, displayed a more accurate knowledge of the rules and rudiments of Welsh grammar. An exhibition, however, was awarded to Mr. Edwards, in recognition of his general proficiency.

In the year 1857, Mr. Edwards matriculated at Jesus College, Oxford, and entered upon his University career, which, however, owing to the indifferent state of his health, which had never been robust, was not as successful as his talents promised or his friends anticipated. The second class which he took at moderations was a keen disappointment to him, and may have tended to discourage him from preparing for honours in the final schools. It is, however, only just to remark, that his medical advisers strongly dissuaded him from that close application to reading which a distinguished position in the schools imperatively demands, but which might have inflicted a lifelong injury on his already too delicate constitution. He often expressed his regret in after-life that it was his misfortune to be debarred from reading for honours in the final schools. But in forming an opinion of his abilities, or his scholarship, based upon his achievements at the examinations, it must be borne in mind that his preparatory training, desultory, and frequently interrupted as it was, as well as the mental prostration and the physical debility which hard study entailed upon him during his academical course, could hardly justify very sanguine expectations for high results in the schools. It was said by Conington, the eminent annotator and translator of Virgil, that he was the best writer of Latin verses of his time at Oxford—no small commendation from so competent an authority. During his residence at the University, he took an active part in the established sports and recreations, and ranked high amongst the athletes.

Ordination and First Curacy.

He took his degree in 1861; was elected Assistant-Master at Llandovery College, and was ordained deacon by Dr. Thirlwall, Bishop of St. David's, obtaining his Title from the curacy of the neighbouring parish of Llansadwrn. Here he preached his first sermon, which, it seems, was chiefly characterized by the amount of matter it contained. He would often relate how he had managed to cram into that single discourse all the theology he knew, and had so completely exhausted his limited store at the first discharge, as to occasion a serious dearth of homiletic ideas for months after.

His father's increasing years and failing health caused him to renounce his sphere of work at Llandovery; and, after a few months' experience of teaching, he was appointed curate of Llangollen. He was admitted to priest's orders by Bishop Short, at St. Asaph, December 21, 1862. Here he commenced his ministerial career, began to develop those powers and gain that experience which combined to make him so conspicuous as a clergyman during the twenty years he was destined to serve the Welsh Church. He had now bidden a final farewell to the dreams of his youthful ambition; he had relinquished for ever the abortive projects and prospects which boyish enthusiasm had doubtless painted in fascinating colours to his active and fertile imagination; he had also experienced the beneficial discipline of the disappointments, the toils, and the pleasures of an educational career. He had entered irrevocably on a life of definite duty, with its stern realities and weighty responsibilities. We could have wished for an authentic record of his feelings as he reviewed at this juncture the vanished dreams of his earlier days, as—

> " Back on the past he turns his eye,
> Remembering, with an envious sigh,
> The happy dreams of youth ; "
>
> (Southey.)

—the hopes which swelled in his bosom, as his active mind scanned the present aspect and the future prospect of that Church, to which he had dedicated his talents, and pledged his faith, and which, during the remainder of his days, he served with unswerving fidelity.

The curacy of Llangollen afforded an admirable sphere for the development of the varied capacities which are pre-eminently required to lay the foundation of a career of ministerial usefulness and success. His father's enfeebled health left him virtually in sole charge of a population of five thousand souls. The parish is bilingual, and demanded full services in both languages. The increase in the congregations which followed his advent to the parish, and rewarded his faithful efforts, and those of his energetic fellow-curate, pointed to the necessity of enlarging and restoring the parish church. He no sooner settled down in his new field of duty than he surveyed the position, and took his estimate of what was required to render the ministrations of the Church more generally efficient and available. With characteristic ardour and enthusiasm, he set about the work of restoration. With the view of obtaining the necessary funds to carry out his plan, an influential and thoroughly representative committee was formed,

His Ideal of Church Reform.

and a well-conceived circular was drawn up by him and printed. In this circular, he says, "During the last thirty years, the parish of Llangollen has undergone a great change. Within that period the village has become a town, and the population has been more than trebled; and thus the church, which was adequate to the want of the parishioners at the beginning of the century, no longer affords the necessary accommodation; for, while the district for which it provides contains nearly 5000 inhabitants, the present edifice accommodates only 350." The plan of restoration provided for an "increase of 300 sittings by the reseating of the present building, and the addition of the south aisle, chancel, organ-chamber, and vestry-room, at an estimated cost of £2950. The church, as enlarged according to these plans, will be a commodious and beautiful structure; and the preservation of the ancient and elaborately carved oak roof, and the other distinctive features of the present edifice, is ensured." There is, perhaps, nothing in these details to justify us in calling special attention to them, as hundreds of churches in the Principality have happily been similarly restored during the last forty years; but they seem to us to supply a striking prophecy and parable of what the Dean in subsequent life consistently advocated, and strenuously promoted, as a policy for the resuscitation of the Church in Wales. In what he successfully did for the outward structure of his father's church at Llangollen, may be recognized his ideal conception of what should be universally effected in the Church of his fathers, not only in material, but also in intellectual and spiritual, reform. That conception was not merely leaving things as they were—the too-prevalent notion of former generations; there was nothing more abhorrent to his active mind than stagnation, whilst everything around was moving and progressing. Nor was it the destruction of what remained, on the plausible pretence of past failure—the policy of Liberationism, which he ever opposed with all the force of his intellect, and with all the earnestness of his soul. It was neither of these; but it was restoration, and enlargement, according to plans which adequately met and satisfied the requirements of a progressive age. Such was his conception; and it will be freely confessed that it embodied the principles, and laid down the limitations, of the extensive reforms which he never ceased to advocate in all departments of Church life.

Here he laid the foundation of that pulpit power and efficiency for which he became celebrated in after-years. The bilingual nature of the parish afforded him favourable opportunities for the development of his talents in both languages. Amidst the multiplicity of duties which the charge of a populous parish and the work of restoration entailed upon him, he found time for elaborate preparation of sermons, which were characterized with freshness and originality. He always entertained the highest conception of the influence and responsibilities of the pulpit, and said on one occasion that he "never heard any one underrating the power of preaching, except those who neglected its cultivation." His discourses were generally delivered without the manuscript, though they did not involve less, but rather more, labour on that account. "Careful and painstaking study of the subject, enables the preacher to produce his best and maturest thoughts; whilst the extemporaneous delivery is the most effectual for presenting them in an impressive style." Such was his ideal of preaching, from the human side. Nor must we omit to record, what is well known to those who were intimate with his private life, that it was his habitual custom to retire to a private room before the commencement of the service at which he was to preach, to hold communion with God in prayer; and he seldom entered the pulpit without thus earnestly seeking the presence of his Master to go with him.

We have before us a printed sermon, entitled "Eight Days in the Camp," which, as far as we know, is the first production of his pen given to the press. It was preached on Sunday morning, June 4, 1865, before the Denbighshire Yeomanry Cavalry, and published by request. It is full of noble sentiment on the duties and privileges of the military profession, expressed in chaste but powerful language; and it doubtless embodies some of those ideas on "the calling of the soldier" which had worked on his mind, and led him to form the resolution of adopting that calling as his own. This sermon is characterized by a lucidity of arrangement, masterly analysis of the subject, descriptive power, fulness of treatment, and directness of application, such as he seldom surpassed in his later days. We will give one quotation, not so much as exhibiting a specimen of his style, as constituting a sound basis of ministerial teaching, thus laid down at the commencement of his career: "From the ruin of eternal unrest, man is saved by Divine grace, through faith in the Name and power of Jesus Christ."

The four years he spent as curate of Llangollen came to an end, but not before he had left indelible marks of his vigorous mind and talents on the outward organization, and the inward life of the Church in the parish. By the strong individuality of his character, the intensity of his enthusiasm, the originality of his thoughts, the impressiveness of his delivery, the charm of his presence, and the peculiar felicity he possessed of imparting the spirit and purposes of his own life to that of others who came within the magic circle of his influence, he was enabled to achieve during what may be described as the probationary period of ministerial life, what he afterwards did more conspicuously, and extensively, when elevated to more responsible positions, and when the sphere of his labours became wider. The effects of his ministrations in Llangollen were seen, not only in the material work of restoration, not only in the increase of congregations and improvement in the services, but also in the warm place he secured in the affections of the people, which he never forfeited. On his promotion to Aberdare, a considerable sum was subscribed in the parish, and presented to him. This sum, with characteristically impulsive generosity, and, we may add, with filial tenderness, he returned to be expended in repairing the national schools—a work much needed at the time of his departure.

His preferment to the important living of Aberdare in the year 1866, with the comparatively short experience of four years as curate, might have been deemed a bold stroke; but the results amply justified the wisdom and foresight of the trustees. Here he threw himself at once with characteristic ardour into the many-sided work of his onerous charge. Such a centre of industry, then in the heyday of its prosperity, gave him abundant opportunities for varied ministerial experience, and the further development of his capacities for parochial organization and pulpit efficiency. Here, in the fullest sense, he came in contact with the masses of his countrymen, whom he always respected, but never flattered. F. W. Robertson, a man of kindred spirit with his own, said once, that "the people of this country stood in danger from two classes—from those who fear them, and from those who flatter them." Dean Edwards belonged to neither of these classes. Throughout his life he had the highest regard for the truest welfare of the working people, and never blushed to claim affinity with them. His highest ambition was to see them returning to the Church of their forefathers, where he was profoundly convinced they could, under favourable circumstances, receive the richest and amplest spiritual nurture. He sought to elevate their social and moral condition, by his eloquent and vigorous advocacy of temperance. He used the influence of his position and talent to secure for them the priceless blessings of higher education..

He interposed the powerful ægis of his polemical skill to protect their character from what he honestly believed were the unjust aspersions of those who were not unnaturally provoked to charge the many with the baseness of the few, who sought to elude the grasp of justice by artful and systematic perjury. But if he was jealous of the people's honour, he was neither blind to their faults nor insensible to their dangers. With candid bluntness, he would often warn them against the perilous experiment of declaring war against capital, and thus "killing the goose that lays the golden eggs." In a speech which he delivered at Llangollen, in January, 1872, on "The Dangers of Political Pilatism," he lays down with fearless impartiality the respective duties and obligations of capitalists and labourers, their mutual dependence, and the essential necessity of close sympathy and co-operation between them, for the internal prosperity of the country. In this address he boldly denounces the ambitious recklessness of political aspirants, who scruple not to excite the envy of the working classes against their employers; and, regardless of the risk of paralyzing the trades and industries on which the life of the nation thrives, aim at the prizes of parliamentary honours. If he disdained to flatter the people in this great speech, it was because he respected their manhood; if he warned them somewhat plainly against possible catastrophes, events have unfortunately happened since its delivery which sadly prove that the warning was not wholly needless.

At the time of his institution, the parish of Aberdare,

embracing within its limits no less than thirty thousand souls, was a centre of industry, where working men and their families had migrated from all parts of Wales. His intense energy, his great capacity for work, his intellectual activity, and his genuine national sympathies, found here a wide and congenial field of usefulness. A careful estimate of the situation revealed to him the utter inadequacy of Church accommodation to meet the spiritual requirements of the teeming population. This he could not endure; and his first move was to set about to do what in him lay to supply the deficiencies. In April, 1867, he printed and circulated a letter to the "landowners, ironmasters, colliery proprietors, and other wealthy Churchmen, interested in the parish," in which, with clearness, force, and fulness, he lays down the needs of the districts, the duties of those entrusted with wealth, and his own responsibilities. "To me," he says, "the National Church has committed the chief place in the ministry of the Word and Sacraments in the parish of Aberdare. I hardly need state that, in those districts in which wealth has been created, the population by an inseparable consequence increases. It is essential to the highest welfare of society that the influence of the Church should advance in parallel progress with the growth of the population." By a masterful analysis of the population, ratable value of the parish, and the deficient Church accommodation in the various outlying districts, he marshals his arguments, and lays down the details of his plan with consummate ability and with telling earnestness. He proposes to establish a Church Extension Association for the parish of Aberdare, the object of which was to be twofold: (1) "To provide the annual revenue for the maintenance of a body of clergy adequate to the wants of the population," and (2) "the formation of a permanent fund for the promotion of church-building in the parish." The result of this appeal was the restoration of the chancel of St. Elvan's Church, the erection of a new boys' school, and a new church at Cwmamman. As the outcome of this movement, may also be mentioned another church at Aberaman, which was subsequently erected by the munificence of Sir George Elliot. An addition to the living agencies was also made, to supply the needs necessarily created by these new arrangements.

In the year 1867, Mr. Edwards was married to Mary, the eldest daughter of Mr. David Davis, a leading colliery proprietor in the neighbourhood. She was a lady of a remarkably amiable disposition, but loved a quiet, retiring life, and in this presented a striking contrast to her active husband. Their wedded life, however, was brief, as Mrs. Edwards succumbed, under a somewhat prolonged illness, in August, 1871, at the Vicarage of Carnarvon, leaving an infant daughter only five months old at the death of her mother.

The Dean's life at Aberdare was one of unremitting toil and activity. In addition to the labour which Church extension and preparation for the pulpit entailed upon him, he now began to apply himself strenuously to the study of the past history of the Church in Wales, and its bearing on her present condition. The aggressive attitude of the Liberation Society, which about that time began to draw special attention to the Principality, induced him to enter on a careful examination of the causes which led to the partial failure of the Church, and to discover remedies for the efficient removal of those causes. To this investigation, which had been hitherto grievously neglected by those who were responsible for the administration of the Church, he brought many qualifications which eminently fitted him for the task. Genuine national sympathies, a keen insight into the peculiarities of the Celtic temperament, of which his own nature largely participated, sincere attachment to the doctrines and constitution of the Church, and, withal, a clear and vigorous intellect, an independence of mind to form his own opinions, and courage to maintain them at all hazards,—all this marked him out as specially endowed to bear an important part in guiding the destinies of the Church through the important crisis which seemed then imminent. The course which he thus early himself took, and recommended to others, was, as we have already indicated, the twofold policy of defence and reform. The former was rendered necessary by the persistent clamour of those who demanded the overthrow of the Church as a national establishment, and the confiscation of her revenues, while the latter was no less called for by the internal abuses and anomalies which generations of neglect had allowed to creep in, and which paralyzed her influence and impeded her progress. He saw threatening clouds gathering thick on the horizon, and began to feel that he was entrusted with a mission to awaken the slumbers of friends, and to repel the assaults of foes. The firstfruits of his study of this question appeared at the time, in a sermon "printed for private circulation," and entitled "The Natural and Supernatural Church Endowments." It is. based on St. Matt. v. 14-16, and contains the keynote of his defence. In the exordium, he traces the argument to the ultimate sources of all obligations; and here we discover the basis of his theology, which he constantly reproduces in his subsequent writings. Indeed, it is a peculiar characteristic of his pulpit discourses, that he almost invariably commences them by establishing the connection that subsists between the lesson enforced by his text and the fundamental truths of revealed religion. "To manifest in our human lives the likeness of the Divine life is the end of our being, in the fulfilment of which alone we find the satisfaction and harmony of our nature." In this quotation we have, from the standpoint of human observation, the objective source and pattern of the renewed life, and its subjective realization and reproduction, as the author conceived them. The sequel is a powerful exposition of his theory on the duty and privilege of employing the highest sanctions and influences of the commonwealth, in its public and corporate capacity, for the support and diffusion of the principles of the Gospel through all the grades and departments of the national life. In support of the dictum that "position has a function in the diffusion of light," he adduces confirmatory examples from different epochs in the history of God's Church, and appeals to the common sense and conscience of a Christian people, not to be deluded by the fallacious reasoning of those who would persuade them to embark on a policy of confiscation, on the specious pretence of making the Church less worldly. "A great and an understanding people will never dream that it can banish worldliness by confiscation. The power of God's quickening Spirit alone can banish the worldly disposition."

About this time he also published his first volume of sermons, "The Victorious Life," the proof-sheets of which he corrected during his recovery from a severe illness. It is not our intention to offer an elaborate criticism of this volume; but we may say, *en passant*, that, while the twenty discourses of which it consists exhibit traces of imperfect treatment, occasional crudeness and redundancy of expression, they are, nevertheless, full of brilliant flashes of thought, and display analytical powers, and a fertility of imagination, of no ordinary merit. They fairly establish his reputation as an original expounder of the Word of God, and as one who had profoundly studied the apostasies of fallen humanity, and the provisions of the Gospel for its final redemption and restoration.

The results of his study of the Church's past history in Wales were given in a powerful letter addressed to Mr. Gladstone, as first minister of the Crown, in 1869. It has been said that this pamphlet supplied the then Prime Minister with much of the materials for his conclusive and crushing reply to the late Sir Watkin Williams, who, encouraged by the fate of the Irish Church, brought forward a motion in the House of Commons for the disestablishment and disendowment of the Welsh Church. Be this as it may, it is a fairly exhaustive analysis of the causes that were responsible for the alienation of the masses from the Church's fold, and a spirited vindication of her right to be governed by chief pastors who are thoroughly conversant with the language, and in full sympathy with the temperament and legitimate aspirations, of the people. In common with all those who are acquainted with the inner life of the Welsh nation, and are anxious for the removal of all impediments to the solid and healthy progress of the Church in Wales, he maintained that a return to the administrative policy which promoted such men as Bishops Morgan and Davies to preside over the Welsh sees, can alone lead to a resumption by the Church of her legitimate position and influence in the Principality.

Under the severe strain of his multifarious engagements, his health gave way, and forced him to seek temporary retirement and rest abroad. When we consider the weight of care and anxieties that pressed upon a mind naturally sensitive, and a physical frame always liable to nervous prostration, we can hardly wonder that the pressure of excessive mental and bodily toil threatened serious consequences. Whatever he undertook, he employed his whole energies in its execution. When he had any work on hand, he would not economize his resources till he saw it accomplished, or was forced by the utter collapse of his powers to abandon it. It would be an accurate description of his life to say that he lived and thought and worked intensely. He drew on precious capital with reckless temerity, and gave little chance to his recuperative powers. His life at Aberdare was prophetic of his future career, both in its triumphs and in its disasters. It was here that he commenced to pursue with painstaking assiduity the study of those questions which he treated with such conspicuous ability, and which brought him fame and popularity in after-years; it was here also that he sowed the seeds of those constitutional maladies which ever afterwards haunted him, grew *pari passu* with the development of his capacities for usefulness, and dogged his footsteps in his progress to distinction, till at last they triumphed over him, and cut him off in the flower of life.

In 1869, Mr. Edwards' tenure of the incumbency of Aberdare terminated. The prominent living of Carnarvon became vacant by the death of the Rev. James Crawley Vincent, who was removed from the midst of his labours when the sun of his popularity was at its meridian height. The vacancy was offered to Mr. Edwards by the Bishop of Chester in the following terms, contained in a letter dated October 4, 1869: "After anxious deliberation, I have come to the conclusion that my duty, as patron of the Vicarage of Carnarvon, cannot, according to the light that I have, be better discharged than by asking you to become the successor of one who seems to have won the confidence, love, and reverence of his parishioners in an extraordinary degree." Mr. Edwards accepted the offer, and Carnarvon seemed to present a sphere more congenial to his talents, and was situated in a climate more conducive to the restoration of his health, which, as we have seen, had seriously threatened to give way. The parish of Llanbeblig, with its eleven thousand inhabitants, is, in some respects, the most important ministerial charge in North Wales, with one possible exception. Considering the nature of the population, the prominent position of the town, and, we may add, its historical associations, it may be fairly presumed that he who deliberately comes to the decision of undertaking so important a charge, especially at a time when the Church is passing through the agonies of her severest trials, accepts his responsibilities as a matter of duty rather than of choice. Carnarvon is the head-quarters of some of the chief actors in a drama, the aims of which are directed to paralyze and thwart the efforts of the Church in extending her labours, and whose plot is intended to culminate in her overthrow. The choice of Bishop Jacobson was a specially happy one. A young clergyman of thirty-two, with a ministerial experience of seven years in populous districts, was appointed to preside over a parish which was the chief provincial centre of the Liberationist and secularist agitators. Carnarvon and North Wales were singularly favoured by the accession of one who had the courage and ability to vindicate the rights and position of the

Church, and repel the hostile advances of those who had entered on a crusade against her. But if North Wales had reason to rejoice at his appointment, South Wales felt and acknowledged the heavy loss it sustained; and the Bishop of Llandaff (Dr. Ollivant), in reply to Mr. Edwards' letter, in which he communicated his decision to his lordship, frankly admitted that he wished very much "that circumstances had been such as to make it possible for you to come to a different conclusion to the one at which you have arrived. For I feel unfeignedly," adds the Bishop, "that this diocese, and your parish especially, will sustain a great loss at your departure."

As we have seen, the same year that saw his promotion to Carnarvon, witnessed also the publication of his "Church of the Cymry," which is headed by the significant motto, "Hic jacet Arturus rex quondam, rexque futurus," so indicative of his own conviction of the Church's historical position, as well as of his confidence in her future. This subject henceforth absorbed much of his time and attention. "We want public souls,—we want them," says Bishop Hacket; and Peter Bayne says, "Unless institutions are souled by earnest and capable men, they have no more chance of prosperous and beneficent activity, than dead bodies have of climbing mountains." The Church in Wales has grievously suffered during the last hundred and fifty years of her history, from want of leaders who combine thorough loyalty to her principles, and a genuine sympathy with the national temperament, and legitimate aspirations of the people. The Anglicizing policy of past generations, which has prevailed too largely in the promotion of the higher dignitaries of the Church, has tended to discourage the due cultivation of the Welsh language, and to crush out the national sentiment from the heart of the ministry. The spectacle has not seldom presented itself of men promoted to high offices who could not minister with decent efficiency in the vernacular. The result has been disastrous. A prohibitory penalty was thus imposed on the healthy development of the most marked characteristics of Welsh individuality, by the uniform selection of men to fill influential positions, who, however estimable and eminent in other respects, were ignorant of the language, literature, and national temperament of the people, and utterly incapable of winning their confidence and sympathy. The native ministry became largely discouraged and demoralized, and the masses were alienated from the Church. We do not, indeed, mean to affirm that the Anglicizing policy is the only cause responsible for the depression of the Welsh Church; but no one acquainted with the religious history of the Principality during the last century, and the beginning of this, will deny that it has been at least the main cause, and the most fertile source of many other subordinate ones. And we venture to say, that no measure of man's device can be more conducive to the reinstitution of the Church in her legitimate position, and her reinvestment with her normal influence, than a full recognition of her rights to have her ministrations performed by men who are practically and profoundly acquainted with the character, language, and religious tendencies of the people. If she is to regain lost ground, and wield successfully her own inherent power, she must proclaim her truths in a style and garb which will recommend them to the vivid imagination and impressible nature of the Welsh Celt. She need not change a single article of her creed, or a single clause of her constitution. The men who seceded from, or, rather, were thrust out of her, in the latter half of the last century and the beginning of this, did not in a single instance express their dissent from her fundamental principles and polity. The Methodist revival, as it is called, broke out within her sanctuaries; the fire was first kindled in the breasts of her own ordained ministers. And this is a sufficient answer to those who insinuate sometimes that a religious revival cannot originate in the Church. Under an administrative policy which ignored the paramount claims of the people to have their language cultivated, and their national sympathies fostered, within the Church of their fathers, their religious instincts were frozen. When they began to melt and flow once more under the vernal breezes of the powerful awakening that broke out within her walls, the same policy withstood the movement, and blindly ejected those who fostered it. The result was dissent, and confusion, and the breaking up of the nation into religious fragments. With the lapse of time, the movement which commenced in the Church, and was professedly designed by its promoters as merely subordinate and supplementary to her ministrations, became crystallized into a separate system.' The influence of the venerable founders of Welsh Methodism, who had uniformly maintained a feeling of profound reverence for the Church, began to wane in the second decade of this century, when the last of them had been gathered to his fathers; and after the death, in the year 1841, of the Rev. John Elias, who had always vigorously withstood the tendency to oppose the Church in the body of which he was an illustrious minister, his successors assumed an attitude of more or less pronounced hostility, till, at the time at which we have arrived in the life of the subject of this memoir, they had cast off almost the last shred of respect for the spiritual mother, to whom they were indebted for their very existence. From the year 1868 may be dated the rise of aggressive political Methodism in Wales; it was then that this body broke loose from their earlier traditions, and formally entered into an alliance with the hereditary enemies of the Church, and the subsequent years of Mr. Edwards' life were largely spent in combating this combination of heterogeneous foes to the life and prosperity of the National Church.

During the first few months of his incumbency at Carnarvon, his attention was chiefly occupied in effecting a readjustment of the income of the vicar, which was rendered practicable by the fact that the rectorial tithes had just then, by the expiry of a lease, fallen into the hands of the Ecclesiastical Commissioners. This work proved to be of a somewhat delicate and complicated nature, and he had the misfortune to differ from some of the details contained in the scheme proposed by the

Commissioners. After some negotiation, however, he was enabled to fix on terms which ultimately met their approval, and which placed the stipend of the vicar on a basis more satisfactory, as being less liable to fluctuation than it had hitherto been. By this arrangement, provision was made for the district of Waunfawr, which was subsequently constituted into a separate incumbency, and annexed to the small parish of Bettws Garmon. A church was also needed at Twthill, to afford convenient accommodation for the substantial and increasing congregation that had been gathered in that part of the town by the combined exertions of lay and clerical agencies. In a short time, St. David's Church was built, and became the home and centre of a flourishing cause. His work of Church extension here and elsewhere involved much toil and anxiety, as churches cannot be built, and living agencies cannot be provided, without funds. To a man of comparatively limited means, whose resources were constantly crippled by such work with which his hands had been full almost since the day of his Ordination, and to one who was endowed with an intellectual and sensitive temperament, the task of continually dabbling in bricks and mortar was neither easy nor congenial.

Nothing is more essential to the happiness and mental repose, and, we may emphatically add, to the ministerial efficiency, of men in such circumstances than genuine sympathy, and ungrudging co-operation. It increases their capacity for work, and inspires courage and enthusiasm. Mr. Edwards was brought here into contact with some who did not understand him, and occasionally into collision with others who could not altogether sympathize with him. But he toiled on with unflagging energy, and soon succeeded in completing his arrangements, and in introducing method and regularity into parochial work and organizations.

It was at this time that he became embroiled in controversies, from which he was not wholly exempt during the remainder of his life. His letter to Mr. Gladstone, of which we have already spoken, drew forth much criticism, both favourable and adverse. A hostile review of it by a leading Welsh Calvinistic minister, in a weekly periodical called *Y Goleuad*, was answered by him, and gave rise to a correspondence of some length. Mr. Edwards took his stand on the principle of Christian unity, and called upon the reviewer and his co-religionists to return to the Church, inasmuch as the internal administrative causes which had occasioned the secession of that denomination had been removed. The controversy was conducted with great ability, courtesy, and fairness, on both sides. The Dean insisted on outward unity, on the broad basis of the doctrinal orthodoxy and the Apostolical constitution of the Church; his opponent, while candidly admitting the Scriptural character of the Creeds and Articles, was content with asserting spiritual unity as essentially sufficient. Whilst we fully admit that the spirit of arrogant pretensions, misrule, and misconduct within, is often responsible for outward schism and secession, and acknowledge the precious reality of spiritual as distinguished from visible unity, we nevertheless find from experience, and from the sad records of Christian history, that there is no more fruitful source of spiritual disunion and discord, no cause more fatal to the healthy and successful development of victorious spiritual unity in the Church of Christ, than the miserable rivalries, created, fostered, and intensified by the interminable divisions by which our outward Christianity has been rent and disfigured. And no appreciable advance can be made towards the attainment of that strong and healthy position of spiritual union of hearts, sympathies, and aims, which all confess to be ideally the best, until earnest souls amongst the different sections of Christians, actively and professedly yearn for the recovery of the priceless blessings of outward unity.

The ecclesiastical reunion of his countrymen was the great aim and aspiration of the Dean throughout his public life. He often discussed the subject in a spirit of candid earnestness. He saw and mourned the infinite loss, both in outward resources and in spiritual power, which Christianity suffers from the rampant spirit of faction that prevails. The flippant sneer in which the scoffer indulges at the expense of our "unhappy divisions," and the unctuous self-complacency with which the professional advocate of sectarianism glories in them, were alike distressing to him; they grieved his heart, and crushed his hopes. He saw, as every thoughtful observer sees, that there stand between us and the initiatory step towards the restoration of Christian unity, a formidable combination of mixed interests, unrelieved and undisturbed by any appreciable aspiration after a higher and better state of things. The last paper he wrote, which is published in this volume, is an honest and liberal attempt to lay down the principles on which the religious wounds of generations may be healed. Even in the din of controversy and the strife of tongues, the contribution of an ardent patriot, Churchman, and Christian, ought to speak to us with authority, recognizing as he does, fully and frankly, the benefits which Nonconformity has conferred on the nation, whilst he does not abate one jot of the prescriptive rights and inherent possibilities of the Church. Surely there is pathos and power in the voice that thus speaks to us as from the grave.

The passing of the late Mr. Forster's Act, in 1870, brought the subject of elementary education very prominently before the country. Churchmen had hitherto borne a noble part in establishing parochial schools in a large number of districts, and had maintained them at a heavy expenditure. The active part which many of the clergy took in imparting religious teaching, based upon Scripture and the Church Catechism, and the influence they acquired thereby, had roused the jealousy of the Nonconformists, who now began to evince an unwonted interest in education, by setting themselves in opposition to the existing voluntary schools, and vigorously supporting a universally compulsory scheme. Whilst the Education Bill was passing through the House of Commons, they used their political influence with the Government to the utmost of their power, to secure a purely secular system. No sadder example of the evil disposition of religious rivalries can be conceived than this, and nothing can be advanced in justification of the efforts the Nonconformists made to extrude the Word of God from our elementary schools. In the recent weighty words of Lord Selborne, "One of the most deplorable effects of religious disunion at the present day is leaving out the teaching of religion, the teaching even of the Bible—which, if you were to look at it even from a purely secular point of view, is one of the most important and interesting books that could be imagined, even if one did not believe in it, but which from my heart and soul I do. If one did not believe in it, to leave it out of the system of education would be like leaving out the principal part from the great drama of life. But these miserable religious dissensions, these odious jealousies, excommunicate the Bible from that thorough teaching in schools which other books taught there are expected to receive." The attitude which the Nonconformists assumed towards the Bible in its relation to the education of the country, is painfully anomalous. They have been credited with a jealous regard for the Word of God, as the sole rule of faith and conduct. In 1870 they practically forfeited their claim to this distinction. The religious Dissenter had gained a high reputation as a man of "one Book;" in the education controversy he damaged that reputation irreparably. We have had some few expressions of regret since; but they have proved unavailing, and the Dissenting bodies stand to this day virtually committed to the principle of secular education. It is difficult to discover any very commendable motives for their conduct in this. Those motives probably lie, as we have before intimated, partly in the jealousy they felt at the zeal which the clergy evinced in promoting the religious education of the children, and partly in their eagerness to save their logical consistency as Liberationists, even at the expense of sacrificing their reputation as advocates of the Word of God. Be this as it may, the side they took in this controversy, and the alliance they formed with the avowed enemies of revealed religion, constituted a serious and startling departure in their religious history, and forced them to support a policy of elementary education little in consonance with their traditionary attachment to the Bible. Events have transpired since in the Principality, which justify the suspicion that the policy so rashly advocated then, has already produced an injurious reflexive influence on themselves, and a baleful effect on the life of the nation. It would be an insult to the position of the leading accredited teachers of a large portion of the country, to say that their advocacy of a system of education from which the Bible was to be excluded as a text-book, did not seriously lower the character of the sacred volume, and impair its authority in the eyes of the people. In a speech delivered in Bangor, May, 1883, the late Mr. Forster, when speaking of this controversy, used the following significant words, with special reference to Wales : "As to secular education in schools without religious teaching, he thought that a mistake.

He thought that this would be found hereafter to be a mistake."

The then Vicar of Carnarvon was the first and foremost in the campaign, which the friends of voluntary schools and a religious system of education entered upon, in opposition to the advocates of compulsory secularism. He met his opponents on every platform, and, in the stirring meetings of that period, he held his own wherever he went. In most of the controversies of his life, it must never be forgotten that he always laboured under two heavy disadvantages. The first that he had to oppose men who attacked the existing state of things, whereas he had "not only to strive with a number of heavy prejudices, deeply rooted in the hearts of men, who think that herein we serve the time, and speak in favour of the present state, because thereby we either hold or seek preferment; but also to bear such exceptions as minds so averted beforehand usually take against that which they are loth should be poured into them." "He that goeth about to persuade a multitude that they are not so well governed as they ought to be, shall never want attentive and favourable hearers, because they know the manifold defects whereunto every kind of regiment is subject; but the secret lets and difficulties, which in public proceedings are innumerable and inevitable, they have not ordinarily the judgment to consider. And because such as openly reprove supposed disorders of state are taken for principal friends to the common benefit of all, and for men that carry singular freedom of mind; under this fair and plausible colour whatsoever they utter passeth for good and current. That which wanteth in the weight of their speech, is supplied in the aptness of men's minds to accept and believe it" (Hooker). The other disadvantage he laboured under was that he had to speak often before a hostile audience. But he shrank not from duty. He found, and others found, that the Dissenting orators were not such formidable antagonists as many had imagined them to be. Those orators had a ready tongue, a large amount of self-assurance, and a fund of stale anecdotes, which they had learnt to relate with dramatic skill; but when their arguments were subjected to a tolerably close analysis, they were found to be pitiably incoherent and inconclusive. They made the most astounding assertions about what they were pleased to call the trifling cost of Board Schools, which can only be said, on any charitable hypothesis, to have been due to their no less astounding ignorance.

This controversy entailed much labour on Mr. Edwards, and overwhelmed him with obloquy, on the platform and in the press. He was constantly exposed to the most virulent attacks; but this was a necessity of his position. "Censure, says an ingenious writer, is the tax a man pays to the public for being eminent. . . . All the illustrious persons of antiquity, and indeed of every age in the world, have passed through this fiery persecution. There is no defence against reproach but obscurity; it is a kind of concomitant to greatness, as satires and invectives were an essential part of a Roman triumph" (Addison). In this controversy he proved himself a ready debater, a formidable antagonist, a master of sarcasm and invective. He would discern at a glance the weakness of his opponent's armour, and unerringly direct his dart into the joints. He raised the Church in the estimation of the public, inspired her friends with courage and her enemies with dread. He was nobly assisted by his brethren, and notably by Canon Evans, his successor at Carnarvon. They had the satisfaction to find that the Education Act, as it emerged from the Legislature, aimed at supplementing, and not at supplanting, the voluntary schools; that religious education was retained in these by the insertion of a conscience clause, and that the exclusion or admission of the Bible into Board Schools was made dependent on the vote of the majority of the ratepayers.

Mr. Edwards' growing fame and popularity added greatly to his labours. He was now called upon everywhere to do battle for the cause of religious education, to defend the Church from the organized attacks of her assailants, and to occupy her pulpits on all important occasions. In addition to this, and to the care of a populous parish, he became a constant contributor to the Welsh Church press. He believed in the power of the press; he longed to see it employed in the service of the Church, and strenuously advocated the policy of securing the co-operation of men of talent and education in its support. And he was not one to advance a theory without acting upon it. He entered into the arena of the public controversies of that time with all the enthusiasm and intrepidity of his soul, and, utterly heedless of the storm of abuse that raged around him, he charged men who had inherited from their religious ancestors the precious legacy of a reputation for exceptional piety and sanctity, with the guilt of advocating a godless system of education, and the spoliation of the sanctuary from mere jealousy at the progress which the Church was making in the country. He wrote leading articles in the weekly organ of the Church in Wales, edited and wrote the major part of the *Amddiffynydd* for two years, and often carried the war into the enemy's camp, by defending the Church from the calumnies and misrepresentations of hostile critics on the pages of the Dissenting newspapers. His success as a leading-article writer was unquestionable. His contributions to the *Dywysogaeth* and *Amddiffynydd* at this time made the Church press a greater power in Wales than it had probably ever been before. The productions of his facile and prolific pen, though anonymous, could hardly be mistaken. The elaborate introduction, the wealth and brilliancy of illustration, the satirical humour, the lucid and masterful treatment of the subject; the frequent occurrence of the double negative and the periphrastic form of the verb; the diction powerful, but not always classical; the style soul-stirring, but not elegant;—all this rendered the paternity of his anonymous contributions to the Welsh press easily recognizable.

About this time he also gave to the world two other volumes of sermons, entitled respectively "The Exile and Return," and "The Babel of the Sects," the latter of which was published in both English and Welsh. These volumes exhibit all the peculiarities of his style, and drew forth high commendation from the reviewers. The following quotation from "The Exile and Return" will supply us with a specimen of his thoughts on the momentous question of national education, which he had profoundly studied, and elaborately discussed on the platform and in the press at this time. "The nation which banishes the Name of God from the schools of its youth, and from its organism of government, in the hope of increasing human happiness and power, has no promise. That liberty which expresses the love of our neighbours, has its root in the love of God. National religion is the guardian of national liberty. Until the nation has learnt to obey the command of Religion, enjoining self-denial and self-sacrifice, saying, 'Take thy growing life, and offer it unto me,' it can never hear the true charter of Liberty, 'Lay not thine hand upon the lad.'" To those who recognize the paramount authority of the Christian religion, and the supremacy of its claims as the Divine guide and guardian of life, these truths appear so axiomatic and incontrovertible, that it awakens sad reflections, when they are forced to observe that the combination of sectarian rivalry and political exigencies render necessary their inculcation and defence, in a country whose people have been credited with an intense reverence for the Gospel, and with an unusual degree of proficiency in practical religion. Is it another instance of "*Corruptio optimi pessima*"? The admission of a false principle opens the doors for others of a kindred nature.

In the year 1874, Mr. Edwards sought to represent the clergy of the diocese as their proctor in Convocation, and was elected without opposition, which shows that his brethren appreciated the great services he had already done to the Church. In a letter he says, "My views upon the ecclesiastical questions of the day are not unknown to my fellow-clergy. If elected, I will offer at all times a conscientious opposition to those who would either add to or take from the Book of Common Prayer, a loyal allegiance to the authority of which I regard as the best basis of unity amongst Churchmen." This is sound policy. At a time when the country is passing through a crisis of educational and intellectual transformation, when secularists and socialists, rationalists and Romanists, are greedily seizing the opportunity for propagating their theories amongst the masses, and when sectarian animosities and political expediency have entered into an alliance for the overthrow of the National Church by the destruction of her organizations and the crippling of her resources, we can hardly offer better or more reasonable advice to all loyal Churchmen than that contained in the above extract. To stand firmly and unitedly by the Prayer-book and the principles of the Reformation seems our best, if not our only, chance of successfully repelling the hostile advances of our foes, and avert disasters. In his short preface to "The Exile and Return," the author says that he " believes that their teaching is drawn from the study of Holy Scripture, as interpreted for English Churchmen by the Book of Common Prayer. He has endeavoured to stand loyally on the undebatable ground of the Church of England, without crossing her borders in any direction whatever." His theological views were somewhat broader than those of the ordinary High Churchman; while, on the Ministry and Sacraments, he differed from those held by the typical Evangelical. He did not speak often in Convocation; but, whenever he did, he did not fail to impress his audience with his striking individuality and independence of mind.

In the year 1873, he had married the second time, to Anne Dora, the daughter of Mr. John Jones, of Treanna, Anglesey. She was possessed of a remarkably buoyant nature, a vivacious and sympathetic temperament, a quick and sensitive intuitiveness. With the affectionate tenderness and never-failing resources of a true and devoted helpmate, she strove to lighten the cares and share the burdens of the life of arduous toil and incessant controversies in which he was now engaged. During the short three years of their marriage, he was at the height of his public activities, and the domestic happiness he then enjoyed doubtless contributed not a little to the efficiency with which he discharged his duties as a parochial clergyman, and defender of the Church. The peaceful repose and harmony of a true home must have afforded him refreshing solace, after the tumultuous excitement of the frequent public meetings he attended. He so fully enjoyed and appreciated the blessings of domestic comforts at this time, that he would often say it was too good to last. And the melancholy presage was too true. At the close of the year 1875, his wife was struck with a fatal illness. During the Christmas season with its hallowed association of Christian joy, a heavy sorrow brooded over his home. The letters which he wrote during the progress of his wife's illness reveal the intensity of his affection, and the strong desire of his heart to retain the precious life which appeared essential to the happiness and usefulness of his own. How he agonized in prayer to God to avert the threatening calamity! How he alternated between hope and fear! How tenaciously his whole soul clung to hope, on the appearance of the faintest symptoms of recovering strength! But his prayers were answered otherwise than he wished; the desire of his eyes was snatched from him, and his domestic hearth was once more mysteriously desolated. He was left to mourn his loss with two infant daughters, the elder two years, and the younger only ten months old at the time of their mother's death.

When the dark moment of bereavement came upon him, with a bruised, broken, and bleeding heart, he resigned himself without a murmur to the wise but inscrutable decree of God. In the following extracts from a letter which he penned immediately after the sad occurrence, we find some of the thoughts that struggled for utterance, when he was bending under the terrible ordeal that shook his being to its very centre, and tore by the roots the living fibres that had grown deep into his existence.

"I hoped as long as there was hope. We did all we could, by the use of earthly means, to save the natural life of my darling Dora. An all-wise and all-loving God has seen fit to take away from me the central joy of my earthly life. His Will be done. 'If I could call her back, against God's Will, I would not do it,' as Archbishop Fénelon said in a similar hour of dark trial. 'While the child was yet alive,' said David, 'I fasted and wept; for I said, Who can tell whether God will be gracious to me, that the child may live? But now he is dead, wherefore should I fast? Can I bring him back again? *I shall go to him, but he shall not return to me.*' I am trying to realize the deep, solemn wisdom of those inspired words. It is a hard task. She was as dear to me as my own life-blood. We had no thought, no task, no aim, no feeling, that we did not share with each other. Before we spoke, our hearts beat together; our minds worked in absolute domestic unison. I have known the greatest joy that earth can give—that of a calm, bright home, and a deep, pure, real love, absorbing all the powers of affection, going down to the roots of my heart, growing up and branching out into every part of my life. This earth has no illusions for me in the future. It may have duties; God grant that I may have strength to perform them. I may be more fitted than I have been, if God wills that I should live, to exhort and console others with the authority of one who has been in the furnace of affliction, and knows by personal experience the purifying power of its great, God-kindled heat. A great preacher has said, 'He who has been long under the rod of God, becomes in a peculiar manner God's possession. He bears in his body marks, and has drops upon him that nature cannot provide. He comforts and exhorts with authority. "He comes from Edom, with dyed garments from Bozrah," and it is easy to tell with whom he has been conversing.'"

He saw his earthly home once more ruthlessly shattered. As he surveyed the wreckage, his bereaved and bleeding heart felt the chill of desolation. He bravely strove to resign himself to a lonely pilgrimage, and to seek home, rest, and happiness only in the performance of his duties. "It would be vain to keep up the fabric of my earthly home, now when God has, in His wise love, chosen to take away its chief corner-stone. I must not rebel. I am only suffering what better men have suffered before me, in that process of chastening by which our Father disciplines and prepares us for rest in the glorious, eternal home, where we shall meet beyond the confines of time, and the reach of change, pain, and sorrow—'for the former things are passed away.' . . . What about the future? It is in God's hands. We can only propose; God will dispose. He is very merciful, and good to us. He will not chasten for ever, nor suffer all His anger to fall upon us."

Referring to his wife's personal religion, he says, "She loved beauty and reverence in religion, and had a strong faith in the mysterious workings of God's sacramental grace. She was no formalist, but a deep, living Christian, loving God's Word. The last sermon she heard from me was about the call that God gives to us to rise above the earthly, lower life, into the high, heavenly life (Rev. iv. 1–3). The voice has said, 'Come up hither.' She is gone up, free from the burden of the flesh. We, as long as we live, must try to go up heavenward, seeking those things which are above, and having our conversation in heaven. . . . God comforts us all. If I live, He will give me work to be my consolation."

He could not endure the idea of living at the vicarage, where he had experienced such crushing afflictions; the tender associations of the past harassed and haunted him. He abandoned the scene of his sorrows, and sought lodgings in the town. He writes, January 6, 1876, "I am feeling a little down to-day, but am wonderfully sustained, when the heaviness of the visitation is considered. 'He uttered His voice, and the earth melted' under my feet. I seem to have nothing to cling to, but the hopes that are far above, coming down out of the opened heaven. . . . I hope I shall be able to go onwards under my heavy burden, in the strength of God, better than I anticipate." Three days after he writes, "I have just been reading a sermon by a famous preacher. Its subject is, 'The Cross of Christ the Measure of the World.' There are high joys of being which cannot be reached until we have been beneath the Cross. 'They that sow in tears shall reap in joy.' Let us hope that we shall have a rich harvest of joy after this tearful season, which God has sent us. . . . If it please God to give me tolerable health, and to spare me from nervous depression, which is my old enemy, I hope to be as happy as I can be under the circumstances. . . . It is a great mercy that God has spared the dear children.

May He continue to bless them in His goodness. They will, if they live, be a comfort and brightness to us all." Four days after this he writes again, "I have been dreadfully depressed, last night and this morning. In spite of all my efforts, memory is very busy, and my heart is very desolate. I found a little comfort this morning in reading the chapter in Bishop Butler's 'Analogy' on the 'Future Life,' in which he argues that death is simply that change of condition that enables the immortal soul to enter upon a higher life. 'Thus, when we get out of this world, we may pass into new scenes, and a new state of life and action, just as naturally as we came into the present. And this new state may naturally be a social one.' To try to realize this truth is, really, the only, or almost the only, efficient source of comfort in the hours that have come upon me."

On February 24, 1876, he writes from London, where he had gone for a change, "Thank God, I feel physically very well. I had a sorrowful night, lying awake long in the early hours of the morning. In my sleeplessness, I composed the sad little verses which you will find on the other side. When a boy, I used to write verses for my amusement. I have not written any before for years." The verses alluded to in this letter are as follows :—

"IN MEMORIAM A. D. E.

"With her my life was full, deep, bright
My heart, my mind, my ear, my sight
All daily drank their dear delight
When she was here.

> The angel came; a dreadful night
> Quenched my best rays of earthly light,
> Breathed o'er my Paradise a blight;
>   She is not here.
>
> "In heart and mind, we two were one,—
> This God's own Sacrament had done;—
> I'm broken now, for I'm alone;
>   She is not here.
> Homeless on earth, I stagger on;
> My step is short, my strength is gone;
> Too soon my day of joy is done,—
>   She is not here.
>
> "Shall I repine, rebel, curse God?
> Shall I not rather kiss the rod,
> And tread the path Himself hath trod,
>   With many a tear?
> Yes, yes! Thank God! I will not wail,
> Now I've new hope within the vail;
> Christ grant in grace I may not fail
>   To join her there!"

The dawn of the year 1876 had brought on a crisis in Mr. Edwards' life. The heavy and incessant labours of the past six years had caused an exhaustion of physical and mental energy. The crushing sorrow which had, for the second time, bereft him of the central joy and support of home, had, as we have seen, been followed by a depression of spirits, which made it difficult for him to continue life's duties with the same vigour and buoyancy as before. Mental and physical nature loudly clamoured for change, and in the providence of God that change came. In the early part of this year the genial Dean Vincent died, and Mr. Edwards was appointed as his successor. The deanery afforded him timely rest from the constant cares of parochial duties, while it left him more at liberty to prosecute his favourite studies and pursuits. He was enabled henceforth, both by the dignity of his position, and the leisure it procured him, to employ his time and talents more exclusively in the service of the Church and nation at large. The great variety and amount of work he did, the posts he filled, and the controversies he engaged in during the subsequent years of his life, prove how well he understood and recognized the responsibilities involved in that position, and the value of the opportunities it placed within his reach. And while his promotion to Bangor brought him timely relief from the depressing associations of a shattered home, it was, at the same time, a well-merited recognition of his past great services. No appointment of recent times in the Welsh Church was hailed with more cordial and universal approbation; letters of congratulation poured in upon him from men of all parties. His past labours and experience, as well as his undoubted abilities, had justly earned for him, as well as qualified him for, the conspicuous position he was now called upon to occupy. He had proved himself to be essentially a man for the times. He had already done work which no other representative of the Welsh Church had done. He had raised the drooping spirits of Welsh Churchmen, and inspired them with confidence in their cause, when their assailants were contemptuously threatening them all along the line. We would almost say that, in the public controversies carried on against the Church, so defiantly, and with such self-confident dogmatism by the Dissenters and their political allies, the Church in Wales would have allowed judgment against her to go by default, had not the Vicar of Carnarvon taken up the challenge. His powerful and well-sustained defence created a public opinion amongst Churchmen, filled many a shrinking heart with courage and enthusiasm, and brought to light the positiveness and firmness of the Church's position. It was no longer to continue a mere passive or negative force in the country. A Church which was nothing more than a negation, could neither justify nor preserve its existence, in the face of the severe scrutiny to which it was subjected. Mere passivity could no more withstand the aggressive phalanx of opponents that had conspired to overthrow her, than untrained and unarmed battalions could resist the assaults of experienced and well-organized veterans. The Vicar of Carnarvon braced himself for the contest, and led the army of defence with unwavering confidence, both in himself and in his cause. He was, indeed, well supported by a faithful band of fellow-workers, and in this cause it may be remarked that he suffered but little from the jealousy or apathy of Churchmen. All cheerfully recognized his leadership. He was applauded throughout the length and breadth of the land, and though it may have been that comparatively few were thoughtful enough to express their appreciation by a sympathizing letter, his name, nevertheless, had become a household word, and was cherished with unmixed feelings of affectionate gratitude and admiration. He was known everywhere in the Principality as "the Vicar;" and his brave words and noble self-sacrifice, in those days of severe trials, were the theme of laudatory comments, and have left indelible marks on the life of the Church, and the minds and hearts of Churchmen. His elevation to the deanery, as we have said, was hailed as a well-merited tribute to one who had rendered such valuable services to the Church, and was looked upon as a sure precursor to higher distinctions. We dare not speculate on what might have been, had his life been prolonged; it was not to be so, and our duty is silent acquiescence in the dark, inscrutable mysteries of what has been. To most of his fellow-countrymen, he seemed to have been marked out, by special endowments and qualifications, to lead and to govern. His commanding presence, his undisguised and undaunted patriotism, his intense but unaffected love for Wales and Welshmen, his unfeigned partiality for our national institutions, his knowledge of the language, history, and temperament of the race from which he sprang, and, above all, his firm attachment to the Cymric Church, rendered unquestionable his claims to be raised in due time to the episcopal throne of one of our sees. But his sun set suddenly and mysteriously, whilst life was yet in its noonday splendour, and his name will go down to posterity as a powerful controversialist, a defender of his Church and nation, a leader of men and master of assemblies, rather than as a great administrator and organizer, though the Church in the diocese of Bangor is largely indebted to his energy and inspiration for some of her most beneficial and successful organizations. The Church in Wales has not outlived her trials. She has not conciliated or vanquished her foes, or surmounted her difficulties. She is still in the throes of her conflicts, but without the faithful and courageous defender that so often stood in the forefront of her battles. He has left her, indeed, but not before he had filled her quiver with arrows, and bequeathed to her faithful sons the rich and rare legacy of a conspicuous example of a life consecrated to her service. We have no wish to paint him as perfect. He partook to a considerable degree of some of the faults and frailties, as well as many of the virtues, of his countrymen. Some of those were constitutional, others were excesses of virtues, and all were aggravated by the constant frictions of his life. He was impulsive and impatient of contradiction; his actions appeared at times tinged with too much self-consciousness and self-assertion, and he was prone to morbid and excessive habits of self-introspection. It may, perhaps, be said that his want of self-restraint, which, if more habitually maintained, would have enabled him to husband his mental and physical resources, may have been instrumental in accelerating the final collapse. His fearless exposure of what he conceived to be the errors, imperfections, or injustices, of systems and institutions which it was his duty to criticize, brought upon him charges of harshness or indiscretion, from those whose natural timidity shrank from drastic measures, or from those who felt the scathing severity of his strictures. His life was largely spent in the heated and turbulent atmosphere of public controversy, which brought him into unhappy but inevitable collision with the prejudices and prepossessions of many of his countrymen, whilst it left him but little leisure for calm reflection, and the cultivation of a judicial frame of mind. Some of the few private papers he left behind him, in the form of confessions, vows, and resolutions, show how painfully conscious he was of these personal weaknesses, how he strove and struggled to overcome, and how earnestly he prayed to be delivered from them. Nothing in the history of the human soul appears to us nobler, nothing better proves the dire reality of the spiritual combat within, than these records, drawn out under the searching eye of God, in the sacred privacy of self-examination and holy communings, where the heart unreservedly spreads out its own failures before its Maker and Judge, and, out of its deepest depths, utters its fervent longings to rise victorious over them. These records are to us invaluable. We read them with living, sympathetic interest. Our own inner history and experience enable us to understand and appreciate them; they reveal to us a life kindred to that with which we have the profoundest acquaintance, struggling, but not yet perfect. But we prefer to count the victories rather than the defeats, and though the day closed before, as we thought, the maturest and most precious fruits were gathered for the Church below, nevertheless the echoes of his voice, the influence of his life, and the force of his example, will live on through many generations, in the grateful recollections, and, let us hope, in the faithful imitation of Welsh Churchmen and patriots.

Mr. Edwards' installation as Dean of Bangor took place on April 6, and in the evening he preached a Welsh sermon in the cathedral for the occasion. Though the promotion set him free from the definite and rigid routine of parochial engagements, he did not indulge in any prolonged relaxation. Work was a necessity of his life. During the eight years he held the deanery, his hands were always full, except, indeed, when he was compelled to rest or go abroad, by illness or physical prostration. The amount of work he did, in lecturing, preaching, and writing, was prodigious. Invitations to preach at harvest thanksgiving meetings, choral festivals, Church anniversaries, and other ordinary or special occasions, crowded upon him from every part of Wales, and from many of the principal centres of population in England. He preached in secluded country churches as well as in large towns, and always succeeded in drawing large congregations. He has, indeed, been accused of sameness in his sermons; but the best answer to such criticism is that the people everywhere thronged to hear him, and listened to his discourses with rapt attention. He gave the best of his time and thoughts to the study and treatment of his subject. We find him again and again complaining in his private letters that preparation for the pulpit, as well as the delivery of his sermons, was followed by languor and exhaustion. He did not content himself with scanning over his subject superficially in a twenty minutes' sermon, as is too often the fashion in these days of self-indulgent ease, but he dug deep into the foundation of his text, and enforced its lessons with eloquence and exhaustiveness. If we may select one characteristic of his discourses, which, perhaps more than others, shows at once the strength and the weakness of his style, it would be his fondness for illustrations. Whether we read his sermons, his speeches, or his leading articles, we cannot fail to observe that what gives that peculiar charm which is scarcely ever absent from his productions, in his fertility of illustrations. It however, led him sometimes to place undue weight upon them, and to force them to perform the function of analogy. The legitimate use of an illustration is, not to supply proofs of a proposition, but merely the elucidation of truth. It cannot be denied that the Dean occasionally overstepped these limits in the employment of his favourite figures of speech, which in the main, however, he used with exceptional power and legitimate effects.

The originality which has often, and, as we think, rightly been attributed to him, consisted not so much in the discovery of what is new, or in bringing to light of what lies hidden in the deep, inexhaustible wells of Divine revelation, as in his presentment of what is already known. We can hardly take up a sermon of his without noticing some striking originality of this kind. He was profoundly observant of the currents of thoughts and actions that surged around him, and he seldom failed to adapt and apply the lessons of his text to the condition of contemporary society. All Scripture was to him the living and authoritative voice of God, replete with messages to us of the present day, as to those who first received them. He saw types in, and drew forth lessons on some Gospel truth, or on the providential dealings of God, from passages in the Old Testament, where few would have found them. For this he was sometimes severely criticized; but if in error, he erred on the safer side, especially in days when the critical spirit betrays tendencies to eliminate the typical, the prophetic, and the supernatural from the older Scriptures. It no doubt requires the faculties well disciplined to draw the limits between what are historical types and what are mere history, between mere temporary details, and facts or events which contain in them the germs of lessons designed for permanent and ever-recurring application. As we have observed, the Dean was fond of drawing out theological and practical lessons from Old Testament events where few would have discovered them, and it may be remarked that he preached oftener from the older than from the later Scriptures. This may be regarded as a legitimate and timely protest against the too liberal and rationalizing spirit which would relegate the Hebrew records to the position of mere ancient history, and would eviscerate them of all higher and permanent ethical teaching and spiritual edification. Old Testament revelation, besides its typical and prophetic import, contains an authentic record of God's providential dealings with nations and individuals. The veil is drawn aside by the Divine hand; the plan and principles whereby God rules the world are laid bare; the events are, so to speak, specimen events in which are revealed the relation of the Supreme Ruler to earthly powers, and the laws of His universal government over His responsible subjects. The Gospel dispensation of the New Testament has not altered, or modified, or annulled the foundation principles of the economy of God's Providence, as revealed and exemplified in the Old. The laws of that Providence are still operative. The only difference is, that their operations are not directly authenticated by supernatural communications or interpositions in our day; we are left to be guided in our interpretation of them by the authoritative records of the Old Testament. The Gospel dispensation left unaltered the laws of Providence, so clearly revealed, so strikingly and profusely illustrated under the old dispensation, and which were founded, not on the temporary and transitory character of the Jewish nation and polity, but on the immutable relation of God to all nations, and communities, and ages, as consisting of moral beings, accountable to Him for their actions, and living before Him in a state of probation. We do not, indeed, affirm that Dean Edwards was not sometimes fanciful in his interpretation of particular passages; but we do maintain that his application of the historical truths and typical lessons of the Old Testament to the condition of society in our own times, is based on sound principles, and is a seasonable protest against the pernicious tendency of modern neology, which, by an exhaustive process of elimination, seeks to divest the older

Scriptures of all permanent and moral teaching, leaving us only the bare, empty historical shell—just as the same spirit of destructive criticism, advancing a step further in its logical development, essays to abstract from the Gospel narrative all the historical and miraculous elements, allowing us only a dry, lifeless remnant of ethical teaching.

The Dean's theological position has been described as a broad High Churchman, and we recollect that, on its being once mentioned to him, he did not repudiate the designation. The fundamental articles of his theology, those on which he laid the most prominent stress in his discourses, were the loss of God's image in the Fall, in consequence of which man incurred personal misery, and deserved eternal banishment from the presence of his Maker; man's restoration to the favour of God, and his reinstitution in all the privileges which he had forfeited, through the redemption and mediation of the Man-Christ, the Incarnate Son of God. The conception of "law" runs through all his writings. Law violated brings its punishment in the derangement of the life or constitution, for the well-being of which it exists. The law of selfishness, isolation, and self-assertion, is death and bondage; the law of self-sacrifice, unity, and self-surrender, is life and liberty. These primary laws he regards as supreme and universal in their operation; in their light he reads the fate of individuals and communities. His system may be sometimes too rigid and exclusive; he may not always take sufficient account of the modifying and remedial power of subordinate laws, which, through the merciful and marvellous intervention of God, are, in the moral and spiritual world, analogous in their beneficent operations to what in the physical world is termed *vis medicatrix naturæ*. His belief in the inspiration of Scripture, as the revelation of God's Will, was firm and implicit. Great controversialist as he was, he rarely introduced controversy into the pulpit, on the great and fundamental verities of the Christian religion. Christ, as the eternal Son of God and the Saviour of man, was the central Figure of his message and ministry. It may be that he dwells oftener and with greater emphasis on His example, than on the culmination of His life in the vicarious death upon the Cross, as the source of man's renewed life; or the completion of His triumph in the resurrection from the dead, as the pledge of the Church's final victory. It may be, as a consequence to this, that he lays greater stress on the Christian's duties than on the principle of faith, whereby alone the life of God in Christ is apprehended and appropriated. But he never fails to point the lost soul to the Saviour, both as the only Name whereby we must be saved—as the Incarnate Word in Whom is revealed the fulness of the Father's love—and as the only Pattern of a life of holiness.

During the first three or four years of his occupation of the deanery, his movements were rapid and almost ubiquitous. He spoke, and preached, and lectured incessantly. The imperfect records of his doings that have been preserved to us in occasional private letters,

Bible Classes and Saturday School. 63

show how varied and heavy his engagements were at this time. He was called upon to preside at literary meetings, at educational establishments, and other movements of a national, ecclesiastical, or philanthropic nature. Every week was crowded with work of a diversified kind, which taxed his energies to the utmost.

In addition to outside engagements, was his work in connection with his own cathedral. With all the energies of his soul, he entered on the double task of setting on foot the restoration of the outward fabric of the "mother church of the diocese," and to initiate movements for its utilization as the centre of diocesan life, which was his ideal conception of what it ought to be. He invited men from all parts of the diocese to occupy its pulpit during the seasons of Advent and Lent, and on special occasions secured the services of preachers of distinction from England and Wales. He conducted a Bible-class for Sunday school teachers in the chapter-room, which was largely attended and highly appreciated. Later on, he started a Saturday "Sunday school," an experiment somewhat novel and hazardous, but which turned out a decided success, and which drew forth words of commendation from Archbishop Tait. Children of all creeds and classes freely and gratefully participated in the opportunity thus afforded for instruction in the Scriptures, and the number of attendances reached over six hundred. Unlike some of our Church dignitaries, he did not consider his position one of mere learned leisure, or dignified ease—a serene altitude, from which to look with silent sympathy and philosophic interest on those who are engaged in the conflict below. He was as ready as ever to offer his powerful aid in militant work. When the Liberationists mustered in full force in the parish he had just resigned, he disdained not to enter once more into the arena of controversy, and lost no time in delivering an exhaustive and crushing reply. A few months before his death, when a feeble attempt at assailing the Church was made by some local representatives of a moribund society, he again replied with more than his wonted vigour, in a speech which bristles with brilliant epigrams and playful repartees. These two speeches fairly exhaust the whole subject, and form a splendid repertory of Church Defence arguments. He was called upon, moreover, to deliver temperance lectures everywhere at this time, and he gained a high reputation as an ardent and powerful advocate of this cause. And whilst these heavy and numerous engagements were pressing upon him, his powerful pen and voice were incessantly employed in pleading for money—now for the Bangor Clerical Education Society, whose income he raised to £700 a year; now for the restoration of the cathedral, which was completed, though not as originally proposed and planned, at a cost of £11,000; and again for the establishment of higher education in North Wales.

In the spring of the year 1879, Dean Edwards was invited to preach at a special English service in St. David's Welsh Church in Liverpool, and in his introduction to the second edition of this sermon, of which we give a reprint in this volume, the author says that he deemed the occasion "not unfitting for briefly reviewing the past and present relation of the Church to the Welsh-speaking population of Wales." Without any comment of our own, we introduce an extract or two, from a highly favourable review of this sermon, which appeared in the *Spectator* for September 20, 1879. " This is a very masterly discourse, which we cordially recommend to the study of all statesmen and Churchmen. The sermon contains some passages of great eloquence." After quoting an extract in illustration of this remark, the reviewer goes on to say, " But it is not as a piece of glowing oratory—and Dean Edwards is a Celt of the Celts—that we value the present pulpit utterance. It is because it supplies a lucid and convincing answer to the question, Why are the Welsh of to-day so largely lost to the National Church? while the author is sanguine enough to believe, as we ourselves also are, that when light shall have been thrown upon the real state of the Welsh Church, when due consideration shall have been given to the fact that Welsh is still the mother-tongue of over a million souls —that is, of nearly five-sixths of the inhabitants of Wales—and that it is the language in which three-fourths of them still worship God, efficacious remedies may yet be found for the mitigation or general absorption of a dissidence which has been occasioned almost entirely by English neglect of the needs and claims of our Cymric brethren. Dean Edwards has succeeded in giving a luminous as well as a most pathetic narrative of the treatment to which the Welsh have been subjected in spiritual matters since the days of the Norman kings." After recapitulating briefly the various fortunes which befell the Welsh Church under a "Welsh dynasty" and the "House of Brunswick" respectively, the reviewer concludes thus: "The story needs no comments, and no subject could more worthily occupy the attention of the forthcoming Church Congress at Swansea, than that which is so ably discussed by the Dean of Bangor in the present discourse. We will only add that we can commend its theology and spirituality, as much as its true patriotism."

When the arrangements for the Swansea Congress of 1879 were made, "The Past and Present Position of the Church in Wales" occupied a prominent place in the programme, as suggested in the above extract. As was to be expected, Dean Edwards was amongst those selected to address the Congress on a subject which he had made his own. His speech on that occasion created a profound impression on the country. It was an effort to rouse the responsible leaders of the Church to a vivid realization of her position. It has been thought to have exaggerated the failures of the Church; and this opinion was subsequently shared by him, as he modified some of the views expressed then, in his last and greatest speech delivered in Carnarvon in 1883, to which we have already referred. But it was characteristic of the man. It bore the impress of his mind. Its epigrammatic antitheses were brilliant; its analyses incisive; its exposures unsparing; its concessions were generous, and its candour almost severe. No other living man could have either conceived or delivered it It was a vivid panorama, covering a long but definite period of history, crowded with details both pleasant and painful, bristling with lessons both of encouragement and of warning—almost an illustration of his own career, the varied events of which succeeded each other with bewildering rapidity. We may be forgiven the comparison, as he criticized the efforts of his own life with the same unsparing severity as he did the administrative history of the Church in Wales, which, it is no exaggeration to say, was equally dear to him.

Few lives of public service have compressed into themselves so many sharp contrasts, so many events of gloom and brightness, joys and sorrows, successes and disappointments, during the short period of twenty years. He used to complain sometimes that his life was a failure. But this was when he brooded with morbid despondency over disappointing results; it was when his analytic, restless mind took its estimate too exclusively from separate facts or events. It is difficult to define, and still more difficult, for earnest souls, to preserve the golden mean between stoical indifference to the results of our labours, and utter despair when those results are found to betray our calculations. The fields do not ripen immediately after the sowing. As in the natural kingdom, so in the moral and spiritual, the active combination of laws and forces, as well as the revolution of the seasons, is necessary for the production of the full harvest; and much of the seed scattered by the most diligent and faithful hand is destined, some never to cut the surface and see the light, some never to reach maturity and to be gathered to the granary. The Dean expected too much from single efforts, into which he at least threw the whole weight of his energies; he had too little faith in a continuous, well-sustained course of action. His impulsive nature, ever anxious for immediate, palpable results, commensurate with the labour and pain spent in the sowing, could not be reconciled to the necessity of waiting for the "due season." "Let us believe," says Landor, "that there was never a right thing done, or a wise one spoken in vain, although the fruit of them may not spring up in the place designated, or at the time spoken." And, says Kingsley—

> "What though thy seed shall fall by the wayside,
> And the birds snatch it? yet the birds are fed;
> Or they may bear it far across the tide,
> To give rich harvest after thou art dead."

This lesson the Dean evermore needed, as a corrective of his natural impulsiveness and impatience, which, combined with the growing despondency that arose from intense mental application, made him sometimes, and notably in his Swansea speech, express strong dissatisfaction at the progress of the Church in the Principality. But he watched that progress with too much jealous anxiety to be always a safe witness. He lived too near the events—he played too large a part in them—to estimate them always at their true value. Moreover, his strong tendency for pungent, epigrammatic sentences led him occasionally to express truth in an exaggerated form. In all his platform utterances, he scarcely laid aside his controversial attitude. He had a keen and ready mind for dissection and analysis; and whenever he detected a fault, or a weakness, he turned upon it the concentrated light of his genius and all the powers of his destructive criticism. To this, partly at least, must be attributed the apparent contradictions of his public utterances. They were not due, as sometimes asserted, to capricious and arbitrary changes of opinion, but to the exclusiveness with which he would deal with his subject, from that point of view which he specially wished to lay before his audience. His style was adapted rather to convince or convict, than to persuade or win. We may be obliged to disagree with him, but we cannot fairly accuse him of inconsistency, before we give due weight to the peculiarities of his style and the necessities of his position. His strong attachment to the constitution and doctrines of the Church, his profound conviction of their historical and scriptural orthodoxy, made him express himself all the more vehemently on what he believed to be the miserable shortcomings of her administration. It may be freely admitted that he viewed those shortcomings too exclusively from the standpoint of a patriotic Welshman; he fixed his eye and concentrated his attack too severely on the tendency to Anglicize the Church, while a broader and more accurate view of the question demanded the ventilation of minor and collateral points of defect. His intense faith in the vitality and vast possibilities of a Church possessed of such a noble history and infinite resources, made him all the more impatient at the too slow progress she appeared to him to be making in winning back to her fold those that had been forced to stray abroad. We may blame his impatience, indeed, but we are compelled to admire his zeal and candour. Whenever he attacked Nonconformity, in its polity or practice, he did so with the same exclusiveness as he exposed the administrative deficiencies of the Church, but he was foremost to admit with gratitude the practical good that had accrued from it. In these days of unreasoning bigotry, the tribute of praise given by an opponent is apt to be taken as unqualified justification, just as discriminating censure, proceeding from a friend, is construed into a wholesale condemnation. Nothing is more liable to misconstruction than the praise of an antagonist, or the blame of a friend. The Dean's impetuosity, his love of epigram and invective, would sometimes carry him beyond the dictates of his calmer judgment, and he often freely expressed his regret at having wounded his victim too severely; for he possessed a nature which was keenly sensitive to the feelings of others. Below those manly features, so expressive of invincible purpose, behind that resolute form, which stepped forward so often to the battle-field as if determined never to retreat till he could proclaim the word of victory, there throbbed, nevertheless, a heart as tender as that of the tenderest woman. It was finely susceptible of kindness, which, with guileless trust and simplicity, it received and reciprocated. His controversial blows were heavy and incisive, but when once delivered, he used to say that he freely forgave and forgot all. Nothing pained him more than the reluctance and refusal of a few amongst those whose actions and opinions he was obliged to criticize and controvert, who were unable to rise above the influence of personal pique, to enter into a renewal of friendly intercourse, when the dust of controversy had subsided.

The Dean's position as a dignitary, as we have already observed, gave him a vantage-ground, which he sought to utilize on every opportunity for pleading the cause and advancing the interests of the Welsh Church and nation. When the authorities of Jesus College, Oxford, resolved to throw open certain endowments originally attached to that college for the exclusive benefit of natives of the Principality, his patriotism was thoroughly roused, and he used all the influence of his position and polemical experience to frustrate the scheme. In the sharp controversy to which the question gave rise, it cannot be denied that the force of fair argument was on the side of the Dean and those who supported him; but the spirit in which the public had learnt to deal with ancient endowments, enabled the originators of the project to sacrifice both the intentions of donors and the advantages of Welshmen to a possible improvement in the efficiency of an institution —a not unfrequent occurrence in these days of cold utilitarianism. It was the Dean's ambition, on the one hand, to be the means of opening the eyes of the generous English nation to the real grievances—the educational and other disadvantages, under which his countrymen were heavily handicapped in the race of life; and, on the other, to be the instrument, as far as he could, of bridging the gulf between the hierarchy of the Church and the masses of the people. He saw, as every impartial observer sees, that the religious disunion of Wales has paralyzed the life of the nation, and has inflicted upon it an injury which it is difficult to exaggerate. It has torn society into fragments; it has created unwholesome rivalries, where the deepest harmony ought to prevail; it engenders and fosters social strifes, and above all, in fact and in spirit, it is a libel on the central principle and final aim of the Christian religion; it

> "Wastes the spiritual strength
> Within us, better offered up to Heaven."

> "Oh, shame to men! devil with devil damned
> Firm concord holds; men only disagree
> Of creatures rational."

The Dean believed that he was entrusted with a mission to bring nearer the fragments into which his countrymen have been socially and ecclesiastically broken. For the attainment of this, he was prepared, as a Churchman, to sacrifice much—even everything except what he deemed to be essential principles. He contended that the Church was the only true centre of religious unity, both on account of her being the mother from whom the sects had originally sprung, and also because she is in possession of the Apostolic polity—a broad but distinct basis of communion, and a fulness of truth. Believing this, he felt keenly the want of sympathy between the masses and the Church. He acknowledged the partial justice of the charge that the latter had neglected the means whereby that sympathy could be generated and fostered, and did what he could to wipe off the disgrace. He endeavoured to influence the people through the press, the pulpit, and the platform, and threw himself heart and soul into popular movements. His Welsh "Commentary on the Gospel of St. Matthew," which he completed in a twelvemonth, and published early in 1882, was an attempt to supply the deficiency in modern Welsh Church exegetical literature; and though he wrote it in too short a time to make it a work of lasting merit, there is much that is highly valuable and useful, both in its critical and homiletical sections.

It will be freely granted that the Dean's efforts, as a dignitary of the Church, to bring her ministrations to bear upon the masses, was a noble example, worthy of more general imitation. The Church will never wield the power she is inherently capable of; she will never duly assert her privileges, and discharge her duties; she will never live down the prejudices that have been so long cherished, nor successfully refute the calumnies that are so assiduously disseminated against her; she will never regain her supremacy over the conscience and affections of the people; she will never vindicate her claims, or effectually convince the nation of the Divine authority of her commission, till the superior clergy, and those who hold her prominent offices, are able to address the masses with fluent efficiency in the vernacular. A feeble imitation of a foreign accent, style, and phraseology, will never make an impression on a Welsh audience, save one of disappointment and dissatisfaction, which will inevitably perpetuate the estrangement which all so deeply deplore. We deem it our duty, in reviewing the life and work of Dean Edwards, to speak with emphasis on this point. No better use can be made of the opportunity, none more in harmony with the aim of his life and the influence of his work. We cannot disguise from ourselves the fact that, with all the warnings and lessons of past generations, we are only tardily awakening to the realization of what appears to be an elementary truth. The system of preparatory training for the ministry has grievously neglected the cultivation of Welsh habits of thought and expression, and has only turned out Anglicized Welshmen—a result most disastrous both to themselves and to the Church. This truth needs to hold a more prominent place in the considerations and utterances of those who seek and suggest remedies for the revival of the Welsh Church, than it has hitherto held. The policy of Anglicizing Welshmen, we repeat, has been as much, or more, the bane of the Welsh Church, as the appointment of Englishmen. It ruins the men, and it ruins the Church; but it is sanctioned and stereotyped, as an analysis of those who occupy higher positions in the Welsh Church at the present moment would disclose; our dignitaries are, as a matter of fact, either Englishmen or Anglicized Welshmen, who, with a few exceptions, are incapable of preaching a Welsh sermon with decent efficiency. The appointment to high offices of men who possess some formal claims to be considered Welshmen, but whose knowledge of the language and the religious temperament of the people is painfully limited, is only an evasion, infinitely worse than an outspoken denial, of the Church's rights. We do not want truths delivered in English idioms from Welsh pulpits—thoughts filtered through English minds, and enfeebled in the process. We want men to hold leading positions in the Welsh Church who can feed the multitude through the pure channel of their own expressive language. We profess to have discovered one of the most grievous mistakes of past administration, in the neglect of giving due scope to the healthy development of Welsh sympathies; we affect to lament our shortcomings, and have expressed our repentance; let us beware of perpetuating the anomaly. Dean Edwards was thoroughly patriotic, and knew that without genuine patriotism the Church could not successfully win her way. English mannerisms and idioms will never restore the confidence of the nation to the Church. We are convinced that the plain truth has not even yet been realized on this important question; it is indisputable that we are still clinging with fatal tenacity to old habits, in spite of the abundant censures we are pleased to pass on the blindness and stupidity of our predecessors.

The position and prospects of the Welsh Church

were ever uppermost in the Dean's thoughts, and he was never tired of adverting to or expatiating upon it. He approached the question from every point of view, and discussed it with absorbing interest, and with astonishing familiarity with its different phases. We remember a conversation we had with him on the subject, on a fine August morning, during one of his accustomed walks, outside the city of Bangor. He plunged at once into his favourite topic. The burden of the discussion turned upon the due preparation of candidates for the ministry. He expressed his strong dissatisfaction with the inadequate training for the pulpit which the Church required and afforded in past days, and mentioned various means whereby the deficiency might be remedied. It was suggested to him that the stiff, stereotyped, unanimated tone, acquired during their academical training by many of our candidates, was unacceptable, and even offensive to a Welsh audience, and had, in the past, done much to estrange the Welsh people from the Church. He fully endorsed this, and replied that he was then doing what he could to instruct the exhibitioners of the Bangor Clerical Education Society, who were under his care during the vacations, in reading Welsh and in the delivery of sermons, in a way that he thought would be acceptable to the Welsh ear. We shall never forget the earnestness with which he emphasized the necessity of a thorough Welsh training for the ministry, in profound sympathy with the Welsh mode of conceiving and expressing their thoughts, and in the Celtic fervour of diction and delivery. He had an uncompromising contempt for the "Dic Shon Dafydd" tendency, which he never attempted to conceal. "In every position, it is contemptible," he would say; "in the ministry, it is simply intolerable." And in this he was surely right.

In days when the Church is passing through new and formidable trials; when the sequence of events discloses new difficulties; when the rapid development of the educational and political, the intellectual and moral, condition of the people ever modifies the problem in its social and religious aspects; when the pernicious tendency to intermingle religion and politics in the pulpit, and on the hustings, is on the increase, and seriously threatens to sap the very foundations of Christian life;—when all this confronts us, it is the urgent and paramount duty of those who are entrusted with the government of the Church, to probe the disease to the very root, and apply themselves with unwearied diligence to the discovery of sound and effectual remedies. The Church must adapt her ministrations to her rapidly changing environments; she must distinguish between essentials and accidents, between what are foundation-truths, never to be changed or tampered with, and those modes of administration which may be wisely and beneficially altered and adapted to meet the requirements of the age. She must promptly remove obsolete excrescences, which the neglect of generations has allowed to fasten on her system, but which sorely hinder the healthy extension of her influence and the consolidation of her work. Above all, she must strive to evoke and foster her own true vitality, upon which alone she can rely for power to carry out necessary reforms. Her standard must be the broad but distinct ground of Christian truth; her aim the permeation of society by the living and life-giving principles of Christianity. It cannot be denied that she is confronted by powerful antagonistic forces; these she must fully recognize, and be prepared to meet, with charity, but with firmness. The great danger that threatens the purity and the power of our Christianity is the tendency we have already adverted to, of making religious questions the battle-ground between contending parties and rival political factions. The real issue is obscured in the heat and dust of controversy; Christian charity is immolated; the high ground of the supremacy of the claims of Gospel truth and progress is sacrificed to political expediency, or the temporary triumph of political parties. This reckless bargaining and bartering, in which the high interests of Christian communities are often the proffered equivalents for political support, evince an alarming degeneracy in the public conception of the sacred character of religion, and produce the effect of lowering it in the estimation of the country. The leading journal was right when, a few months ago, it described our age as one in which a "cowardly fatalism and a base opportunism are rampant;" and the description receives no stronger confirmation than in the disgraceful bargaining that goes on between religious and political leaders. The plague spreads through all grades of society. The identification of politics and religion by those who are pledged to the doctrine that they are separable and are to be separated; the novel practice of settling disputes, and paying debts, by methods that are utterly subversive of law and order, and that in the name of conscience and religion, will inevitably result in moral confusion, which will imperil the very essence of Christianity, as well as the stability and efficiency of our national institutions. The restless spirit of political ambition, in alliance, defensive and offensive, with religious bigotry, is sweeping over the country like a noisome pestilence; and nothing but the true, self-sacrificing spirit of the Cross will purify the atmosphere, and stay the plague. In the cultivation of this spirit lies the safety, as well as the duty, of the Church.

In the summer of 1882, the city of Bangor was visited with typhoid fever of a malignant type, to which the Dean fell a victim on August 4. The incessant strain to which his constitution had been subjected, the heavy sorrows of previous years, the consumption of vital energies by these, and the mental work and worry of controversy, and the steady progress of nervous depression—which, as we have seen, he calls his "old enemy," in 1877—rendered him an easy prey to this terrible epidemic. He was utterly prostrated; his life hung critically in the balance for days, and was more than once despaired of. But his previous habits of abstemiousness, careful nursing, and medical treatment, enabled him to pull through successfully. He recovered, indeed, but his emaciated form, and the utter prostration of his system, showed that the victory was only partial. He never after regained his normal vigour or capacity for work, though he rose on a few occasions to the full measure of his former efforts. We find him henceforth constantly complaining of being completely done up, after any unusual exertion. He became more restless, more despondent and dissatisfied with the work of his life. Writing September 16, immediately after his recovery, he says, "My spirits are very depressed, and I am in that state in which difficulties assume large proportions. Everything worries me." For the purpose of recruiting his shattered constitution, and in obedience to the recommendation of his physician, he paid a visit to America and Canada, as soon as he could safely leave home. Instead of resting, however, he preached and lectured in several towns on the Western continent, and employed his time in writing an account of his voyage, and his impressions of America, which he communicated to the Welsh press. After his return, he threw himself with his accustomed energy to the support of a movement which was then on foot, whose object was the establishment of a university college for North Wales; and this cause owes his memory a heavy debt for the invaluable services he rendered in collecting its funds, in selecting its *locale*, and in framing its constitution. His advocacy of a system of higher education on a secular basis, exposed him to the charge of inconsistency from many of those who had previously co-operated with him in strenuously opposing a similar system of elementary education. To this charge, he offered a reply in a speech delivered in Bangor, before the members of the "Menai Literary Society," on February 12, 1883; and since those who accuse him of inconsistency, when asked to substantiate their charge, generally refer to his conduct on this question, we offer no apology for the following somewhat lengthy extract from that speech:—

"Superficial critics have supposed that it is not consistent for an opponent of secularism in the elementary schools, to be an advocate of unsectarianism in colleges. The two cases are not analogous. In the elementary schools, thousands of children are gathered together from houses in which negligent, ignorant, irreligious parents may have neither the will nor the ability to give them moral and spiritual instruction. If religious knowledge is not offered them in the schools, there are many who fear that they may never obtain it elsewhere. It seems to many of us practically impossible to make effectual provision for their religious instruction outside the school. But the difficulty that we think insuperable in the case of hundreds of thousands of children between the age of five and thirteen, does not exist in the case of a few hundreds of youths between seventeen and twenty. To exclude religious instruction from the elementary schools is, in the judgment of many of us, to endanger the religious life of coming generations. To confine the college to secular teaching, is practically compatible with the fullest security for the religious training of the students.

"I have not formed this view suddenly. Twelve

years ago, I was invited to support the Aberystwith College. I declined to do so, on the ground that it was not a national and unsectarian institution, although its promoters claimed for it those attributes. I explained the conditions under which I considered it possible to establish such an institution, in a letter published on November 25, 1870, in the *Western Mail*. I used the following words: 'All intelligent Welshmen must sympathize with the promoters of this movement, in their desire to obtain ample means of high education for the middle classes of Wales, whose comparative poverty excludes them from the advantages of Oxford and Cambridge. If it were possible to induce the various religious bodies in Wales to rebuild their colleges in one central town, Wales might hope for the advantages of a university. The lectures and examinations of the university might well be confined to strictly secular subjects, while the religious discipline and teaching in the inner life of each college would be regulated in accordance with the religious principles of the society to which it belonged. Thus the fire of religion on the domestic altar would burn unquenched. At the same time, the intellectual life of the middle classes of Wales would be quickened by the competitive culture, in one centre, of the most gifted youths of Wales—all meeting in the unsectarian lecture-rooms, and unsectarian examination-halls. Thus, gradually, the intellectual powers, now grievously wasted, would find their true exercise.' The views which I expressed twelve years ago, are the views which I endeavoured to express at the Chester Conference, in the following words of the amendment which I proposed: 'That the buildings, in order to secure the unsectarian character of the college, shall be strictly limited to the purposes of secular teaching and examination, and to housing the principal and professors, no students being permitted to reside within the walls.' This principle is enforced by the Departmental Committee (Report, page lxvii.), in their recommendation that, in the colleges, no provision be made 'at the cost of the foundation for boarding and lodging the students.'"

"Consistency is the bugbear of little minds," says Emerson. Without, however, subscribing to this somewhat cynical dogma, it is impossible to deny that, in practical life, especially in an age of endless conflicts of opinion, the alternative often lies to practical men, between incurring the charge of inconsistency and retiring into sullen isolation—between exercising a modifying, salutary influence on popular movements, and their total surrender into the hands of an opposing faction.

The private life of the Dean was simplicity itself. As a rule, he kept regular hours; he lived on plain diet, and was a most rigid total abstainer. In private conversation he was irresistibly fascinating, and communicative to a fault. Even the most diffident could not but feel at home in his company. He was fond and full of anecdotes, which he would relate with unaffected enjoyment. His abrupt and open manner, the sweet smile that played on his lips, and the indefinable charm of his presence, never failed to impress deeply those who came under his influence. He was a man of frequent and fervent prayer. He used to speak in terms of loving tenderness and appreciation of the simplicity, comprehensiveness, and sweetness of the Church's Liturgy, and he read the Morning Service in a railway carriage when travelling. His extemporary family prayers, says one who knew him well, were amongst the best things he ever heard from him. A colonial archdeacon, who had joined in family worship at the deanery, asked him for the manuscript of his prayer, and was surprised to find that it was unwritten. A gentleman whom the Dean visited during a severe and prolonged illness, asked him some questions respecting God's disciplinary chastisement of His people, and the mystery of pain and suffering. "I was somewhat disappointed," said his inquirer afterwards, "at the little help the Dean was able to give me, as we talked together; but when he knelt to pray at my bedside, I found that he had understood all my difficulties, and his prayer brought me great relief." We find from his private correspondence that his children were seldom absent from his thoughts and prayers. When he sends a birthday or a new-year's gift, he adds, "I have not forgotten to implore God's blessing to rest upon my darling." As an instance of his tender thoughtfulness, we would mention the fact that, for more than a twelvemonth after the death of his wife, he never omitted to write daily to her family, as she was in the habit of doing. His gratitude to those who showed him kindness was deep and sincere. His will, which is a perfect model of brevity and clearness, is touchingly expressive of his implicit confidence in the fidelity of those to whom he commits its administration, and the guardianship of his children. With a keen susceptibility, he enjoyed the beauties and grandeur of external nature. He used to say that the scenery around Bangor was to him the loveliest on earth, and often, when overworn with the languor and fatigue of the desk, he sought and found reinvigoration and refreshment in a ramble over the surrounding hills. And after his short but eventful day of toil and suffering, he sleeps tranquilly in his favourite spot, only a few yards from the beautiful church erected to his memory, by the munificence of one who valued his friendship, and appreciated his services to the Church and nation.

On December 20, 1883, the Dean delivered his speech against the Liberationists at the Guild Hall, Carnarvon, under the presidency of Colonel the Hon. W. Sackville West. With this, the public work of his life ended, if we except the exhaustive essay he wrote during his last voyage to the Mediterranean. The nervous depletion caused by the fever of the previous year, his persistent activities under physical exhaustion and mental depression, and the supreme effort he made in the preparation of that speech, which took nearly three hours in delivery, brought on an utter collapse of his powers. A terrible gloom spread over him, which deepened as he found himself unable to perform his work. Insomnia was the consequence, which robbed him of the rest he so imperatively needed, and cut off from him the last chance of restoring and replenishing nature's exhausted resources. "There is no fact more clearly established in the physiology of man than this," writes Dr. Forbes Winslow, "that the brain expends its energies and itself during the hours of wakefulness, and that these are recuperated during sleep. If the recuperation does not equal the expenditure, the brain withers." The Dean went on a voyage to the Mediterranean in quest of health. Even then he did not rest. He employed his mind, weighted with depression and weary with toil as it was, in writing an elaborate review of the causes that led to the failure of the Church in Wales, the suggestion of means of bringing it into harmony with the national sentiments and sympathies, and of effecting the ecclesiastical reunion of his countrymen. It illustrates his morbid craving for work, and the unflagging interest he felt to the last in the subject of this paper. But he was taxing his overworked faculties, when they were demanding complete rest. His letters during this voyage alternate between hope and despondency; but the former diminishes and the latter grows as the days pass by. Writing from Genoa, February 11, he says, "I have had a very serious illness during the last six weeks. In January, I was in great danger of paralysis, and I have to thank God's mercy for my escape. I hope (D.V.) to be fairly well, when I return in April. You imagine that the cause of my illness was mental anxiety. But it was not. I have been suffering from pure physical and nervous exhaustion, brought on by overtaxing my system during the year after the depletion caused by the fever." Writing from Ancona, February 20, he again says, "I have been and still am very, very ill. I have not much hope that I shall be equal to any work for many long months to come. I am prostrated quite in my nervous system, and can only hope that God in His mercy will give me relief in some form or other. But I must try to bear my burden patiently." In similar strains are letters of later dates, the despondency deepening till his return. "I am returning now, very little improved in health," he writes, March 19. "I sometimes feel that I shall never again be the man I have been during the last few years. But this I must leave in God's hands, and must try to bear my lot with resignation." The next two months have nothing but a record of gloom and depression, occasionally relieved with noble expressions of resignation to the Will of God, and culminating on May 24, at his brother's house at Ruabon. So ended a life which experienced the reality of Carlyle's aphorism, reminding us that "every crown is, and on earth ever will be, a crown of thorns;" and the history of whose quest after earthly bliss might well be given in the words of Houssaye, "Happiness is always the inaccessible castle, which sinks in ruins when we set foot in it"—

> " . . . a bubble on the stream,
> That, in the act of seizing, shrinks to naught."

As soon as he lifted to his thirsting lips the cup of earthly happiness, it was suddenly and inscrutably snatched away, and dashed to the ground. Domestic comforts were no sooner bestowed, than they were withdrawn; bodily health was no sooner established, than it was again ruthlessly shattered; mental depression was no sooner chased away by change of scenery, climate, or occupation, than it returned with additional malignity. The chastisements of God's hand were heavy upon him; the happiness that comes of earth, like the mirage of the desert, appeared only to vanish away at the first approach, and his experience, too, might have been sung—

> "But even while I drank the brook and ate
> The goodly apples, all these things at once
> Fell into dust, and I was left alone,
> And thirsting, in a land of sand and thorns."

We have often regretted, since his decease, that he could not be induced to indulge longer and oftener in such mental relaxation as would at the same time afford him genuine pleasure, and also divert him from the stern realities that occupied him almost without interruption, and kept his faculties at full tension. It has been observed that the mind which deals habitually with the awful problems of the Christian ministry, and dwells with concentrated reality on its practical issues, labours under an absolute necessity of a regular and complete relaxation, if it is to withstand successfully the double pressure of anxiety from within, and labour from without. The Dean seemed to have an innate antipathy to a systematic rest. Whenever he was persuaded or compelled to abandon for a time the sphere of his activity, the restlessness of his mind absolutely forbade him to enjoy the respite. Though he would change the scene, he could not be prevailed upon to lay down his harness, even for a season. True it was of him—

"Cœlum, non animum, mutant qui trans mare currunt."

He had become so inured to a life of bustling activity, that neither the dictates of reason, the advice of his physicians, nor the entreaties of friends, could persuade him to recruit nature, even when it had sunk almost to an absolute state of exhaustion. So morbid had his craving for work become, that, whether he could be tied to bodily rest by the stern mandate of his medical adviser, or allowed full freedom in the pursuit of his favourite studies and occupations, it had become only too evident, to those who intimately knew him, that his constitution was being rapidly undermined. He had so long and so persistently disregarded the faithful monitions of nature, that his frail bark had gone beyond his control. And while his noble activity and conscientiousness in the discharge of his duties furnish those who come after him with a rare example of self-dedication in the service of his Church and country, his untimely end speaks with a terrible emphasis, to warn those who may be rash enough to disregard the claims of mental and physical nature. Whether we persist in doing work whilst she is loudly clamouring for rest, or deny the regular relaxation due to her when she is faithfully and successfully discharging her functions, we are simply exhausting precious capital, and labouring to hasten on a state of confusion and derangement, which will peremptorily decline any rest save that of death and the grave.

The widespread sorrow which the news of the Dean's death evoked throughout the Principality, from men of all creeds and parties; the letters of sympathy which his family received from persons of eminence, and from public bodies in England and Wales; the tone of genuine respect and appreciation of his talents, patriotism, and services which pervaded the press of all shades of opinions; the pathetic references to the sorrowful occurrence made in the pulpits of both churches and chapels; the vast concourse of people that had come together from all parts of the country, to pay their last tribute of respect on the day of his funeral;—these are eloquent testimonies to the fact that his marked individuality, the efforts and achievements of his life, had secured for him a strong and distinguished place in the esteem and affections of his countrymen. For the moment, all criticism was suspended, controversial hostilities were forgotten; there was but one feeling predominant in the hearts of the vast multitude that followed him to the grave; there was but one sentiment on their lips—it was unfeigned sorrow at the irreparable loss which the Church and nation had sustained. As we joined the mournful procession, the mind irresistibly, and almost unconsciously, fell into recounting our gains and losses. The nation has lost in him a sincere patriot; the Welsh Church a devoted son, and her most valiant defender; the pulpit a bright ornament, and his friends one whom they loved and admired. But though they have lost him, they still love to think of him, as in private conversation he discussed, with sparkling wit and vivacity, those interesting subjects which occupied his thoughts with unwearied interest; or as he stood on the platform to plead, with chivalrous enthusiasm, the cause of the weak against the strong; or in the pulpit, as he delivered the message of the Gospel, with that wealth of illustration and metaphor, in which lay much of the secret of his power over assemblies, and the charm of his style. They will never forget his powerful, if not melodious voice, as he rang out with telling emphasis, and sometimes with overwhelming force, the eternal verities that had taken a firm grasp on his own soul. They will recall, with tender feelings, the rapid glance of his piercing eye, and the scathing irony that played on his lips, as he proceeded, with terrible earnestness, to depict and denounce the slavery of sin; or the pleasant smile that lit up his toilworn countenance, as he set forth the attractiveness of virtue, or the greatness of God's love. They will fondly call back to memory the hand that played restlessly with the eye-glass, whilst the other held the surplice with a firm grasp, indicating the severity of the strain on mind and memory, as he marshalled his arguments one by one, and with cumulative force prepared for the final attack, or the closing appeal. They will ever love to recall those manly features that never quailed before a hostile audience, while supporting an unpopular cause; how he exercised his logical acumen in analyzing the propositions, exposing the fallacies, dissecting and shattering the arguments of an opponent, with ruthless severity, and yet with perfect good-nature and self-possession; how he employed his rhetorical skill, as he prepared the way, now with generous compliments, now with candid admissions, for the final onslaught, which culminated in the complete discomfiture of an unfortunate antagonist. Yes, they have lost him; but the work he did, the words he spoke, and the man he was, will not allow the picture soon to fade from the memory. Gratitude forbids us to forget his services, wisdom his words.

Such, then, are the encouragements, such the warnings, of the career whose outlines we have ventured feebly, but lovingly and reverently, to trace. Human life is a mighty force, or rather a combination of forces, whose workings are only less mysterious to us than the inscrutable decrees of God, and whose interactions are often too subtle for our observation and analysis. As we follow its development through shadow and sunshine; as we endeavour to estimate the various influences that combine and co-operate to shape and control its destinies; as we gather together our impressions, and attempt to arrange and reduce them into a living, harmonious picture, we feel that they are, after all, but a little more than a few shadowy generalizations, drawn from the mere surface of that which we seek to portray. The living, acting, thinking essence, is hidden beneath and inaccessible; the lineaments only, and the evanescent colouring, are visible to us. Nevertheless, the words and actions of life, and its purposes, as far as they are discernible, reveal to us the strength of intellect, the depths of convictions, and the nobility of soul, which are expressive of its exalted origin; its great achievements and greater aspirations reveal to us the grateful, responsive efforts of man to cultivate and improve the gifts of God, and to give them back in faithful service to Him Who has bestowed them. Nay, in the blurs and blotches by which the picture is disfigured; in the failings and failures by which life is inevitably marred; here also we recognize the truth of God's revelation, and the essential facts of human nature—even the imperfections it inherits at its entrance into the world, as well as those it contracts in its onward passage through the dusty road of life. As we take a final survey of the record, from its commencement to its close, our gratitude is kindled for its many brilliant examples, and for the rest we are content to say—

> "Judge not! the workings of his brain,
> And of his heart, thou canst not see;
> What looks to thy dim eye a stain,
> In God's pure light may only be
> A scar brought from some well-won field,
> Where thou wouldst only faint and yield."

THE CHURCH OF THE CYMRY.

A LETTER TO THE RIGHT HON. W. E. GLADSTONE, M.P.

Carnarvon, January 22, 1870.

RIGHT HONOURABLE SIR,

I venture to address to you, as the First Minister of the Crown, the following observations upon the past history, the present state, and the future prospects of the Church in the Principality of Wales.

I feel that the recent course of public events, and the action which the representative of a Welsh constituency has announced his intention of taking in the next session of Parliament, render it unnecessary that I should trouble you with any lengthened statement of the reasons which induce me to invite your attention to the subject. It is not unknown that the religious life of the Cymric people of the Principality has for many years presented peculiar aspects. But I am profoundly convinced that the real causes which have produced in that religious life those features which call forth the regret of the well-wishers of my country, have never yet become so fully and generally known, as to reach the heart and, I will add, the conscience of the noble, generous, justice-loving people of England. It is true, in 1834 those causes were unfolded in a work which, in the fulness of its historical and statistical information, in its just appreciation of the national temperament, social conditions, and religious feelings of the Cymric people, and also in its exhaustive review of ecclesiastical patronage in Wales over a lengthened period, has left but little to be desired. A generation has passed away since that statement was made.[1]

Many of the more flagrant abuses of the Church in Wales have been swept away. But the more subtle forces hostile to the life and growth of that Church are still unremoved. The aspect under which they present themselves to-day is in many ways changed. To call your attention to the present operation of those causes, and at the same time, as far as the space of a letter will permit, to trace the effect of the same forces, as they have appeared continuously, various in different ages as to form, but ever identical in spirit, in the religious and ecclesiastical history of this ancient people down a long line of centuries, is the object which I have in view.

Now, there are but few, I think, who, knowing Wales well, can venture to doubt that accurate statistics would show that seven-tenths of the native Cymric population of Wales are alienated from the Church of their forefathers. At the same time, that Church, as existing in Wales, inherits in a large measure the spiritual forces

[1] An essay on "The Causes of Dissent in Wales," by Arthur J. Johns, Barrister-at-Law.

that have been found in all ages to exercise the most authoritative influence over the souls of men. She is strong in the undoubted inheritance of the spiritual authority of original mission to the ancient people who for more than two thousand years, with little admixture of blood or change of characteristics, have inhabited the valleys of Wales; strong in the traditional glories of that ancient British Church which, thirteen centuries ago, in the restless audacity of Pelagius on the one hand, and in the spiritual stature of her great patron saint on the other, manifested within a century evidences of the highest intellectual activity, and of the most exalted saintliness of character; strong (although the southern dioceses have been sorely despoiled) in the possession of no inconsiderable resources bequeathed by the piety of our ancestors, and in the fact (usually so conducive to the welfare of dioceses) that her benefices are for the most part in the gift of her chief pastors who have thus peculiar advantages for quickening the pulsations of Church life in their ability to recompense the merit of their clergy; strong in all the power of extending the range of her spiritual influence that belongs to the high position of national establishment; strong in her claims to the gratitude of a people who owe to the learning of the native Bishops the possession in their own language of that version of the Holy Scriptures which, in the judgment of no incompetent scholars, has been pronounced to be among the finest versions of Western Europe; strong especially in the powerful forces of reverential sentiment that attract towards her portals the hearts of an imaginative and affectionate people, whose holiest memories are linked with her history, and whose ancestry through more than fifty generations sleep beneath the shadows of her sanctuaries.

And yet, notwithstanding this august inheritance, other forces have been at work sufficient to neutralize its influence, and to alienate from her fold seven-tenths of the Cymric population of Wales so completely that they rarely seek her ministrations, rarely receive her teaching of the true and lively Word, rarely bow before the Divine Shechinah in her sanctuaries.

Whence has this grievous alienation of a deeply religious people arisen? To that inquiry I shall endeavour to give the true answer—an answer the truth of which is acknowledged by nine-tenths of the intelligent inhabitants of Wales, and which, if her clergy had not been overawed by powerful influences, would long ago have been spoken in the ears of those who are responsible for the direction of her destinies.

Can it be said that the Nonconformity of the Cymric people is attributable to their unwillingness to accept the dogmatic teaching of the Church? It cannot. There prevails among the Nonconformist societies of Wales the utmost indifference, and, I may add, ignorance concerning systems of dogmatic teaching. Their religion consists in a strong faith in rudimentary Christian morals, in the influences that flow from the ordinances of prayer and praise, in the diligent reading of the Scriptures, and in the frequent hearing of impassioned sermons which treat vaguely of the hidden spiritual life, but rarely contain any reference to objective truths. They have, as might be expected from the semi-educated character of many of their religious teachers, no knowledge of theological definitions, and consequently no convictions upon them strong enough to influence their lives, or their choice of religious systems. The various Nonconforming religious societies are regarded by the ordinary Welshman as merely rival religious seminaries having equal authority to teach, and advertising their educational programmes in the hope of securing a share of that public patronage, which is represented as having been too long the monopoly of one ancient establishment. Of the higher mysteries of sacramental grace, and of sacramental authority derived in the lineage of Apostolical Orders, from organic connection with the objective manifestation of the Divine Humanity, they have rarely any conception. Consequently, in reference to these truths, they have no strong convictions either in a negative or positive direction.

In the anarchy of unauthoritative ministrations, and in the Babel of rival sects, the average Welshman is guided very much by accidental influences in the choice of his religion. The accidents of birth, association, and locality have generally induced him to attach himself to his favourite denomination. But so free is he from the obligations of dogmatic conviction, that on migrating into a different district in which some other sect is in the ascendant, the change of place is not seldom accompanied by a change of religious profession. The Church also to some extent shares this happy immunity from the condemnation of her dogmatic principles. Her shortcomings are, it is true, not unfrequently the theme of Dissenting eloquence. But her revenues, her spiritual sterility, and the social characteristics of her clergy, are more frequently attacked than her spiritual principles. All who have had any insight into the inner life of Welsh Nonconformity, can bear unhesitating testimony that the alienation of the people from the Church is not due to any hostility to her dogmatic teaching. From the first general rise of Welsh Nonconformity in the eighteenth century, through all its variations, down to the present day, its power has been the protest of the Cymric people, not against the essential doctrines and sacraments of the Church, but against the cold, alien, mechanical forms of thought, feeling, and diction in which those doctrines have been preached, and those sacraments have been administered, to the souls of an impassioned race. That such is the case, every observer, qualified for judgment by knowledge of the people and of their language, and unbiassed by partiality towards an opposite conclusion, cannot fail to testify. That such was the case in the beginning of the eighteenth century, when the secession of the Cymric people from the Church in any considerable numbers originally began, is established by the testimony of the Rev. Griffith Jones, Rector of Llanddowror, one of the ablest and best clergymen who ever adorned the Welsh Church, of whose widespread and lasting influence upon the religious life of his country I shall hereafter write at greater length. Early in the last century he wrote these words—

"I must also do justice to the Dissenters in Wales, and will appeal for the truth of it to all competent judges, and to all those themselves who separate from us (except only such who have hardly any more charity for those they differ from than the Church of Rome), that it was not any scruple of conscience about the principles or orders of the Established Church that gave occasion to scarce one in ten of the Dissenters in this country to separate from us at first, whatever objections they may afterwards imbibe against conforming. No, Sir! they generally dissent at first for no other reason than for want of plain, practical, pressing, and zealous preaching, in a language and dialect they are able to understand; and freedom of friendly access to advise about their spiritual state. When they come (some way or other) to be pricked in their hearts for their sins, and find, perhaps, no seriousness in those about them, none to unbosom their grief to, none that will patiently hear their complaints, and deal tenderly by their souls, and dress their wounds, they flee to other people for relief, as dispossessed demoniacs will no longer frequent the tombs of the dead. For though the Church of England is allowed to be as sound and healthful a part of the Catholic Church as any in the world, yet when people are awakened from their lethargy, and begin to perceive their danger, they will not believe that there is anything in reason, law, or gospel that should oblige them to starve their souls to death for the sake of conforming, if their pastor (whose voice, perhaps, they do not know, or who resides a great way from them) will not vouchsafe to deal out unto them the Bread of Life."[1] If, then, as this testimony proves concerning the eighteenth century, and as the testimony of every unbiassed witness will prove concerning the present time, the Dissent of the Cymric people is not an intellectual revolt against the doctrines and sacraments of the Church, nor yet against the forms and ceremonies of its liturgical worship, where those doctrines are preached and worship is ordered in a manner accordant with the natural temperament of the people, in what direction are we to look for the cause of their alienation? Those causes, as I have already intimated, will be found, not in the spiritual treasures of the Church, but in the earthen vessels to which they have been committed; not in the doctrine and ritual of the Church, but in the faltering accents, and in the cold, heartless, unimpassioned forms of thought, language, and gesture in which the true and lively Word has been preached, and the sacraments and other rites and ceremonies of the Church have been, not duly and rightly administered, by an episcopate and clergy whose speech in every act of ministration within the sanctuaries of the Cymric Church bewrayeth them as the agents of a worldly policy at variance with the first dictators of that Spirit Whose mighty impulses carried the life-giving inspiration of the infinite self-sacrifice of Calvary home to the hearts of nationalities;

[1] "Welsh Piety" for 1841.

whose alien forms of thought, feeling, and action bespeak a presence vouchsafed not "in the fulness of the blessing of the Gospel of Christ," but in pursuance of an earthly policy which, instead of blessings, has breathed upon the Cymric Church the deadly breath that has left it wellnigh empty and waste, a wilderness and a desolation. To minister with authority, the heralds of the Divine self-sacrifice must not make their advent among a people as the avowed agents of the policy of selfishness.

In order fully to understand the nature of those forces which have produced this great desolation, it is necessary to review the national history of this ancient people, and to trace under different forms of national life, in different ages, the operation of the influences which on the one hand have cherished, and on the other have enfeebled, the spiritual life of the Cymric Church.

For two thousand years the Cymry of Wales, in identity of language and race, have been in possession of their poor but beautiful country. It is true that some of our more modern neighbours have sought to deprive us even of lineage and history. But fortunately these are beyond the reach of the most vigorous rapacity. In every age of their history, this ancient people have presented the same national character, identical in its genius through all the variations in the fluctuating forms of the outward life and manners. In every age of their history they have loved poetry, music, and social communion; and in every age they have submitted themselves to the supreme domination of the noblest religious ideas of the time, and have recognized in the prophet and priest of religion the highest guidance of the human life. In the first century, when the waves of Roman conquest first broke upon their shores, they displayed the same characteristics that we witness to-day. They were a brave and warlike people,— national gifts that enabled their Silurian king, Caractacus, to withstand for nine years the forces of the greatest military power of the ancient world. But they were then, as now, pre-eminently a religious people. The Druidical creed and cultus, received throughout Britain, found its most enlightened professors and its most devout votaries among the Cymry of Wales, and built its Jerusalem in the Cymric island of Anglesea. The exact nature of the ethical teaching and religious faith of the Druids can be hardly seen clearly in all its lines through the mists of antiquity. But enough is known to indicate that Druidism was among the highest of the Gentile religious systems, and retained no inconsiderable measure of the primeval truth.

Where history is silent, the ancient Cymric language speaks. In that language are found, as the fossilized forms of the intellectual life of a distant age, terms which recall many of the ethical and metaphysical ideas of the Druidical system. A scholar of some reputation has, in an elaborate essay,[1] demonstrated that these terms are in singular harmony with the terminology of that "Philosophy of the Conditioned," which finds a reception in the philosophical faith of the most reverent and not least profound thinkers of this age. In a

[1] "Gomer," by John Williams, late Archdeacon of Cardigan.

system which taught that man has in his being a trinity of natures—animal, intellectual, and spiritual—in accordance with the Pauline "body, soul, and spirit;" that man born in the consciousness of his lowest nature is destined to rise through a succession of transmigrations into the consciousness of a higher and immortal life,—by losing the image of the earthy to bear the image of the heavenly; that the most comprehensive purpose of the Creator is the good of all His creatures, and therefore His highest Name, Love; that suffering and death, by the virtue of their moral discipline, work together for man's highest good by hastening his transmigration into the higher forms of life; that, although absolute truth is not attainable by him until he shall have transmigrated through all the intermediate forms of life, man is ever bound to seek truth and hold it against the world, a doctrine extant in the old Cymric proverb, "Y gwir yn erbyn y byd;" was the system of a people who were in an eminent degree "seeking the Lord, if haply they might feel after Him, and find Him,"—a system which dimly and imperfectly revealed to human souls not a few nor the least important of those truths, which only found their perfect manifestation in the Divine-human life of Him, "in Whom are hid all the treasures of wisdom and knowledge."

What, then, was the attitude of the Cymry towards their most authoritative religious system in that age? They were its most loyal, faithful votaries. We read of no dissent from Cymric Druidism. The Romans were not tempted to thrust upon the people "alien" professors of Druidism, and its ethical teaching and religious rites were administered in a tongue "understanded of the people." The same Cymric island of Anglesea, which in this century has produced the most powerful and influential preacher of Welsh Methodism, was also the most venerated sanctuary of Druidism. In that early age the masses of my countrymen received with enthusiastic reverence the teaching of their religious instructors, and yielded themselves with loyal devotion to their guidance and inspiration. So in their political and social life to-day the Cymric people regard their religious teachers as their true and natural guides, and recognize in their counsels their highest inspiration. Events have shown that the influence of the Nonconformist preachers in our own day is great, and I am bound to express my belief that, in the main, it is based upon the grounds of instruction and moral authority.

In the day when he sought the subjugation of the warlike national spirit of the ancient Cymry, Paulinus attacked the centre of their inspiration—their religious system—but he carried out his policy wisely and well; he adopted no half-measures; he did not enfeeble the Druidical system by thrusting into its hierarchy Roman aliens. The massacre of the Druids on the shores of the Menai was the logical development of the policy that seeks to destroy the life of a nationality through the religion of its people. To-day the teacher of religion wields over the minds of the Cymry an influence as paramount as ever. For ages English rulers, in that insularity of spirit which makes them intolerant of the existence of any nationality but their own, have recognized the wisdom of Paulinus, but have not been so "thorough" in the execution of his policy. They have not massacred the religious teachers of Wales, but they have driven them out of the Church of their forefathers. Beholding the miracles which the religious influence has effected among the Cymry, they have sought to wield that influence for the destruction of the Cymric nationality, by sending into Wales alien Bishops and clergy who have enjoyed the revenues, but have not wielded the influence of the religious system. The revenues and the influence are not indissolubly united. That religious influence which finds the sources of its power in the deepest affections and national sympathies of a people, is a Divine gift which cannot be bought for money or secured by statecraft. To-day Providence, in the cry for disendowment of the Welsh Church, is dispelling the Simonian delusions of those who, in the pursuit of a selfish policy, dared to tamper with the spiritual rights of the Church, by the stern rebuke, "Thy money perish with thee, because thou hast thought that the gift of God may be purchased for money." That the alien Episcopate would perish with the revenues of the Cymric Church, is a probability upon which I think it unnecessary to enlarge.

How devout was the loyalty of the Cymric people to the influence of their native instructors, the priests and teachers of Druidism, the pages of Tacitus abundantly demonstrate. How, then, did a people, who had been so full of enthusiastic devotion to the highest form of religion previously revealed to them, subsequently bear themselves towards the earliest heralds of the perfect manifestation of the mystery of the Divine Life, which had been hid from ages and generations? The concurrence of historical records, ancient tradition, and probability leads us to the conclusion that the Name of Jesus Christ was preached among the Britons in the earliest decade of the second half of the first century; and that the progress of Christianity in supplanting the old faith was rapid and decisive. The Silurian king, Caradog (Caractacus), after his nine years' contest, was finally conquered about the year A.D. 57, and, with a large number of his more distinguished subjects, was taken captive to Rome. In the workings of overruling Providence, the Apostle of the Gentiles, present in the great imperial city, into which then ran the conflux of all nations, was with all the might of his inspired genius extending among the various classes of Roman society the knowledge of the faith. That some of the British captives, with that eagerness for the knowledge of spiritual truths which has ever marked their race, embraced the doctrines of Christianity, and became on their return the missionaries of its truths to their countrymen, seems to be fairly established.[1] The high authority of Stillingfleet and Burgess may also be quoted in support of the tradition that, on their return, they were accompanied by Aristobulus, mentioned in the sixteenth chapter of the Epistle to the Romans. This tradition is confirmed by the record in the Greek

---

[1] *Vide* "History of Wales," by Jane Williams.

martyrology that Aristobulus was ordained by St. Paul as a Bishop of the Britons. It is even said that his name in its British form survives in the Deanery of "Arwystli" in North Wales. But whether we accept these traditions and historical conjectures or not, there can be little doubt that before the close of the first century, or at an early date in the second, Christianity had made very considerable progress among the Britons. The high ethical teaching of the Druids transmitted orally by that mnemonic system of which the most ancient "Triads" are said to be remains, combined with their dogmatic assertion of the future existence of the soul, had doubtless made the ever-religious Cymric mind eagerly receptive of the tidings of the life of Him Who had "brought life and immortality to light." That the power of the Divine Kingdom had penetrated into the unconquerable recesses of Cymric independence before the close of the second century, the correspondence of Lleurwg (Lucius), King of Gwent and Morganwg, with the Bishop of Rome, as recorded by Bede, is sufficient proof, when confirmed by that sublimely terse testimony of Tertullian: "Britannorum inaccessa Romanis loca, Christo vero subdita."

During the third and fourth centuries the Church seems to have had absolute sway over the religious mind of the Cymric people, and Wales became of Christianity, as it had been of Druidism, the chosen sanctuary. The Romans, who, when the necessities of war were past, never in heathen times offered unnecessarily violence to the religious sentiments of subject races, but rather adopted their divinities, extended the same wise policy towards the Cymry as soon as they were finally conquered, and permitted the free development of the Cymric Church into the forms of life suited to its nationality. There is no trace of an alien Roman Episcopate having been forced by imperial authority upon the ancient British Church. It is possible that the scantiness of her early endowments secured to her this freedom, and enabled her, in the presence of rapacity, to sing the thankful songs of spiritual liberty in her ancient language, and in a voice free from the foreign accents of intruded ecclesiastics.

That the Cymric Church in that early age had no inconsiderable development of intellectual activity and of moral culture, is evident even to a superficial student of her history. In the economy of the Divine Providence, the wilful, self-assertive spirit of a restless subjective individualism has in various ages been a sign of intellectual movements, and its cyclical manifestations seem to recur by a hidden law through the workings of which the clearing of the ecclesiastical atmosphere, and the quickening in the grasp of a stronger consciousness of the Church's life and truth, are secured. "For there must be also heresies among you, that they which are approved may be made manifest among you." From this point of view, the Pelagian controversy, which had its origin in the subtle and daring intellect of the Cymro, Morgan, is no mean evidence of the life of the Cymric Church. The intellectual force and persuasiveness with which his opinions were asserted, had so far extended their influence throughout Christendom in the second decade of the fifth century as to call forth the controversial energies of St. Augustine, and to require for their suppression the formal condemnation of the Council of Carthage. The energy with which this great controversy was carried on for more than a century, until the Pelagian tenets, condemned at the Synod of Llanddewi Brefi in A.D. 519, were finally exploded out of the Cymric Church at the "Synod of Victory" at Caerleon in A.D. 529, is no insufficient proof of the intellectual freedom of the Cymric mind, and its activity in the sphere of theological science, in an age when the Saxons were still groping in the darkness of heathenism. The colleges of Henllan, Mochros, Caerleon ar Wysg, Llancarfan, and Caerworgan (now Lantwit Major), founded by Archbishop Dyfrig (Dubritius) in the fifth century, still in their ruins bear eloquent testimony to the thirst for intellectual culture that characterized the ancient Cymry. How little they have been permitted to gain in this respect, since their destinies have been merged in the composite national life of other races, the miserable destitution of Wales as regards the means of the higher education, and the cold repulse of her late appeals for the advantages of an university, are a painful evidence.

If the mental activity of the Cymric Church of the fifth century is evident in the misdirected subtlety of the renowned heretic whose intellectual brilliancy caused no slight perturbation in the religious atmosphere of Christendom, moral grandeur, and allegiance to the eternal supremacy of the spiritual life, are not less strikingly represented in the historic figure of her greatest Archbishop and patron saint, whose graces have cast their sweetness down the centuries. In the traditional glories of the Cymric Church under the then uninvaded primacy of St. David's, nourished by the ministrations of her native clergy, and illuminated by the influence of those ancient seats of learning whose ruins are still the most interesting scenes of Gwent and Morganwg, the Cymric Churchman of the present day thinks that he beholds the lineaments of the higher and holier forms of Church life, which the enthusiastic faith of his race (now running wild in the spiritual anarchy of religious dissensions) might, under the happier auspices of ecclesiastical truth and justice, and in the free energy of native development, have presented as a noble spiritual fabric pointing heavenwards amid the earthly tendencies of the materialistic age in which we live.

In the earlier part of the sixth century the darkness which had been casting its shadows over the closing decades of the fifth, began to thicken around the Cymric Church, and to dim the brightness of its early rising. A long period of war, tumult, and desolation was at hand; and the vision of peace and spiritual freedom that had blessed the early Christianity of Wales, was about to give place to scenes of civil servitude and ecclesiastical oppression. The Saxon invasions, and the wars destined to last over 136 years, and to result in the conquest and absorption of the Loegrian Britons of England, had begun; and although the waves of conquest submerged not the Highlands of Wales, they soon began to cast a poisonous spray over the life of the Cymric Church. The influence of the heathen grossness of the Saxons—an influence strengthened by their earthly successes—had doubtless a deadening effect upon the spiritual life of Wales. They who have lived in districts in which secular success is represented in the earthly energy of social leaders, powerful in the possession of wealth and the employment of material resources, but groping in the darkness of a godless animalism, and have watched the extent to which the withering influence of their immorality projects itself, as marked by the lowered tone and degraded tastes of the district that lies beneath their shadow, will be able to realize the debasing effects upon the life of the Cymric Church wrought by the wassail-loving brutishness of Saxon heathenism. The direct effects of this violence of Saxon warfare as witnessed in the destruction of the monastery of Bangor-is-Coed, and the massacre of its monks, were great; but it is probable that the indirect effect of those projected shadows of Saxon heathenism were even greater. Hence in the records of Gildas that period in the life of the Cymric Church is described as a time of spiritual desolation. At the same time, the testimony of that monk, who wrote in a spirit hostile to the independence of the Cymric Church, and in support of the pretensions of Augustine and of that papal usurpation which the Cymric clergy resisted with so much steadfastness, is to be interpreted in the light of our knowledge of his animus.

Very soon after his arrival for the conversion of the Saxons, Augustine sought that renowned interview with the seven Cymric Bishops, at which, with true Romish arrogance, he ignored the primacy of the British see of St. David's, and demanded submission to the authority of the Roman Church. The attitude of Augustine was also held by Laurentius his successor in the see of Canterbury, whose demands for spiritual submission the Cymry met with a firm refusal. Having thus had its origin in the beginning of the seventh century, the struggle for the primacy of the Cymric Church between the then rival sees of St. David's and Canterbury continued with varying and indecisive results until the twelfth century. The demands of Augustine and Laurentius were the first germs of that policy of ecclesiastical aggression and Episcopal intrusion, which has but too faithfully been pursued through twelve centuries, and the fruits of which are visible in the religious anarchy of Wales, and the present prostration of its ancient Church.

When we pass on to the period of the Norman conquest, we find that the same policy of subordinating the spiritual vitality of the Cymric Church to a political purpose was carried out with all the fierce energy of the Norman princes. The bishoprics, deaneries, canonries, archdeaconries, and wealthier benefices of the Cymric Church were rapidly filled by Norman ecclesiastics whose avowed mission in Wales was not to cast out the spirit of sin, but to extinguish the spirit of the Cymric nationality; not "to banish and drive away all erroneous and strange doctrines," but to use all diligence, by means of blasphemous anathemas and excommunications, in hastening the extinction of the Cymric language. The people of Wales heard these new apostles, not speaking in *their* tongue the wonderful works of God, but by a blasphemous hypocrisy trying to use the ordinances of the Church as a means for the extinction of that ancient tongue. So strenuously was this policy pursued, that in 1107 three out of the four Cymric sees were occupied by Norman ecclesiastics, while Gruffydd, Bishop of St. David's, the only Cymro upon the Episcopal Bench, was deprived of the privileges and authority pertaining to the primacy of the Cymric Church. Then, as in our day, the ministrations of aliens in language and blood were regarded by the Cymry as an outrage upon their national self-respect, and a violation of their national rights. It is recorded in the pages of Giraldus and Roger of Hoveden, that Hervey, the Norman Bishop of Bangor, could only maintain his Episcopal position by surrounding himself with a body of armed retainers to defend him against the sheep of his pasture; and that finally the popular indignation became so strong that he was compelled to resign his see, and to take refuge in England. So true was it, even in that age, that the peer must bow to the popular will—"Trech gwlad nag Arglwydd." During all this time, the object of these ecclesiastical aggressions, in the Norman as in the Saxon period, was to subjugate the Cymric Church to the authority of the see of Canterbury, and to deprive the see of St. David's of those ancient rights which had pertained to it as the oldest of the three archbishoprics created in the Roman provinces of Britain. The object was at last accomplished by a gross act of ecclesiastical jobbery. In 1115, Gruffydd, Bishop of St. David's, died, and in September of that year King Henry appointed his Chancellor, Bernard, to fill the vacant see, who was ordained priest on the 18th, and the following day consecrated Bishop of St. David's. The express object of this appointment was the introduction into the citadel of the Cymric Church of an ecclesiastical Sinon, who should facilitate its subjugation by accepting the jurisdiction of Canterbury, and subjecting the see of St. David's to the Primate of the English Church. These acts of aggression, however, though carried out by the overwhelming superiority of English power, were not borne by the Cymry with that long-suffering meekness which has characterized their demeanour under a long series of national insults in later generations. In 1237, Prince Owain ap Gruffydd ap Cynan led the men of Gwynedd in a successful attack upon the Flemish settlements in the south. The first result of that Cymric victory, and the revival of national spirit, was the instant expulsion of the Norman intruders from the bishoprics and other ecclesiastical offices in the Cymric Church. But the policy of usurpation, though checked for a time, was by no means relinquished. In 1176, the bishopric of St. David's again became vacant, and the canons of Mynyw nominated Gerald de Barri (Giraldus Cambrensis), of Cymric blood, to the vacant see; but the king, true to the vain policy of trying to crush the national spirit of Wales through its Church, obstinately refused to sanction the appointment. Finally, a Norman dignitary, Peter de Leia, was consecrated Bishop of St. David's; but after four years his Episcopate became so intolerable to the people of his diocese, that he was compelled to seek refuge in England. In 1196, Giraldus was again elected by the chapter to the bishopric of St. David's; but again the Archbishop of Canterbury refused to sanction their choice. This election of Giraldus is memorable in the annals of the Cymric Church, as having called forth from the Welsh princes a powerful and eloquent appeal to the Pope in demand of a national Episcopate, and against the intrusion of alien ecclesiastics, which for centuries has been working the ruin of their Church, from which I venture to quote the following extract:[1] "The Archbishops of Canterbury, as if it were a matter of course, send among us English Bishops, ignorant alike of both our customs and language, and who can neither preach the Word of God to the people, nor receive their confessions except through interpreters. These Bishops arriving from England, love neither ourselves nor our country; but, on the contrary, vex and persecute us with a hatred rooted and national; they seek not the good of our souls, but only aspire to rule over, and not to benefit us. For which reason they do not often labour among us in discharge of their ministerial functions, but whatever they can lay hold of, or obtain from us, whether justly or unjustly, they take away to England, and there live luxuriantly and waste-

---

[1] *Vide* "The Literature of the Cymry," by Thomas Stephens.

fully upon wealth derived from the monasteries and lands given to them by the kings of England. From thence, like the Parthians who discharge their arrows while flying, and at a distance, they excommunicate us as they are desired to do so. Whenever an expedition is preparing against us in England, the Primate of Canterbury suddenly lays under an interdict that part of the country which it is proposed to invade. Our Bishops, who are his creatures, hurl their anathemas against the people collectively, and by name against the chiefs who take up arms to lead them to the combat. So that whenever we take up arms to defend our native land against a foreign enemy, such of us as fall in battle die under ban of excommunication."

This touching appeal reveals (in addition to the outrageous wickedness of their excommunication) the inability of the alien dignitaries of the Cymric Church in that age to deal directly and personally with the sorrows and yearnings of the soul; the inability "to patiently hear the complaints" of the penitent "and deal tenderly by their souls and dress their wounds," of which Gruffydd Jones wrote in the eighteenth century. These direct ministrations of personal communion are in a peculiar degree a spiritual necessity of the Cymric temperament; and the want of them in later times, as I shall hereafter show, has had a powerful influence in alienating the people of Wales from the Church.

The Pope, however, was either unable or unwilling to afford any deliverance to the Cymric Church from the oppressions which it suffered. Fresh acts of aggression were continually repeated, in order finally to crush out of that Church, as far as possible, every recollection of its ancient independence. Every influence was employed, every opportunity was craftily seized, to accomplish this result. In 1188, Baldwin, Archbishop of Canterbury, with great pomp, made a solemn progress throughout the four Welsh dioceses, for the alleged purpose of preaching the Crusade and inciting the Cymry to enrol themselves among the soldiers of the Cross. But in addition to the object of enlisting military votaries, it is probable that the object of gaining access to all the principal Welsh churches, and celebrating Mass with solemn state in such a manner as to impress practically upon the minds of clergy and people the reality of his ecclesiastical supremacy, had no slight influence in inducing his visit. His preaching was attended with great success. That the Cymric people in that age were animated by all that religious ardour which characterized the race in Druidical times, in the early brightness of the Primitive Church, and which in all its ancient fire survives to-day in the misdirected enthusiasm of the numerous sects into which the misgovernment of the Church has divided my countrymen, is significantly demonstrated by the fact that the white Cross, as the earnest of enlistment, was accepted from the hands of an alien Archbishop by not less than three thousand Cymric warriors. Not in one day, nor in one age, did the cruel policy of ecclesiastical intrusion succeed in quenching the light of the ancient British Church, and alienating the ardent devotion of a religiously enthusiastic race. But there are manifest indications that, even in that early age, all their devotion to the Divine attributes of the Church was insufficient to enable them to regard with respect her greedy representatives, who, under the pretence of leading souls to feed upon the pastures of the Word and Sacraments, came as wolves in sheep's clothing, to batten upon the revenues that the piety of the ancient Cymric princes had bequeathed. Those who can read the pages of Ionas Athraw, Sion Cent, Lewis Glyn Cothi, Dafydd ap Gwilym, and other writers who have revealed the inner mind of the Cymry between the eleventh and the fifteenth centuries, will find that the clergy did not possess over the minds of the people that influence which a religious system in accordance with their sympathies could not have failed to exercise. It is recorded that in the twelfth century the ministrations of the Church were so unpopular, that the bards endeavoured, not without some success, to supplant her teachings by the propagation of a kind of anti-Christian natural theosophy which was virtually a revival of the old Druidic tenets. But the influence of this movement does not seem to have been of long continuance. The mighty verities and Sacraments of the Church still found in the people earnest votaries, while the alien Norman clergy were evidently the objects of general and not undeserved contempt. That paramount influence over the Cymric race, which has in every age been wielded by some recognized body of popular teachers; which in pre-Christian times was wielded by the Druids; which in the first five centuries, and more or less during the sixteenth and seventeenth centuries, seems to have been in the hand of the Church; and which is now in no small measure enjoyed by the ministers of the various Nonconforming societies, was during a lengthened period, and especially in the twelfth and thirteenth centuries, in the hands of the bards. During those times this popular class, being in the ascendant, exercised so potent an influence in arousing the national spirit of their countrymen, and in directing their policy in aggression and defence, that in order to ensure the subjugation of the country, the English monarch was compelled to resort to measures hardly less ruthless than those which his Roman prototype twelve centuries before had adopted towards their ancestors on the banks of the Menai. The cruel policy of Edward I. towards the bards is but one of the cyclical repetitions of the massacre of the Druids—a policy that survives (milder in form but identical in spirit) to-day in the efforts with which, in this money-worshipping age, all the coarse forces of social scorn, literary ridicule, and ecclesiastical aggression are seeking to destroy the inextinguishable characteristics of the ancient and undying nationality of the Cymry. That the persistent efforts of injustice are about to work out their own punishment; that Canterbury is about to suffer the penalties of its ancient injustice to St. David's,—those seers who foresee the course of ecclesiastical events in the coming years will perhaps be able to predict. That the forces which have long been dormant in the religious attitude of the Cymric people, are destined to exercise a commanding influence in shaping those events, and are at present threatening to be no slight source of weakness to the English Establishment, is certain. The influence of the religious genius of the Cymric race, crushed by long oppression, retired into its own wild fastnesses; but to-day it is rising from the tomb that recalls the epitaph, "Hic jacet Arturus rex quondam, rexque futurus"—words significant of the imperishable spirit of Cymric nationality.

As it indirectly bears upon the ecclesiastical treatment of the Cymric Church, I cannot refrain from alluding to the scornful and depreciatory language which the English press habitually applies to the literary and intellectual capacities of my countrymen—language which I regret to know has occasionally fallen from the lips of statesmen. This estimate of Cymric intellect has perhaps found its most offensive expression in the plea justificatory of English ecclesiastical intrusion, that the Cymric people does not produce men who rise to the Episcopal height of intellectual and moral stature. Hereafter I shall illustrate the motive of that assertion by evidence abundantly sufficient. I have no intention of penning a florid eulogy upon the intellectual merits of my race. But scorn unmerited provokes self-assertion otherwise unnecessary. We have no reason to complain of any judgment that has been passed upon us by learned philologists who have studied our ancient language. The language that we deprecate is that of flippant writers in the "press," whose ephemeral lucubrations would be of small importance, did they not contribute to form that public opinion to the imperial control of which our destinies in Church and State are now subject. Such an assertion as the declaration recently made in a weekly Review, that the ancient language of Wales is but a "barbarous language, more like the cries of brute beasts than the speech of reasonable men," is of course utterly unworthy of an educated writer, and unlikely to deceive an educated reader. But such declarations pass for truth among classes not powerless, and contribute to form that public opinion which rules the empire, and of which statesmen do but fulfil the dictates. We are quite willing to leave the intellectual claims of our race to the judgment of men of wide culture who have learnt our language. The wealth of that language in ethical and metaphysical terms cannot be denied,—a wealth not improbably due to the philosophical speculations of the Druids. Undoubtedly the works of Aristotle and Plato can be adequately rendered in the Cymric tongue, without borrowing many foreign words. Can that be said of the language of those who scorn my countrymen? Are not English writers compelled to express ethical and metaphysical ideas in the borrowed terms of Greece and Rome? The modern poverty of a language that only enabled the translators of the English Authorized Version to translate terms so different in significance as $\phi \upsilon \sigma \iota \kappa \upsilon \varsigma$ and $\psi \upsilon \chi \iota \kappa o \varsigma$ by the same word "natural," and which compelled them to render $\pi \nu \epsilon \upsilon \mu \alpha \tau \iota \kappa o \varsigma$ by a word of Latin origin, because their own native word "ghostly" was so stained by the earthy associations of Saxon superstition as to be incapable of expressing the highest conception of life, should silence the voice of English scorn concerning a language which is unusually rich in the capacity of expressing moral and spiritual ideas.

The English language seems to reveal the truth that the genius of the English race is more practical than spiritual, more prone to dwell upon the natural than the supernatural life, more energetic in the domain of physical than of metaphysical truth.

On the other hand, the Cymric language proves that the Cymric people for long ages, and especially in the ages when the development of their native life was unrestrained, have been a people habitually capable of grasping moral and metaphysical conceptions.

For five centuries before the oldest of modern European languages was sufficiently formed to be capable of a literature, there existed in the Cymric language a literature which, when the number of the people is considered, will be despised by none but those daily and weekly scribes who evolve their estimate of it out of their own consciousness. German scholars have within the last few years made the intellectual activity of the Cymric race, of Wales and Brittany, in the Middle Ages, a field of research. No man of Cymric blood need be ashamed of the result of their investigations. The Arthurian legends, which, by the force of the eternal truths of humanity embodied in them, gave the most powerful impulse to that awakening of the European intellect which expressed itself in the Romance Literature, are pronounced to have been the creations of the imaginative genius of the Cymric people. Those legends, as has been observed by a recent writer, are the earliest expression among modern nations of man's yearning after ideal greatness which afterwards breathed so strongly in the spirit of chivalry. Found in the earliest efforts of almost every European nation, they effected a literary conquest of the West not less complete than the religious conquest which the genius of Mohammed effected in the East. The names of the heroes, the names of places, in those legends bear testimony to their Cymric origin. Around the Cymric names, Arthur, Merlin, Caerleon, Caerdigan, Caerdual, the imagination of Cymric genius has thrown an imperishable halo. In all the literatures of Europe, Arthurian allusions are found; Shakespeare, Milton, Dryden, Parnell, Gray, all show traces; and the greatest living English poet has sought the inspiration of his muse at this fountain. I may, then, use the words of Alain de L'Isle in 1181, and ask, "Quousque Christianum pertingit imperium, quis, inquam, Arturum Britonem non Loquitur?"

The Cymric origin of these legends will also be in harmony with the experience of those minds who can take a generous view of the modern characteristics of the Cymric race. The imaginative genius of the Cymric people of Wales and Brittany between the sixth and twelfth centuries found expression in the efforts of bardic rhapsodists who created the "Mabinogion," and in them gave birth to the Arthurian legends. The same imaginative genius in this prosaic work-a-day nineteenth century finds its expression, with an imperishable identity, in the somewhat too copious effusions of the bards of the modern Eisteddfod. The ancient bardic "Session" has afforded a favourite topic for the ridicule of a press that makes Mammon a divinity, but so orders his worship as to exercise a large toleration towards the villanies of the turf and the brutalities of the prize-ring. But surely a mind of classic culture can view the Eisteddfod with other feelings than those of prosaic ridicule. He will feel in its presence as he would feel in sight of Helicon or Castalia. While the typical English "Philistine" would doubtless seek to learn the value of those classic fountains by making a chemical analysis of their waters, and, finding in them neither iron, nor sulphur, nor saline, would self-complacently pronounce them worthless, the cultivated spiritual mind takes another estimate. To the money-making nineteenth-century utilitarian, the Eisteddfod seems contemptible in the aspect of its objective homeliness. But more cultivated spirits will, at the least, regard it as the memorial that marks in the history of genius the holy place at which that fountain of Cymric imagination bursts forth, which, afterwards gathering tributary forces in the minds of every land, flowed on to fertilize and beautify the intellectual wilderness of mediæval Europe. In the recollection of their past history, it is more than the patience of a people less choleric than the Cymry could endure, to be told, when the intellectual standard of their native clergy has, by long and systematic proscription, been somewhat depressed, that they are incapable of producing men who can rise to the Episcopal stature.

After gallantly struggling for more than two hundred years against the overwhelming power of the Norman kings, Wales, on the death of Prince Llewelyn ap Gruffydd, and the capture of his brother, Prince David, was finally subjugated to the English Crown. In 1283, Edward I., true to the ancient policy of making the religion of the Cymry an instrument for ensuring their political subjection, caused that, simultaneously with his own triumphant progress as secular conqueror throughout the Principality, Archbishop Peckham should make a solemn visitation of the Cymric dioceses, and formally take ecclesiastical possession of the vanquished territory. Throughout the greater portion of the fourteenth century, the Cymry, exhausted by their long struggles and their intestine feuds, seem to have settled down into quiet submission to the authority of the English Crown. For a short time only, during the Scotch wars of Edward II., the men of Gwynedd, provoked by the tyrannous exactions of the Lord Justiciary, arose in arms under Sir Gruffydd Llwyd ; but the insurrection, being merely local, was soon quelled, and the land enjoyed comparative rest for eighty years. In 1399, on the accession of King Henry IV., began that feud between Reginald Lord Grey de Ruthin and Owain Glyndwr, which once more plunged Cymru into the miseries of sanguinary border warfare and tumultuous unrest. The English king and nobles were warned against offering provocation, by tyrannous injustice, to a chieftain whose personal qualities gave him so great an influence over the minds and hearts of his countrymen. But they despised the counsel of conciliation, and, haughtily answering that they were not "afraid of those barefooted scrubs," entailed upon themselves a harassing border warfare, which the intrepid Cymric chieftain, by dint of bravery in the field, and skilful combinations in council, maintained for sixteen years, and at its close died in his daughter's house, defiant to the last and unsubdued. During this struggle the English Parliament passed a series of laws against the people of Wales, the effects of which, as recorded in Rymer's "Fœdera," are summarized by a most accurate and painstaking writer[1] in her newly published "History of Wales." "The Parliament which met in January, 1401, passed a series of the most oppressive and cruel ordinances ever enacted against any people; prohibiting the Welsh from purchasing lands, from holding any corporate office, and from bearing arms within any city, borough, or market town; ordering that in lawsuits between an Englishman and a Welshman the former should be convicted only by the judgment of English justices, or the verdict of all the English burgesses, or by inquests of English boroughs and towns of the Lordships, in which the respective suits lay; disfranchising all English burgesses who were married to Welsh women, and forbidding Welshmen to assemble together for conference without licence from the local authorities and in their presence. No provisions or arms were to be received into Wales without special permission from the king or his council. No Welshman was allowed to have the

[1] Jane Williams (Publishers: Longman and Co.).

charge of any castle, fortress, or place of defence, even though he might be its owner, nor to execute the offices of lieutenant, justice, chancellor, treasurer, chamberlain, sheriff, steward, coroner, or any other office of trust, notwithstanding any patent or licence to the contrary. These tyrannous statutes likewise forbade Welshmen to bring up their children as scholars, or to apprentice them to any occupation within any town or borough of the realm."

It is of interest, in considering the present state of the Cymric Church, to note how, in this last struggle of the nationality for political independence, the spiritual officers of that Church were made instrumental in subduing the national spirit. The burning of the cathedral at Bangor, and of the cathedral, Episcopal palace, and canons' houses at St. Asaph, in North Wales; and the destruction in the same year (1402) of the castle of the Bishop of Llandaff, and of the house of his archdeacon in the south, were indications of the popular hatred of the Cymric people towards a system which degraded the spiritual officers of the Church into instruments for the accomplishment of a selfish earthly policy. The writ of Henry IV., addressed to Guy de Mona, Bishop of St. David's, commending to him and other English noblemen the charge of the various castles erected throughout the country to frown down the national aspirations of my countrymen, is an historical record of Episcopal subserviency to that exaggerated anti-national policy which has succeeded in alienating from their ancient Church one of the most religious of

European peoples. Before the close of the fifteenth century, a virtual change of dynasty brought with it to the Cymric people the dawn of happier days, in the accession of a sovereign whose rise was the resurrection of Cymric kingship. On August 22, 1485, on the field of Bosworth, through the valour of his Cymric levies, aided by the timely defection of the Stanleys, the grandson of Owain ap Maredudd ap Tewdwr ascended the throne of England, and became the founder of a dynasty not the least distinguished in English annals for intellectual capacity and imperial strength of will. For several centuries the Cymric people and the Cymric Church had been subjected to political treatment, the cruel injustice and the short-sighted oppressiveness of which the most judicial of English historians has thus described: "As to the Welsh frontier, it was constantly almost in a state of war, which a very little good sense and benevolence in any one of our shepherds would have easily prevented by admitting the conquered people to partake in equal privileges with their fellow-subjects. Instead of this, they satisfied themselves with aggravating the mischief by granting legal reprisals upon Englishmen."

During the reigns of the Tudor princes, the Cymric people for the first time began to experience in the affairs of the Church and State some taste of that "fair play" of which Englishmen are always boasting, in language that amounts to something like national cant, but which they have by no means always exhibited in their appreciation of the natural rights and sensitive national feelings of the Celtic races who have been united to their destiny. That the Cymric people in the sixteenth century, under fair and generous treatment, evinced that same order-loving loyalty which marks them in these days, may be gathered from the testimony of Sir Henry Sidney, then Lord President of Wales, who, in a letter to Sir Francis Walsingham, dated March 1, 1583, speaks of his presidency as his "great and high office in Wales,[1] a happy place of government; for a better people to govern, or better subjects, Europe holdeth not."

At this period a mighty force called into existence, in the moral and spiritual life of the nation by the invention of the art of printing, was beginning to produce powerful effects. Through that force and the consequent multiplication of books, the masses were gradually growing up into full possession of those treasures of the written Word, which in previous ages had been dealt out to them by the then monopolists of learning, their "tutors and governors" in the Church. That new force gradually led to the reconstruction in its outward aspects of the Church in this land. In the previous generations the clergy had been engaged as priests in the administration of the Sacraments and other rites and ceremonies of the Church more conspicuously than as prophets or public teachers in the preaching of the Word. The multiplication of the Scriptures wrought gradually in the sixteenth century a mighty change by

---

[1] *Vide* Churchyard's testimony to the integrity of the Welsh of the sixteenth century.

which the prophetical office became so prominent as to obscure the functions of the priestly office, by which the Sacraments were almost forgotten in the absorbing study of the newly opened Word, by which the pulpit became so enlarged in the reformation of the Christian temple as partially to exclude from view the eternal witness of the Altar. In our own day we are beholding a reaction the force of which, while it dims no single ray of the enlightenment diffused by the opening of the written Word, promises, when the wine of a new religious movement shall have passed through its period of fermentation, to exhibit gladdening results in a nobler, fuller, higher Church life, by unveiling to this generation the long-hidden soul-subduing glory of the Shechinah of the Altar, and multiplying once more the Divine Bread of sacramental grace. In the times of the world the darkest hour precedes each new dawn. In the generation immediately preceding the new light of the Reformation, the religious state of the Cymric people seems to have been devoid of intelligence and low in moral tone. A celebrated enthusiast of the period, John ap Henry or John Penry (who suffered in Smithfield), in "His Exhortation unto the people and Governours of Her Majesty's people in Wales," speaks of the same people, whom Sir Henry Sidney at the same time was eulogizing as second to none in Europe, as sunk in grossest ignorance and barbarous irreligion. But his exaggerated language must be received with a due allowance for the extravagance that characterized the utterances of the Puritan preachers, whose minds, coming into the new light of the written Word after the darkness of ages, seem to have been unable to bear its brightness, and to have been excited into a mania of enthusiasm that disturbed the balance of the moral judgment, and caused them in their vituperations to lose sight of charity, and in their fierce callings down of fire from heaven to forget what manner of spirit they were of. A sour-minded Puritan, recognizing no truth save in his own interpretations of the written Word, hearing no music save in the repetition of his own shibboleth, and seeing no beauty or comeliness that he could desire except in the reflection of his own morbid mental and emotional states, would in our own age, while fixing his eye exclusively upon the drunkenness, worldliness, and scepticism that are its worst features, doubtless be able to write in terms equally bitter and sweeping of its low estate. But such men are the caricaturists—the weeping, not the laughing, caricaturists—of their times. The Cymric Church, which in that age produced, among its laymen, Sir John Pryce, of Brecon, who first translated into Welsh the Lord's Prayer, Decalogue, and Creed; William Salesbury, who produced the first Welsh translation of the Psalms and Gospels and Epistles (as used in the Communion Office), and afterwards of the entire New Testament; and Rowland Heylin, and Sir Thomas Middleton, who in 1630 published the portable Welsh Bible for private use among their countrymen; and on the other hand, among its native clergy, such men as Bishop Morgan, who in 1588 completed a translation of the entire Bible from the Hebrew and Greek; and Bishop Parry, who in 1620 revised it as it now exists —one of the noblest versions in any living language; and Vicar Prichard, who will ever be remembered as the author of that volume of sacred poetry, "The Welshman's Candle," which for generations, side by side with the Holy Volume, has been found on the humble book-shelf of almost every Welsh cottage,— could not have been in that miserable state described in the exaggerated caricatures of Puritan fanatics— caricatures which their more designing successors in our own day find it profitable to reproduce for the purpose of strengthening the anti-Church prejudices of the ignorant.

One of the most important consequences of the Reformation, in its bearing upon the Cymric Church, was that for a time it rendered it impossible for the Government to appoint to the Cymric sees alien Bishops ignorant of the native language. If the desire had existed (which did not exist in the Tudor times) to remind the Cymry, through the Church, of their national subjection, it would have been difficult, in an age when the translation and exposition of the Scriptures was so prominent a work, to have appointed to the Cymric dioceses dignitaries contemptuously ignorant of the Cymric language. It is probable that to these requirements of the time, combined with the Cymric sympathies of the Tudor dynasty, the Welsh Church owed the temporary removal during a hundred and fifty-six years of that unfair proscription which before and since has persistently excluded men of the Cymric race from the Episcopal Bench. In the period between 1558 and 1715, forty-three native Welshmen rose to Episcopal thrones, and seven more men of Cymric blood.[1] During

[1] The following list of the forty-three prelates of Cymric blood and birth, raised to the bench between 1558 and 1774, is due to the antiquarian research of the late Rev. — Jenkins, of Kerry, and placed by his representatives at the disposal of the learned author of the essay on "The Causes of Dissent in Wales."

	NAME.	SEE.	BIRTHPLACE.	DATE OF DEATH.
1.	Thomas Gray	St. David's and York	Pembrokeshire	1568
2.	Richard Davies	Bangor	Denbighshire	1581
3.	Rowland Meyrick	Bangor	Anglesey	1565
4.	Nicholas Robinson	Bangor	Carnarvonshire	1584
5.	Thomas Davies	St. Asaph	Carnarvonshire	1573
6.	Marmaduke Middleton	Lismore and St. David's	Cardiganshire	1592
7.	William Hughes	St. Asaph	Carnarvonshire	1600
8.	William Morgan	Llandaff and St. Asaph	Carnarvonshire	—
9.	Richard Parry	St. Asaph	Denbighshire	1623
10.	R. Vaughan	Bangor, Chester, and London	Carnarvonshire	—
11.	Henry Rowland	Bangor	Anglesey	1616
12.	Lewis Bailey	Bangor	Carmarthenshire	1631
13.	David Dolben	Bangor	Denbighshire	1633
14.	Edmund Griffiths	Bangor	Carnarvonshire	1637
15.	Hugh Jones	Llandaff		1574
16.	William Blethin			1590
17.	Morgan Owen		Carmarthen	1644
18.	Hugh Lloyd	Llandaff	Cardiganshire	1667
19.	Francis Davies	Llandaff	Glamorganshire	1674
20.	Godfrey Goodman	Gloucester	Denbighshire	1655
21.	John Williams	Lincoln and York	Carnarvonshire	1650
22.	Thomas Howell	Bristol	Carmarthenshire	1646
23.	George Griffiths	St. Asaph	Carnarvonshire	1666
24.	Robert Morgan	Bangor	Montgomeryshire	1673
25.	Humphrey Lloyd	Bangor	Merionethshire	1688
26.	Humphry Humphrys	Bangor and Hereford	Carnarvonshire	1712

The Church of the Cymry. 135

the subsequent hundred and fifty-five years, on the contrary, hardly a single Welshman has been permitted to rise to the Episcopal dignity. To what is this exclusion attributable? Are we to be told that the native ability which claimed elevation so frequently between 1558 and 1714, has never manifested itself between 1714 and 1869? The contrast establishes unmistakable proof of a deliberately continued proscription, which has produced a most depressing effect upon the moral and intellectual calibre of the native clergy, and which in its duration has been most

27.	John Evans	Bangor and Meath		—
28.	John Lloyd	St. David's	Carmarthenshire	1687
29.	Edward Jones	St. Asaph	Montgomeryshire	1703
30.	John Wynne	St. Asaph	Flintshire	1712
31.	Lancelot Bulkely	Dublin	Anglesey	1650
32.	Griffith Williams	Ossory	Carnarvonshire	1671
33.	Lewis Jones	Killaloe	Merionethshire	1646
34.	Richard Meredith	Ferns and Leighlin		1597
35.	Robert Price	Ferns and Leighlin	Merionethshire	1665
36.	John Salesbury	Man	Denbighshire	1573
37.	John Meyrick	Man	Anglesey	1599
38.	George Lloyd	Man and Chester	Carnarvonshire	1615
39.	John Phillips	Man and Chester (translator of Bible into Manx)	Anglesey	1663
40.	Hugh Bellot	Bangor and Chester	Denbighshire	—
41.	W. Lloyd	Llandaff, Peterbro', and Norwich	Merionethshire	1709
42.	W. Glyn	Bangor	Carnarvonshire	—
43.	Maurice Griffith	Rochester	Carnarvonshire	—

Seven other prelates of Cymric race and name, though born in England, died between 1685 and 1717, amongst whom was William Lloyd, of St. Asaph, one of the seven Bishops sent to the Tower.

significantly coeval with the growth of Cymric Nonconformity.

In the seventeenth century the religious state of the Cymric Church was for a time disturbed by the commotions of the revolutionary period. In 1650, special commissioners were appointed to investigate its condition, and to reform it upon the Puritan model. These commissioners ejected from their benefices a large number of the Royalist clergy, and proceeded to realize the Puritan ideal of the perfect Church, by making priests of the lowest of the people, and promoting to the vacant benefices the noisy village theologians who happened to be gifted with the power of vociferous exhortation. Their efforts, however, did not leave any very lasting impress on the Cymric Church, and at the restoration of the monarchy, in 1660, the desirability of recognizing knowledge in addition to zeal, as a qualification for the ministry of the Church, was once more admitted.

At an earlier date in the century a Puritan clergyman, named Wroth, a man of some earnestness and ability, was ejected from his benefice for disobeying the commands of his Ordinary, and became the original founder of Nonconformity in Wales. His modern successors have striven without success to prove that he was ejected not so much for irregularity as for excess of religious zeal. It is worthy of remark that a far abler and more distinguished man (to whom I have already alluded), Rhys Prichard, Vicar of Llandovery, and author of a volume of poetry that will bear comparison with the very best efforts of George Herbert, evinced zeal as great in the cause of religious revival, and exercised a far wider religious influence than Wroth and his Puritan brethren, and yet died a dignitary of the Church, and so much venerated that Bishop Bull expressed a desire to be buried by his side. That Wroth and his Puritan fellows were infected with the licentious spirit of religious disorder so prevalent in their times, and had no cause to complain of the treatment they received, may be inferred from the fact that the Nonconformity of which they became the founders, representing no force but the disorderly tendencies of a few earnest enthusiasts, made no progress for two generations. In 1700, the Nonconforming religious societies of Wales were few in number, and contemptible in influence. At that date the total number of meeting-houses throughout Wales was but thirty-six.[1] During the preceding hundred and fifty years, that had witnessed the fierce growth of Puritanism, which for a time despoiled the Church and overthrew the throne, the Cymric Church, then mainly ruled by native Bishops, had weathered the storm and retained the affections of the people. At the beginning of the eighteenth century Welsh Dissent was not only insignificant in its extent, but very low in its spiritual vitality —a proof that independent religious societies enjoy no immunity from those periods of depression that seem to recur cyclically in all the spheres of human energy.

During a period of religious deadness and indifference, it is quite possible that even under an alien Episcopate

[1] *Vide* "History of Nonconformity in Wales," by Thomas Rees.

the Church of Wales might have been so ruled as to retain the nominal allegiance of the people. In calm weather, under the government of an unqualified pilot, whose experience is scanty, eye untrue, hand unsteady, a vessel *may escape* wreck. But when the sleeping winds and calm waves have been awakened out of their repose, the wreck of the vessel, followed by the tossing hither and thither of her disorganized fragments, will show the nature of his pilotage. In the eighteenth century such a change was about to disturb the surface of religious indifferentism in Wales. In the annals of the Cymric Church, the year 1709 is made memorable by the ordination of Gruffydd Jones, afterwards Rector of Llandowror, in Carmarthenshire. This remarkable man was, in the order of Providence, destined to call into action new forces in the religious state of the entire Principality. Now, the calling forth of new religious forces is always ordained for "the fall and rising of many"—for the bursting of the old bottles, and the adaptation of new forms of religious habit capable of giving expression to the energies of the quickened spiritual vitality. To subject the machinery of an engine, defective in construction, to the pressure of increased steam by the addition of more stimulating fuel, will end in its disruption. The same addition of power in an engine of true construction, would only give to it the propulsion of a nobler and more rapid advancement. The first of these similes must be employed to illustrate the state of the Cymric Church, under the guidance of an ineffective alien Episcopate, during the years of that eighteenth century which witnessed so remarkable a revival of religious light and warmth among the people of Wales. The close of the seventeenth century left them devoid of the means of education, unable to read, and therefore excluded from that fountain of light which, in the study of the newly opened Scriptures, had begun to diffuse its rays.

At an early date in the eighteenth century, Gruffydd Jones, who was marked by the intense religious fervour of his race, and by a high degree of intellectual power, looked abroad, with the eye of a patriot, upon the religious and social state of his countrymen. He found that, notwithstanding all their earnestness, his ministrations produced no quickening, enlightening effect. His experience taught him soon that mere preaching, however eloquent and forcible, conveys to peasant minds but vague notions, which produce no fruits; that the seed of the Word, falling on the uneducated mind, falls on the hardened surface of the wayside, to be quickly swallowed up by the absorbing influences of the lower animal life. In the light of this experience he adopted a system of catechetical instruction; and at this day several of the admirable manuals upon the Lord's Prayer, Decalogue, and the Creed, of which he became the author, are extensively used in the Principality. But this was not his greatest work. Finding that his countrymen were unable to read the Holy Scriptures in their own language, he established by his own energy, without the aid of the Bishops and dignitaries of his day, a system of circulating schools.

According to this system (a remnant of which still survives in the Welsh Bevan Schools), a school was maintained in one parish for a period of six months, and then opened for a like period in another parish destitute of educational means. This educational system, founded and maintained by the unaided energy of a simple Welsh clergyman, numbered at one time 200 schools, which contained an aggregate of 8687 contemporary scholars. It is recorded, on unquestionable authority, that within a period of twenty-four years no less than 150,212 of his countrymen (constituting more than a fourth of the then population of Wales) were taught to read the Scriptures in their native Cymric language, in these schools established and maintained by the unaided exertions of this native Cymric clergyman—one of a body who are incapable of developing such intellectual and administrative power, we are told, as have adorned the Episcopal Bench in the Welsh Church during the 150 years of its decline! Few men, in any age or country, in so humble a position, have exercised a nobler or a wider influence. Few teachers and philanthropists have passed away into eternity cheered by the review of richer results of their life-work, than the absolute certainty of having exercised an enlightening and ennobling influence upon more than fifteen myriads of souls.

The increase of knowledge was accompanied by an increased warmth of religious zeal, expressing itself in a greater hunger for ministrations of religion. These effects are recorded in numberless letters of thankfulness, addressed to Gruffydd Jones by the clergy from different districts of Wales. An extract from a letter written by the Rev. P. Thomas, curate of the large parish of Gelligaer, will show the nature of results that were general: "Our Churches in general in this neighbourhood are now near as full again of auditors as they used to be before the Welsh Charity Schools circulated about the country. Their ministers endeavoured before, both by fair and rough means, to bring the people under the droppings of the sanctuary, but all in vain; but now (blessed be God) our solemn assemblies are thronged."

Throughout Wales in that generation there was a rapid diffusion of religious knowledge, calling into action new and strong spiritual forces in the awakened zeal and earnestness of the ever-religious Cymric people. Those forces could not have been quelled save by the extermination of the people. They were destined to seek expression in objective forms of religious habit. That was the time when native Bishops, able to take a true view of their dioceses—ἐπισκόποι in power as well as in name, "seers" taking the spiritual oversight as well as enjoying the material revenues of their "sees," having native sympathy with the fervour and zeal of the Cymric religious temperament—would have been able so to order, renew, and enlarge the Church's machinery, as to comprehend within her organization those newly evoked spiritual forces, which, under the mechanical, inelastic, routine government of Bishops alien in language and feeling, and not seldom absent in body, burst the Church's bounds, and are now threatening to return with Volscian allies to work her grievous ruin.

Those blind "seers" were not left without warning. The man who had the zeal and energy to call forth the forces of religious revival (the true Cymric Archbishop of his time) had also the genius to foresee the conditions essential to their healthy and regular action. His recorded words are these: "The poor have now in many places a stirring among them; they have a thirst for knowledge, and if they have it not in the Church, they will turn about and apply to some others. To refuse the necessary means of instruction would tempt them to look upon it as a step towards reducing them again under the yoke of bondage, which their forefathers had been some time subject to in former days,—or as the foreboding of threatening popish darkness."

When these dormant forces had been extended throughout Wales by the schools and catechetical instruction of Gruffydd Jones, awakening the spiritual yearnings of an ever-religious people, the men who were destined to fire the train, and to give expression to their ardent religious emotions, were not long wanting. The hour was come when a more earnest religious life was to be quickened in Wales, and the men appeared. In 1735, Howell Harris, a layman who had been educated for the ministry of the Church, began to preach in his own neighbourhood, and after a time to visit other districts throughout Wales, in which large concourses of people assembled to hear the appeals of his impassioned eloquence. With a voice terrible in its religious earnestness, from lips touched by the live coal off the altar of supreme self-sacrifice, that sounded like an echo of the Hebrew prophets or the Baptist's cry, he called his countrymen out of the lethargy of sensuality and worldliness into the consciousness of that eternal spiritual life, in the communion of which alone man can find the final rest of his being. The effect of his preaching was very great. It attracted the eager attention of thousands of his countrymen; and in whatever district he appeared, there "went out to him all the region round about."

About the same date, a man still more remarkably gifted with the attributes of the prophetical office appeared, in the person of Daniel Rowlands, a clergyman of the Church. Rarely, if ever, in modern times, has there appeared a preacher of greater power, if power is to be estimated by its effect in arousing the soul to a consciousness of the frailty of the lower natural life, "of the earth, earthy," and to an overwhelming conviction of the supreme importance of the eternal spiritual life manifested in the Divine-Humanity of Him Who is "the Lord from Heaven." Whitefield and Wesley attracted no greater crowds. In a remote village of Cardiganshire, again and again on special occasions, did twenty thousand people, many of whom came from districts distant several days' journey, assemble to hear his preaching.

These two men became the founders of Welsh Methodism. In order to extend the revival of religious earnestness among their countrymen, they trained a large number of lay-preachers, called "cynghorwyr," *i.e.* exhorters, who itinerated throughout the country delivering addresses, not essentially different from those appeals which congregations in London have lately heard from the lips of earnest clergymen. The effects of this prophetic movement were great, rapid, and widespread. What was the attitude of the alien Bishops? Utterly unable to sympathize with the *un-English* Celtic fervour of the Cymric people, unable to appreciate the necessity of satisfying the spiritual hunger of their souls by more frequent preaching of the true and lively Word, and more faithful ministration of the Bread of Life, the Bishops and their several retinues of "alien" clergy frowned upon the movement, and ultimately expelled from their positions in the Church, Rowlands and other clergymen who had joined it.

At the same time, it must not be forgotten that the avowed object of Harris and Rowlands was not to create a schismatical society, but to produce a revival of religious life within the communion of the Church. To the end of their days they retained feelings of affectionate loyalty to the Church, which inherits the Divinely given inalienable rights of original mission to the people of this land. The dying request of Harris was that he should be buried in the chancel of Talgarth parish church, beneath the spot on which he stood when he first realized the consciousness of intense faith in that Life which he sought to reveal to others. Among the last words of which there is authentic record, uttered by Daniel Rowlands on his death-bed, were these: "True religion has begun in the Church, and into the Church it will ere long return."

The lasting influence which these two men produced upon the religious mind of their country was great, but not comparable either in value or extent to the influence which Gruffydd Jones, without forfeiting his position in the Church by ignoring Episcopal authority, exerted in the work I have already described. His influence, in its calm self-restraint and subjection to authority, was nobler and higher than the excitement of the self-deceiving enthusiasm, which degenerated into the assertion of a lawless spiritual individualism. As the educator of his countrymen, and as the preacher whose earnest appeal, in the church of Llanddewi-Brefi, first called Rowlands himself out of a life of irreligion, Gruffydd Jones must be regarded as the creator of the religious movement which Harris and Rowlands afterwards directed, and which they will hardly escape the charge of having in some degree misdirected. That they exerted an immediate influence for good, no unbiassed mind can deny. That their influence was unmixed with evil pregnant of fatal after-results, and unstained by the taint of earthly self-assertion, no calm judgment will pronounce.

Sixteen years had not elapsed after the date of their first preaching, before those features of schismatic religious energy, which contains the seeds of its ultimate dissolution in the irresistible tendency to further schismatical subdivisions, began to appear. In 1751 a bitter feud arose among their followers. For twenty years they were internally divided into sections bitterly hostile, who were known as "Rowlands' people" and "Harris' people." The "carnal" element in Nonconforming religiosity—viz. its invariable self-assertiveness, that ultimately leads its votaries to repeat in various forms the tendencies of the Corinthian schismatics, who called down upon themselves the stern Apostolic rebuke, by calling themselves "Paul's people," and "Apollos' people"—appeared among my fervid countrymen (whose temperament has such especial need of the sobering influence of healthy Church authority) in virulent strength. It can hardly be doubted that the experience of these self-destructive tendencies in the spiritual life of their followers enabled Harris and Rowlands to realize in Church authority the Divinely appointed guardianship of unity—a realization which found expression in their last and most solemn moments.

Early in the history of Welsh Methodism there also appeared no slight symptoms of that impatience of the supernatural, and that tendency to lose all vital grasp of the living verities (the realization of which ever accompanies full conception of the central truth of the Incarnation), which sooner or later develops itself in all religious societies; that, denying the spiritual authority of Apostolical Orders, and cutting themselves off from the communion of the Church, lose sight of the truths of sacramental doctrine, and the spiritual food (essential to the highest development of spiritual life) of sacramental grace. In 1771 the sect was openly divided into Arians and Calvinists. Fortunately the Church, in her Creeds, Formularies, and ministrations, although causes entirely untheological have alienated the Cymric masses for a time from her fold, still bears to the verities of the Incarnation a testimony sufficiently influential to restrain the spread of Arianism, which now, in Wales, exists overtly only in the very insignificant sect of the Welsh Unitarians. Thus the candlestick of the Church, although grievously impaired by the worldly policy of her rulers, still retains its doctrinal stability (unlike the movable tapers of schismatic teaching), and "giveth light unto all that are in the house." That the great body of Welsh Nonconformists (inheriting the restless subtlety of Pelagius) still retain an implicit faith in the doctrines of the Incarnation, to the explicit denial of which their rejection of Apostolical Orders and sacramental truth logically leads, is undoubtedly due to the traditions of truth, which eighty years have not sufficed to intermit, and still more to the indirect influence of the Church's central light, which has never failed, although her earthen vessels have often been grievously defiled and marred by worldliness, to present in them, through the Formularies, Creeds, and Sacraments, the essential treasures of the primitive faith.

I must briefly notice the work of one of the most remarkable men that have influenced the later life of Methodism in Wales. Thomas Charles, a graduate of Oxford, educated to Holy Orders, unable to distinguish the eternal life of the Church that underlies the frail forms in which it is presented on earth, unable to see the spiritual life of the Church, except as embodied in ministers then often carnal and worldly, joined the Methodist Society. He will be long remembered with reverence in Wales as the founder of the Methodist Sunday schools, which have imparted much scriptural knowledge, and in which the strength of the Methodist system, while devoid of Orders and Sacraments, mainly consists. In a larger circle he will be known as the original mover in the formation of the British and Foreign Bible Society.

What was the attitude during this time of the Bishops towards these earnest, if mistaken men, and the work which they were doing? They failed to recognize in it any elements of truth and good. They attributed (with the miserable narrowness of those who of old sat in the chair of authority and monopolized the keys of knowledge) to the evil spirit of disorder not only the divisions they threatened, but also the undeniable good which they effected. Some of these Bishops were personally good and earnest men. Others were like that notorious prelate (the Bishop of Bangor) who for seven years never once entered the diocese. But all of them, alike aliens in language and feeling, were incapable of dealing with the difficulties of the crisis. Religious forces that might have given a noble spiritual vitality to the Church, revived the warmth of its early love under the primacy of Dewi, and exalted, in the power of a living organic religious unity, the whole character of my countrymen, were lost to the Church, and suffered to expend themselves in the wild gyrations of endless schismatic divisions and subdivisions. It is difficult to resist a conviction that Bishops of Cymric blood and temperament, having that mysterious power of sympathy which identity of race alone can give, partaking in some degree of that truly national fervour which characterized the Methodist leaders and their followers, might have developed a policy of conciliation that would have retained Methodism within the communion of the Church, and saved my country from the social strife and envying, the sectarian bitterness and hatred, that now poison its moral atmosphere.

Even as it was, the influence of the Episcopal office long retained its hold upon the minds of the masses. In 1739, at Machynlleth, and in 1741, at Bala (now two strongholds of anti-Church feeling), this influence subjected Harris to threats of personal violence, as a schismatic transgressing Church order. So strong was the traditional influence of Church order and authority over the minds of the Methodists themselves, that for sixty-eight years they steadfastly resisted every temptation to secede from her Communion, and never entertained a thought about the possibility of the Blessed Sacrament being validly consecrated by the hands of ministers not authoritatively ordained to the functions of the priesthood. Had the Bishops of the Church possessed enough knowledge of, and sympathy with, the fervid religious feeling of this society to discern the signs of the times, the danger of the grievous schism might have been averted.

During the first decade of the present century, when Harris and Rowlands, and the clergy who had originally led the movement, were dead, the lay-preachers, or "cynghorwyr," began to exhibit a more definitely schismatical spirit, to clamour for formal secession from the Church, and to assume authority to consecrate the Sacrament. The proposal, first openly made at one of the Associations or Quarterly Assemblies of the Methodist congregations, was received with a feeling akin to horror, and the ambitious descendant of Korah was ordered by the chairman to leave the assembly. But after a long agitation the "cynghorwyr," in 1811, succeeded in carrying the Methodist Society into a schismatical position by a vote ordering that lay-preachers should be permitted to consecrate the Sacrament. Since that date the greater number of the Welsh Methodists have continued to deprive themselves of sacramental order, and to feed their souls upon a religious rite, which, unconsciously testifying to the truth, they describe as having no validity except as a commemorative ceremony and a badge of membership. There are few Welshmen who believe that this fatal catastrophe in the religious history of my countrymen would have happened if the Cymric Church had been ruled by native Bishops. The grave responsibility must, therefore, rest in no slight degree upon those statesmen who insisted upon appointing to the Cymric sees prelates unqualified for the discharge of their spiritual functions, and whose political mission has egregiously failed.

It is true that English Bishops in England adopted a policy equally fatal in dealing with the founder of English Methodism. But surely it is no slight confirmation of the view I have enunciated, that the head-quarters of English Methodism are also found among the *Celtic* population of Cornwall, long subjected to the Episcopal supervision of the virtually alien Bishops of Exeter. If, therefore, a bishopric of Cornwall is to be founded, as an earnest Churchman I will venture to express a hope that, upon the same principle, the application of which I claim to Wales, a man of Cornish race and temperament may be appointed to guide the religious life of our kinsmen.

During the last fifty years, that schismatic spirit which led to the secession of the Methodists has been acting as a powerful solvent upon all the larger fragments of religious unity in Wales. At the present time my countrymen are divided into a greater number of sects than I am able to enumerate. Calvinistic Methodists, Wesleyan Methodists, Baptists, Lesser Baptists, Independents, Unitarians, Primitive Methodists, and even, I regret to add, Mormons, have a share in the religious allegiance of the people. That there is, however, a spirit beginning to move upon the chaotic surface of this religious anarchy—a spirit destined, under favourable circumstances, to give form and beauty to Cymric religious life by the development of a strong Church revival, is the conviction of many thoughtful far-seeing men. An earnest Cymric Churchman can hardly fail to weep in spirit over the present religious aspect of his ancient country. Its people are torn by the evil spirit of internecine division into hostile jealous sections. In making a common assault upon the Church, these sections find it mutually convenient to affect a belief in the existence among them of a unity of spirit underlying the endless variety of their organic forms. The existence of such a unity is imaginary. The religious aspect of Wales to-day cannot be more clearly illustrated than by recalling its political aspect in the twelfth and thirteenth centuries. On a few great occasions, in the prospect of an English invasion, the Princes of Gwynedd, Powys, Dyfed, Gwent, and Morganwg managed for a few weeks to unite their forces. But no sooner was the object of their common hostility withdrawn, than those fierce chieftains devoted their warlike prowess with equal energy to the destruction of each other, and the devastation of their common country. That such is the result of Cymric schisms to-day, having no bond of union save in destructive hostility towards the Church, and devastating the nobler moral beauties, and laying waste the higher fruits of the Spirit, no one who knows the inner life of Wales can deny. True to the history of their race, my countrymen still display strong religious yearnings and great intellectual activity. They circulate in the native language nine weekly papers, eighteen monthly magazines, and two quarterlies, the majority of which are almost exclusively read by the working classes. But it is no exaggeration to state that these papers, although professedly religious organs, are, with a few honourable exceptions, printed in the gall of sectarian bitterness, and that their special mission at the present time is to endeavour, under very discouraging circumstances, to stir up a spasmodic agitation for the disestablishment and disendowment of the ancient Church, to which, for seventeen centuries, my country owed its knowledge of Christianity. To perpetuate a policy that makes the removal of the Church's candlestick, by the destruction of her material organization, even a distant possibility, involves a grave responsibility. If the mission of the Church of Christ is to restore man to the image and likeness of God's countenance, and if unity be one feature in that eternal countenance, then it follows that a people who have lost well-nigh all moral consciousness of the obligations of religious unity, have, notwithstanding their Bible-reading, one of the rudimentary lessons of religious truth yet to learn. At present the universal visible unity of Christendom seems as far removed from the region of possibility as that universal international peace for which the Peace Society expresses its aspiration. But both these unities are revealed ideals destined to be realized in the future of humanity. The distance of that realization does not lessen the necessity laid upon each individual of striving, as far as in him lies, to hasten its fulfilment. The distance of the unity of Christendom no more justifies the individual in habits of schism, than the distance of universal peace justifies the individual in disregarding the obligations that flow from the ideal, by breaking the peace of his neighbourhood.

That the schism, finally consummated in 1811, has had an injurious effect upon the spiritual life of the Calvinistic Methodist Society (the most numerous of the Welsh Nonconforming societies), although it has not as yet greatly lessened the number of its adherents, can hardly be doubted by an unbiassed observer. The prevailing tone of the Methodist congregations is less distinctively religious and more political than in the past generation. Twenty years ago no announcement of a religious meeting failed to attract a large assemblage. Now, throughout the Welsh towns, the annual meetings of the Bible Society (proud as the Methodists are of its Welsh origin) are attended by scanty numbers; harangues upon some social or political grievances have a far greater fascination. This is one of many symptoms indicative of the fact that the simple, fervent, unworldly piety of the original Methodists has given place, in some measure, to the partisan zeal of a jealous sectarianism.

At the same time, the influence of the Nonconformist ministers is still very considerable. I will venture to write a few words concerning a class of men who, since the election of 1868, have been the objects of excessive praise and of excessive depreciation. As a body of public teachers they have faults and defects, not few, nor difficult to perceive. Their knowledge is necessarily partial and scanty; their experience and views of life narrow; they almost always seem to regard the Incarnation as having first displayed its power in the sixteenth century, and as having been virtually inoperative in Wales until their own sect arose in the eighteenth; their feelings are strong, and their prejudices are sufficiently violent to make their language and conduct at times somewhat unscrupulous. But they have also many great and admirable qualities. They are industrious, zealous, generally moral, have a great thirst for knowledge, and many of them are gifted with abilities of a very high order. Their faults are in a great measure attributable to the system upon which they depend for maintenance. The author of the very able essay on "The Causes of Dissent in Wales," wrote of them thirty-five years ago in these words: "From the days of the Sophists of Athens down to those of the Mendicant Orders in the Romish Church, experience is but little in favour of ethical teachers dependent on the breath of popular favour. Instructors thus circumstanced have generally been found prone to sacrifice truth to novelty, to the varying passions, the prejudices, or the morbid ingenuity of their audience. The operation of a similar influence is but too strongly apparent in the religious economy of the Dissenters of our own times; ethical novelty was never more industriously pursued in the schools of ancient Athens, than it is in our days in the chapels of our modern separatists."

At one time the influence of the Dissenting teachers in Wales was greater than it is now. In the earlier part of the century they were regarded by a simple peasantry with feelings of reverence and warm affection. What was the source of those feelings? I think their poverty and humble social position gave them a great measure of their influence. In those days that poverty presented an honourable contrast to the worldliness of many of the Bishops and higher clergy. To illustrate the nature of this contrast, I must write a few lines concerning some of the features of Church patronage in Wales. I shall not dwell at any length upon the subject, as it has been exhausted in a work to which I have more than once alluded. To give, however, to those who are unacquainted with the subject some idea of the extent to which native intellect and ability have been proscribed during the last hundred and fifty years, I will briefly state a few facts which cannot be questioned. During a period of eighty-five years, throughout which the Welsh sees were mainly filled by Welshmen, and the Welsh people attached to the Church, the number of native clergymen holding the higher preferments was sixty. During a subsequent period of the same length, in which Nonconformity reached its present proportions, under English Bishops, the number of natives holding any of the higher preferments was only ten. As recently as in 1834, Church revenues in the county of Montgomery, to the amount of £13,930 per annum, were enjoyed by sinecurists and absentees, almost without an exception relatives of the alien Bishops; while the aggregate incomes of the working resident clergy amounted to only £8511 per annum. Early in the present century a Bishop of St. Asaph had managed to confer upon himself and those of his own household £23,679 per annum, while the entire body of resident working clergy divided amongst them £18,391 per annum. This prelate was sent into Wales to preach to its people the doctrines that flow from the reality of the Divine-Human self-sacrifice of Calvary. The law has now made these gross scandals impossible. But sad it is to think that there have been Bishops who were not, in these matters, a law to themselves. The secret is to be found, perhaps, in the nature of their position. The position of a richly endowed Bishop, having nominal oversight of a diocese, the language and feelings of whose people he does not understand, carries with it an influence deadening to the moral sense, and especially to the higher impulses of the spiritual life. Hence, doubtless, the gross exhibitions of worldliness which I have described.

The eloquent denunciation of this worldliness of Church dignitaries in a past generation, illustrated by the poverty of their own lives, secured to the Dissenting preachers that moral power which even the semblance of self-sacrifice sometimes produces. These Church abuses have been in later years removed; and their removal has proportionately lessened the influence of those whose eloquence was employed in denouncing them. But as long as the policy is maintained of sending into Wales Bishops alien in language and feeling, the Cymric people will not forget the wrongs they have suffered, nor learn to regard the Church as anything but an engine wielded, in the name of religion, to crush out their national spirit, and to outrage their national self-respect.

To return, however, to the Nonconformist ministers. Although their influence in Wales is still great, there are not wanting signs that they are destined to experience the fate of their historical predecessors, the itinerant preachers of the Mendicant Orders of the pre-Reformation Church. The words in which Blunt has described the gradual wane of the influence which those once powerful instructors exercised over the masses, are not inapplicable to the growing experience of those modern teachers, who, while professing a peculiar pride in their dependence upon voluntary contributions, are compelled to have recourse to concerts, tea-meetings, lectures, lotteries, and other undignified sources of revenue, to supplement the results of popular liberality. "Indeed, the frailty of human nature soon found out the weak places of the Mendicant system. Soon had the primitive zeal of its founders burnt itself out; and then its censer was no longer lighted with fire from the Altar; a living was to be made; the populace was to be alarmed, or caressed, or cajoled out of a subsistence. However humiliating may be the truth, experience has sanctioned it as a truth, that an indigent Church makes a corrupt clergy."

There is a very prevalent popular fallacy which has in no slight degree conduced to the popularity of the mendicant teachers of religion in all ages. The populace, seeing their teacher poor, are apt to jump to the conclusion that he must therefore be unworldly. They forget that these professors of unworldliness are almost invariably from the humblest ranks of life, and that to them the position and emoluments of a preacher afford a worldly *rise*, often greater than the highest Church preferments afford to the educated members of the wealthier classes. Hence worldliness gives the false call into the ministry of the Dissenting societies no less than of the Church. The only difference is a social, not a moral one. The falsely called Dissenting minister is usually a worldly peasant; the falsely called clergyman a worldly gentleman. This fallacy runs through all those superficial commonplaces talked about the poverty of the Church in her origin. That kind of language bespeaks a covertly Socinian conception of the Person of our Blessed Lord. To many unconscious of their Socinianism, He appears only as the *poor* Man, known as the carpenter's Son. They forget the endowment of infinite power manifested in the water made wine, the bread multiplied, and the corpses reanimated. In the combination in His Person of infinite command of material wealth, with infinite unwillingness to use it for selfish purposes, we find a guidance to a true conception of the perfect state of the Church's organization. The Church, which is the extension of the Incarnation, is then in her true relation to matter when endowed with the command of material resources, but also animated, in the persons of her ministers, by that Divine spirit of self-denial which teaches them not to use those resources for their own physical aggrandizement or indulgence, but for furthering the welfare of humanity, so that men be constrained to say, "They save others; themselves they cannot save." Also in the ministry of the Apostles, *endowed* as they were with supernatural powers, we behold the Church placed in the same position, rich, yet for others' sake making herself poor. Very deeply, however, is this fallacy seated in the popular mind. And so the populace are ever apt to mistake poverty in circumstances, which ought not to be an attribute of the clergy, for that nobler attribute—poverty in spirit—which no true clergyman can ever fail to manifest. Hence, in different ages, the temporary popularity of the teachers recommended by their mendicant position. But fallacies are ever destined to be refuted by the logic of experience.

This fallacy, however, as I have said, has, in its day, contributed to the popular power of the Dissenting preachers of Wales. I would not write harshly of a class of men who have done much good, and exhibited many noble qualities. To assert, however, that they are free from the faults to which the system of maintenance upon which they depend exposes them; to say that they never cajole, never mislead their hearers, never retain their allegiance and their contributions by making exaggerated statements to perpetuate their prejudice against the Church, from which they have schismatically seceded, would not be true. But that they also number among them many excellent men, some of rare natural ability and of great oratorical power, which, with due culture, would have made them worthy of holding high places among the clergy of the Church, is equally true.

Within the present year Welsh Calvinistic Methodism has lost its greatest preacher[1] of this generation. The leading representative of a sect which denies the necessity of Episcopacy, he was a witness to its truth by exercising over his countrymen more than Episcopal influence. Of humble parentage, owing all to self-

[1] Henry Rees.

culture, he was endowed with natural gifts that would have made him remarkable in any assembly of men. A head and face of Apostolic power; a native dignity of presence worthy of a prince of the Church; a keen analytical intellect, and a surpassing power of sacred oratory combined with deep religious faith, and a blameless life, secured to him an influence over the minds of his countrymen that has fallen to the share of no Bishop in Wales during the last hundred and fifty years. He wore no mitre and enjoyed no revenue, but he was, for all that, in his day the successor of St. David in his authority over the religious mind of his country. Had he, under happier auspices, received the culture of a scientific theology, and the knowledge of sacramental truth, he would have become a prelate whose eloquence would have borne comparison with that of the most gifted occupant of the Episcopal Bench. Through a long life he held himself aloof, with a singular dignity of character, from those paths of political agitation and sectarian bitterness into which so many Nonconformist ministers have wandered. Why was that man tempted to feed his soul upon the half-truths of an obscure sect, and his genius lost to the Church? An Episcopate alien in language and in feeling supplies the answer.

Although no candid clergyman can deny that, in the presence of a Church organization defectively worked, the Nonconforming societies have effected a valuable supplementary work in the scriptural instruction of large numbers of the Cymric people, it would be wrong to attribute to their system a religious stability capable of

M

resisting the strong earthward attraction that lowers in all schismatic bodies the tenets of high spiritual truths. If it were possible that the candlestick of the Church in Wales should be removed, and the negative systems of Nonconformity substituted, no sober man can doubt that in a few generations the masses of this quick-witted impulsive people would be in danger of sinking into some of the various gradations of Socinianism, or even into some of the lower stages of naturalism. The position of Nonconformist faith is like "an inclined plane, upon which individuals may make a safe stand, but generations cannot." It is, therefore, of supreme importance to the welfare of my country that the causes which alienate its people from the Church should be removed. What are those causes? The influences of an alien Episcopate productive of a clergy in its own likeness.

The regeneration of the Church of the Cymry, by the restoration of the masses into her fold, can assuredly be effected by none other than native Bishops and native clergy. I have already dwelt upon the marked differences of natural temperament that distinguish the Welsh from their English neighbours—differences requiring corresponding differences in the modes of religious teaching and ministration. It requires no arguments to prove that the presence in Wales during a hundred and fifty years of Bishops incapable of performing Episcopal functions in the language of the people, has been an indecent violation of the principle of the twenty-fourth Article, and an undeserved outrage upon the national sensibilities of the Cymric people. If space allowed, I should have no difficulty in showing how signally these "Fathers in God" have failed in creating an influential clergy. Gruffydd Jones, early in the last century, wrote of the gulf that separates them from the masses in these words, "The common people being of a different language, and unable to make known their grievances, their lordships are therefore obliged to credit the testimonies and to see with the eyes of others." Now, in such a country as Wales, it always must be that a very large proportion of the clergy will be drawn from the ranks of "the people." Ignorance of the language and feelings of the people, therefore, implies ignorance of the antecedent associations of a large number of their clergy. To this cause is it due that many young men from the lower social strata, furthermore defective in natural abilities, are not seldom admitted into Holy Orders. In a word, the Bishops and pastors of the flock, ignorant of the people and their language, instead of being able "faithfully and wisely to *make choice* of fit persons to serve in the sacred ministry of the Church," are compelled to lay hands suddenly upon unfit men.

But indirectly in their influence upon the clergy, the withering effects of the "alien Episcopate" are painfully apparent. The native clergy, subjected for generations to systematic exclusion from the higher positions in their profession, and depressed as ecclesiastical Helots, have lost confidence, self-respect, and moral tone. Their numbers are now but rarely recruited by the ablest and most high-spirited of their countrymen. Knowing that for the higher offices of his native Church no Welshman need apply, Welshmen of spirit have not failed to seek professions in which their nationality is no barrier to their honourable and legitimate advancement.

Furthermore, English dignitaries appointed to Cymric sees, in entering (as in many cases) for the first time a country virtually foreign to them, have generally brought with them a retinue of English adherents. These clergymen have, as a rule, been gradually placed in the most commanding positions of the diocese. They naturally have the reputation of being especially "in the confidence of the Bishop." Each of them in his sphere exercises a most painfully cowing influence upon the surrounding native clergy, many of whom, being poor men with families, have the best of reasons for sinking all independence of spirit. These rectories and vicarages (many of them occupied by excellent men, who have every qualification for ministerial success, save knowledge of the people and their language) are centres of influence not dissimilar to the influence which the Norman castles, whose ruins dot the country, were erected to exercise in depressing the national spirit of the native chieftains. The cowed spirit of the natives has been abundantly evident in the patient endurance of a proscription that has degraded them and ruined the influence of the Church, and poisoned and embittered the entire social atmosphere of Wales. They could not venture to give expression to their feelings of indignation.

But in another way the effects of the "alien Episcopate" have tended to make the native clergy uninfluential. The "Father in God" in the course of time moulds his clergy into his own image. Hence even the native clergy, save a few stronger natures, gradually lose their Celtic characteristics of manner and diction. The Cymric fervour, indispensable to effectual ministrations in Wales, is rarely found in the churches, but is as rarely wanting in the chapels. The average Cymric clergyman (especially if he is in the favour of his Bishop), ministering in the native language, is not himself, but is a feeble imitation of an Englishman. The native genius of every people must be developed in freedom according to the law of its own individuality.

In another relation, also, the clergy lose their influence in consequence of their denationalized sympathies and Anglicized forms of thoughts and feelings. The Cymry are a social, warm-hearted, affectionate people, fond of the excitement of large assemblages and the quickened sympathy of social gatherings. The cohesion of the Dissenting congregations depends in no slight degree upon the "Gyfeillach," the weekly reunion of religious friends. A clergy affecting, in imitation of their leading dignitaries, a contempt for the Cymric language and people, and an indifference to Cymric tastes, very soon lost their influence over a warm-hearted people, who sought the satisfaction of their yearnings in systems which extended to them a larger sympathy.

Moreover, not a few of the Anglicized clergy (especially those most deficient in culture) have assumed airs of social superiority, while at the same time losing sight of the very real and inalienable ground of higher authority which they possess. If the clergy have any claims to the allegiance of the people superior to those of the Dissenting preachers, those claims rest not upon their social distinctions, nor yet upon the establishment of the Church, but upon the original mission of that Church, and their own Apostolical Orders. Too many Welsh clergymen, however, losing sight of these momentous attributes, have preferred to regard themselves as better-paid, better-clad rivals of the sectarian preachers. Naturally, therefore, do the masses fail to realize in the clergy any greater difference than that which distinguishes the workmen of a Government dockyard from those of better-managed private yards. This ignorance of fundamental Church truths, when combined with social arrogance, and bitter, though feeble, denunciations of Dissent, has contributed to weaken the influence of the clergy in Wales.

I must briefly allude to a prevalent opinion concerning the present weakness of the Church in Wales. The Bishops and clergy, seeing the masses alienated from her fold, generally attribute it to the want of material resources for the erection of schools and churches, and the provision of additional ministrations. They conclude, therefore, that the co-operation of the gentry and landowners would, by the contribution of money on the one hand, and by the exercise of social influence on the other, conciliate the native population, and restore them to the Church. Thus they too often put their trust in princes, and confine their attention to the thin upper crust of society in Wales. Not seldom has it occurred that religious services in the parish church are provided for a few English families, forming, perhaps, a fifth of the population, while the four-fifths native Welsh are entirely neglected. So much has this been the rule among the higher clergy in Wales, that Mr. Gilbert Scott, in his report upon the Cathedral of St. David, thought it necessary to use these words : "God forbid that in the Church of the patron saint of Wales the Welsh should be neglected. Though an Englishman, I am ready to cry heartily, "Wales for the Welsh!" and to add, "The Church of Wales for the Welsh, and *à fortiori* the Cathedral of St. David's for the Welsh."

Now, I would by no means underrate the valuable influence for good of the higher classes in Wales. But that influence can never restore to the Church the affections of a people the cause of whose alienation is to be found in the violation of their national sympathies. On the other hand, if the Church can regain the attachment of the religious Cymric masses by the efforts of a native clergy and Episcopate, she will not want (all experience teaches us) the support of the rich and noble, who now make the estrangement of the people an excuse for withholding their contributions from her Altars. The Church, whenever it cannot be said that the "common people hear her gladly," is not in her true position.

At the same time, it is a great evil that the social princes of a country should not worship at the same Altars before which the masses adore the Life. That separation destroys the health of the social system which arises from the living mutual sympathy of all classes, and the performance by all, in the light of the one faith, of their relative duties. Alienated in religion from the masses, the social leaders forget the duties of sacrifice, sympathy, and benevolence, and the great verity of the essential equality and brotherhood of humanity, that underlie the necessary distinctions of social sphere and position. Alienated in religion from their social leaders, the masses are apt to become narrow, jealous, and discontented levellers. The Church, when she becomes the representative of a class, is but a mutilated form of the mystical Body of Christ.

The probability or improbability of the extinction of the Cymric language as a living tongue does not affect in any way the necessity of a native Episcopate and clergy. I have already alluded to the differences of temperament (requiring differences in the ministrations) that mark the Welsh and the English. It is an acknowledged maxim among the Welsh Nonconformists that the pastorate of even an English-speaking congregation of Welsh race cannot, with any hope of success, be confided to an Englishman. Hence the question is not seriously affected by the extinction or non-extinction of the Welsh language. The national temperament will survive if the national language becomes extinct. But that extinction is not likely to be accomplished for some generations. To-day the ancient tongue is the living language of 700,000 Cymry. The policy hitherto employed to destroy it has assured its longer existence. Nonconformity, the creation of that policy, is intensely Celtic, and its influence tends to prolong the use of the

Welsh tongue. The irritation excited in its behalf by the ungenerous means used to extinguish it, has only tended to defer its extinction.

While no rational man can doubt the necessity of extending universally the knowledge of the English language among the Cymric people, the necessity of quenching the national spirit may well be questioned. Every respect has been studiously paid to the spirit of Scotch nationality. Is it fair that the equally ancient Cymric nationality, more strongly marked, as it is, by the retention of its national language, should be crushed out? True sentiment and true expediency alike declare, I believe, against a policy so ungenerous, so expressive of the worst attributes of the English national temper—attributes which, above all others, have had the effect of involving the empire in strife and perplexity. The millionnaire who acquires an old estate, finding upon it a single tower, sole remnant of its ancient castle, does not demolish that memorial of the past, but so arranges his modern edifice as to bring it into harmonious relations with that time-honoured fabric that has weathered the winds and rain of a thousand years. The Cymric nationality is the oldest feature in the life of the British people, connecting it with the annals of that ancient race which inhabited this island before the Roman empire had risen to its height. Surely every generous sentiment (rarely at real variance with practical wisdom) dictates that this ancient, loyal, industrious, and order-loving people should, within the obvious limits compatible with the imperial welfare of the entire British people, be permitted to cherish the traditions and to develop the free impulses of their distinct national character. The truest utilitarianism will also be found in harmony with the dictates of this sentiment. It is, I believe, a maxim of modern strategy, that two or more columns moving from different bases upon a common centre, strike with a more irresistible impact than a combined host moving in one body. This principle would teach the wisdom of permitting the nationalities that form the united people of the British Isles to develop, within due limits, their own distinct, characteristic, national energies. The fiery dash of the Irishman, the fierce perseverance of the Caledonian, the strong, patient resolution of the Englishman, and the spiritual yearnings and quick sensibilities of the Cymro, can all contribute distinct motive impulses that will enable the empire to move onwards for the expulsion of the Canaanitish ignorance and debasement that disfigure some scenes of its life, and the development of a nobler religious spirit, and to march into fuller possession of the promised land that flows with the milk and honey of a healthier social system, a more general enlightenment, and a more harmonious national life.

The Scotch people are not unreasonably proud of their strong national life. To what is their success in its development attributable? Dr. Chalmers has traced it to three causes: The ecclesiastical endowments of Scotland have been enjoyed by a native clergy; every parish has had its parochial school; the more gifted youths have been able to obtain the benefits of a high education in the three national Universities. The Cymric people are only beginning to enjoy the second of these advantages, while the first and the last have been persistently withheld from them.

It has long been a maxim of statesmen to ignore the distinct nationality of the Cymric people, and to treat Wales as a part of England. This cannot be a wise policy, based as it is upon a subjective figment. The distinct national character of the Cymry is an objective reality—one of the living forces in the imperial life of the British people; and it is a force which cannot be wisely ignored. The generous policy which recognizes the wisdom of not ignoring Irish ideas in the government of Ireland, encourages my more patient countrymen to hope that their modest demands for a national Episcopate and a national University will not be long refused.

Every principle of justice and truth dictates the wisdom of appointing to the Cymric sees men of Cymric race and language. That my countrymen could be reconciled to the Church of their fathers by native Bishops and clergy, cannot well be doubted by those who have studied their history. The withdrawal of the ban that has excluded the Welsh clergy from the higher positions in their native Church, would rapidly have the effect of raising their moral and intellectual standard, by adding to their number some of the ablest and most high-spirited of their countrymen.

That native Bishops would be able to assume an attitude of conciliation, and to organize a system of clerical education, by which the fine natural talents now lost to her would be devoted to the service of the Church, is equally certain. They would, in their public utterances and ministrations, be able to strike with effect the strong chords of national feeling; and the whole force of the powerful sentiment of nationality would no longer be, as it now is, arrayed against the life of the Church. I must add that I write concerning a system. I would not pen a line that could reasonably hurt the personal susceptibilities of the English prelates who preside over the four Cymric dioceses. The prelate appointed to the last vacant see in Wales, though not a Cymro, is a Celt, and has consequently much more sympathy with the Welsh temperament. His Celtic sympathies, joined with the fact that he had acquired the Welsh language, and laboured in one of the chief parishes of Wales in such a manner as to win the profound and affectionate regard of all classes, have combined to render his appointment more popular and his Episcopate more successful than it would otherwise have been. Two other living prelates in Wales have wisely shown a just regard for the national sentiments of the people, and have endeavoured to qualify themselves for their positions as rulers of the Cymric Church, by attempting to acquire the Cymric language. But their meritorious efforts have not materially added to their power of reaching the minds or influencing the hearts of the people. The Cymric language is a language of which the grammar, though difficult, is easier than the pronunciation. For an adult to acquire that pronunciation in such a degree as to enable him to address a Cymric audience with fluency and authority, is almost a physical impossibility. Now, the Cymry, like several other Celtic tribes, have a great love of oratory, and are gifted in a remarkable degree with the natural gifts of the orator. Hence, to them, addresses entirely wanting these attributes are peculiarly distasteful. The sermons, however grammatically composed, which are read falteringly, with a most unmistakable foreign accent, and an utter want of native force and fire, are peculiarly ineffective, fall on the ear without reaching the heart, and have a tendency to alienate the people from a Church which unnecessarily subjects them to the necessity of hearing her most authoritative utterances in foreign forms of thought, feeling, and diction. I appeal to an Englishman, animated by the love of justice, and ask him to imagine how the most illustrious German or Frenchman, arriving in an English diocese, and diligently studying grammar, dictionary, and vocabulary, until able to perform the feat of reading in broken English an address upon the subject that most powerfully stirs the emotions of men, would be received. Would a series of such arrivals, extending over a hundred and fifty years, to the exclusion of all the native clergy, be tolerated with patience? No! His success would be no greater than that which has attended the efforts of the English prelates in Wales. What that success has been, the present position of the Church in Wales abundantly testifies. The living Bishops of the Welsh Church are prelates so illustrious in ability and character, that I cannot venture to praise, much less to speak evil of them. That they would have eminently adorned the highest position in the Church in their native land, all Welshmen believe. But in Wales they have signally failed. When such men have failed, there are few Englishmen, I believe, who would presume to hope for success. That native Welshmen of inferior attainments would be incomparably more successful in ruling the Welsh Church, is a conviction which few Welshmen do not share.

It is sometimes asserted that the clergy of Wales do not number men of sufficient attainments and ability to fill the Cymric sees. That the general average of intellectual culture among the Welsh clergy may be lower than it ought to be, is perhaps true. But that depression is obviously due to the effect of that long proscription under which they have suffered. The race which gave Dr. Owen to one side and Archbishop Williams to the other, can hardly be said to want native aptitude for theological science or ecclesiastical administration.

Indeed, for proof of Welsh administrative talent, I venture to point with confidence to the admirable organization of the most numerous of the Welsh Nonconforming societies. When the materials at their disposal are considered, the founder and present guardians of that organization must be acknowledged to have achieved no contemptible result. Within a very short period, a single individual is known to have recently collected for the erection of the Methodist College at

Bala, no less a sum than £25,000—a financial success to which no diocese in Wales under an English Bishop (especially if we bear in mind that the wealth of Wales is mainly in the possession of Churchmen) can be said to have presented any parallel. Welshmen, admitted to the Episcopate of their native Church, will not be found wanting in theological or administrative ability. They have a right to demand a trial of their power. If it is true that 'Ἀρχή τὸν ἄνδρα δείξει', it is also true that political and ecclesiastical oppression tends to conceal the capacities of a people.

The depreciatory estimate which Englishmen are sometimes pleased to express of Welsh qualities, is not, I think, in a slight degree attributable to a strange ignorance of the Welsh people. Throughout this letter, I have frequently used the word "Cymry" in preference to "Welsh." The name "Welsh," "Wealhas" (the Anglo-Saxon equivalent to "strangers"), is singularly significant of the attitude of Englishmen towards us and our country. We are still *strangers*. While Englishmen study the language and customs of distant nations, they have in their own island an ancient people of whose inner life they know nothing. In the sixteenth century a quaint writer protested against this attitude towards Wales—

> "It is great blame, to writers of our daies,
> That treates of world and gives to Wales no praise;
> They rather hyde in clowde (and cunning foyle)
> That land than yeeld right glory to that soyle."
>
> (Churchyard.)

May we hope that the day will come when this

ignorance shall give way to a warmer appreciation; when my countrymen shall no longer be known to their fellow-subjects as "Wealhas"—by a name which recalls English coldness and indifference—but by the name that recalls the significance of their ancient origin and their national characteristics?

The Cymry are proud of England—proud of being united to its august destinies. They demand in return some degree of justice and consideration. They demand that aliens in language and race be no longer appointed to the sees of the Cymric Church. The selection of an Englishman, who has had the industry to investigate some of the mysteries of Welsh grammar, is not the concession which they demand; nor is it the concession that will remove the causes that threaten to throw upon the Cymric Church, in the present year, the fierce light of Parliamentary discussion. They demand that men of Cymric race and language be appointed to the Cymric sees. They demand that the evil policy which for a hundred and fifty years has degraded the Church in their land from her high and holy mission into a mere instrument for extinguishing their ancient national spirit, be deliberately reversed. They demand that within all the limits not incompatible with true imperial interests and the welfare of the people, they shall be permitted in Church and State to cherish the traditions of their ancient race, and to develop the characteristic gifts of their strong-featured nationality. They demand that the temples of their religion, the influence ever most dominant in their lives, be regarded as the holy places of prayer, truth, and love, and no longer defiled by the unworthy associations of an ungenerous policy, which, while it has signally failed in its earthly object, has broken up the religious unity of their country, disturbed the harmony of their social life, and, instead of the genial concord of a religiously united people, has created bitter envying and strife.

The Cymric clergy have heard of the tidings of Parliamentary discussion upon the state of their Church with feelings of pain not unmixed with satisfaction. While feeling a painful apprehension that many short-comings will be revealed, they rejoice in the prospect that many grievous wrongs done in the ecclesiastical obscurity of Wales will be brought at last to the light, and judged by the generous English nation as they deserve. They are not much moved by the dread of disestablishment and disendowment. Bitter experience has taught them that there are wrongs that wound the spirit of a people more deeply, and paralyze the spiritual vitality of a Church no less completely, than the loss of ancient revenues. Proud of her august traditions in the past, they have no fears for the destiny of their Church in the future. At the same time, they feel assured that, in an age of which a gross materialism is the worst feature, nothing less than a supreme imperial necessity could induce a wise statesman to devote revenues bequeathed for the quickening and support of the spiritual life, to material purposes, however noble, that do not rise beyond the sphere of the lower physical being of man. Whatever may be the events of the future, the Cymric clergy, with strong feelings, in which they are joined by not a few of the foremost Nonconforming teachers, demand that the justice so long denied to the Cymric Church shall, in future appointments, not be withheld.

Encouraged by their knowledge of the generosity of your character and the breadth of your sympathies, my countrymen venture to believe that your ears will not be deaf to demands the justice of which cannot be denied.

I have the honour to be your most obedient Servant,
HENRY T. EDWARDS.

WALES AND THE WELSH CHURCH.[1]

IT is not easy to understand the inner life of a people distinct in race, traditions, and language. It is given to some nations beyond others to go out of themselves, and to occupy in thought and feeling the point of view from which men of a different race regard life. The imperial English race, among its many glorious gifts, can hardly reckon this power of self-forgetting sympathetic insight as its own. Some of its greatest difficulties have their origin in this defect. The inner life of the Celtic and Roman Catholic four millions of Ireland has been a closed book, not only to the people of England, but also, and perhaps in a greater degree, to the million and a half of Teutonic race who have formed the dominant class in Ireland. Social nearness sometimes creates moral distance. There are probably no people in the empire further removed from the mind and heart of the Irish Celts than the Protestant Teutons who have dwelt in local proximity to them, while separated from them by the moral gulf of distinct national temperament, traditions, and aspirations. How

[1] This Essay was written in the spring of 1884.

to bridge this gulf is the great problem of English statesmanship to-day. The recognition of its existence is pretty nearly all that has been accomplished. For generations the English people were unable to realize the existence of the Irish nature. But by much chastening they have been taught that the national character of the Celts of Ireland is a fact that cannot be superciliously laughed out of existence—a force that statesmen must take into account unless they desire to shatter the fabric of our imperial unity.

The educated Welshman, who has a real and not a pretended mastery of the Welsh language, who by reading the Welsh journals and literature, and conversing freely with the million of Welsh-speaking tradesmen, farmers, quarrymen, colliers, and labourers in the language of their hearts and homes, can enter into their thoughts and feelings, is continually reminded that the inner life of Ireland is not the only mystery as yet unmastered by the English mind. And as in Ireland, so in Wales, the resident Anglicized classes, ignorant of the native language and out of sympathy with the people, are the greatest strangers, separated by the deepest gulf of prejudice and dislike from that curious survival—the distinct inner national life of Wales.

In earlier ages the geographical features of Wales were a mystery which the English rulers had not mastered. In recording Archbishop Baldwin's progress through Wales in 1188, to enlist soldiers for the Crusade, Dean Hook has written—

"The interior of Wales was as little known as the

interior of Africa at the present time. It was a country which had never been explored by Anglo-Saxons or by Anglo-Normans. An opportunity for surveying the country was now offered, which was not to be lost."

The interior topography of Wales is no longer unknown to Englishmen. The geologists of England have carefully surveyed its mountains, rocks, and vales. The railway has revealed to the English tourist the mysteries of the Wye, the Towy, the Tivy, the Dovey, the Dee, and the Conway, and opened to his gaze the secrets of Snowdonia. But it is still true that the more important "interior of Wales," namely, the social and religious life of the Welsh people, is as little, indeed often less known, than the social and religious characteristics of the Zulus, Basutos, and Bechuanos. But the veil is about to be lifted. A crusade, different in aim from that of the twelfth century, is about to offer "an opportunity for surveying the country . . . not to be lost."

The Liberationist agitation and the Parliamentary discussion about to be turned upon Wales will throw a somewhat fierce light upon the hitherto hidden life. The unselfish Churchmen of Wales do not regret the approach of that light. They know that, if it will disclose painful wounds and weaknesses, it will also expose the false pretences and the self-interested shams by which the ancient Church of Wales has been brought to the verge of ruin.

Mr. Dillwyn, the respected member for Swansea, has given notice that, in the next session of Parliament, he will call attention to the anomalous position of the

Church in Wales; and it is understood that measures are being taken by the Liberation Society to elicit, by means of an organized agitation, an expression of Welsh public opinion in favour of the motion. This assault is regarded by some as peculiarly ominous. It will be remembered that a similar motion, proposed annually by the same honest and consistent politician, preceded the disestablishment and disendowment of the Church of Ireland in 1869. Mr. Dillwyn possibly hopes to repeat the triumph of his earlier days, and to win a success denied to Mr. Watkin Williams, when in 1870 he submitted a similar motion to the consideration of the House of Commons. But it is difficult to suppose that so experienced a politician can anticipate the possibility of dealing with the four Welsh dioceses, an integral portion of the province of Canterbury, separately from the Church of England. Although hardly expecting any direct results from his movement, Mr. Dillwyn may well believe that it will not be fruitless. A skilful general often leads a portion of his forces out of his camp, and feigns an attack upon some point in the position of his adversary, though well aware that he cannot by his partial movement occupy the ground that he threatens. But the march has its uses. It exercises the troops, increases their confidence, and perhaps worries the enemy. These are solid advantages, unless they happen to be counterbalanced by the fact that, if there be a skilful leader in the opposite camp, they put him upon his guard, and enable him to recognize and to strengthen the weak points of his position.

The analogy between the Welsh Church in 1883 and the Church of Ireland in 1869 is more apparent than real. It is true that in Ireland, during the existence of the Established Church, the Roman Catholic Nonconformists outnumbered the members of that Church by four to one. Those who assume to speak on behalf of the Protestant Nonconformists of Wales claim for them a similar majority. What the relative numbers of Churchmen and Nonconformists in Wales really are, it is very difficult to determine. No reliable statistics are forthcoming. But it cannot be questioned that as the Roman Catholics in Ireland, so the worshippers in the Nonconformist chapels in Wales, form a very considerable majority of the entire population of Wales. But there the analogy between Ireland and Wales ceases. The Irish Roman Catholics were a homogeneous body occupying the same position, and all separated from the Established Church by the same deep gulf of conviction and feeling. Very few ever crossed that gulf. But in Wales the separation of the Nonconformists from the Church is more apparent than real. There are thousands who have departed, not from the Church, but from the clergy. They object not to her creeds or her forms of worship, but to the lifeless ministration of the clergyman by whose inefficiency they may happen to be afflicted. They often avail themselves of the occasional offices of the Church, though preferring to avail themselves of the eloquent preaching in the Nonconformist chapels on the Sundays. Thousands who at one time of life and in one place of residence are Nonconformists, when they move into another district blessed with a more efficient parish priest, are found to conform. A very large number of the Nonconformists in almost every district of Wales are glad to attend their parish church on the occasion of harvest festivals, choral festivals, or when some clergyman of special eminence happens to occupy the pulpit. Such occasional conformity by no means proves that they do not value the system and ministration of the chapels, which they habitually attend, but it does prove that they are not entirely alienated from the Church of their fathers.

So shrewd an observer as Mr. Dillwyn, therefore, can hardly have failed to realize that the mental attitude of the vast majority of Welsh Nonconformists towards the Church is essentially different from that which the Roman Catholics of Ireland occupied towards the Church disestablished in 1869. There are some who think that the wisdom of the Irish disestablishment has hardly been conclusively demonstrated by the results. Even those who most warmly commended the measure, as an act of justice, must sorrowfully admit that the beneficial fruits which they expected have been somewhat slow in ripening. The state of Ireland is hardly such as to encourage those who propose to apply to Wales, under conditions essentially different, that policy which, when carried into effect under circumstances that seemed to offer the fullest justification in theory, has hardly been justified by the practical results.

But as the question of the Welsh Church has been seriously raised, it is to be hoped that it will be discussed by all parties in a candid, earnest spirit, without violent prejudice or unnecessary acrimony. It is a question of momentous importance, not only to the Welsh people of to-day, but to all coming generations. It behoves all patriotic Welshmen to realize solemnly the principle that ought to guide them, and the aim that ought to inspire them in determining, as far as it rests with them, the fate of the ancient Church of their country. The highest and most lasting good of the Welsh people is the object at which Churchmen and Nonconformists alike ought to aim. If it can be shown that the disestablishment and disendowment of their Church will tend to promote the unity and happiness, the intellectual enlightenment and moral elevation, of the Welsh people, it will be the duty of Churchmen to rise above the power of prejudice, to acquiesce in a change which they have distrusted, and to adapt themselves with manful courage and self-sacrifice to the new conditions. On the other hand, if there is reason to believe that the Church, which is the oldest institution of this ancient people, though unpopular and forsaken by the masses during recent generations, still offers noble possibilities of infinite good that no modern system or combination of systems can give; that the grievous evils which have afflicted her, and made some of the Welsh people impatient of her existence, are not inherent in her system, but abuses which they have power to remove; that she is capable of a reform and revival which, without impairing the noble energies that have been developed by the free genius of Welsh religion in the Nonconformist societies, will give to the higher life of Wales a spiritual harmony, a moral elevation, a social happiness, and an intellectual progress that cannot be equally assured by any other influence,—then it is to be hoped that the patriotic Nonconformists and earnest Liberals of Wales will resist the temptation of yielding to the not unprovoked instincts of resentful sectarian rivalry, and the not unnatural desire of a party triumph. It is most earnestly to be desired that violent, unreasoning declamation may be avoided on both sides, and that this grave question may be considered by Welshmen in the calm, dispassionate spirit of unselfish religious patriotism. It will be the duty of Churchmen freely to admit all the weaknesses and shortcomings of the Church in the past, although they may honestly believe that she has the capacity of reform, and the power of conferring blessings that Wales cannot afford to lose. It will also be their duty to recognize candidly and unreservedly all the beneficent service that the Nonconformist bodies during the last hundred and fifty years have rendered, and to-day are rendering, the Welsh people. At the same time, the nobler sort of Nonconformists, while confidently assured of the inestimable service which their systems have conferred upon their country, will not fail to ask whether those systems are qualified to render all the service that is needed, and whether there may not be certain forms of influence essential to the highest progress of the Welsh people which the ancient Church, duly reformed, is specially qualified to exercise, and which will be for ever lost, in a great measure, if she is violently removed from the position that she has inherited.

That the position of the Church in Wales is anomalous at present, all honest men must admit. There are two alternative policies offered for the removal of the anomaly—the policy of disestablishment and disendowment, and the policy of reform and comprehensive revival. In order to decide between these two methods, it will be necessary to consider—

I. The condition of the Welsh people.

(1) Their distinct nationality and language.

(2) Their religious life.

(3) Their social state.

(4) The average morality prevalent among them.

(5) Their educational state and intellectual development.

It will be necessary, also, to bear in mind—

II. The governing influences that have long been, and are still, moulding the character of the Welsh people.

(1) The pulpit and platform.

(2) The diaconate, or "Sêt Fawr," which may be translated "the seat of the elders."

(3) The Sunday schools.

(4) The native press and literature.

(5) The Eisteddfod, or congress of bards and musicians.

III. It will be necessary to consider what work the Church of Wales, if efficient, ought to have done under these conditions, and to trace the causes that have disabled her from adapting herself to the genius of the

Welsh people, and from wielding her share of the influences that dominate their life.

IV. After such an investigation, it will be possible to consider more effectually the comparative advantages that Church disestablishment and Church reform seem to offer to the Welsh people.

It is natural to individuals of strong wills and firmly fixed ideas to be impatient of other types of character, and to think it desirable that men should be remodelled after their own mould, and conformed to their own image. This tendency also exists in powerful, strong-willed nations. Perhaps there is no nation in which it exists more strongly than in the English. A vigorous Englishman, in his natural unchastened state, has a noble contempt for types of life not exactly conformed to his own, and judges without much delay that all things un-English are unjustifiable.

The distinct nationality and language of Wales have for centuries been a sore trial to the patience of the English people. The Welsh national type is more strongly marked and more tenacious of existence than either the Irish or Scotch. The survival of the language through so many centuries, within two hundred miles of London, notwithstanding persistent efforts made by the rulers in Church and State to consign it to death, is a proof that Welsh nationality has an extraordinary tenacity of life. The fact almost suffices, even in this sceptical age, to win credence for the ancient prophecy that has for centuries been on the lips of Welshmen in the verse—

> "Eu Nêr a folant,
> Eu hiaith a gadwant,
> Eu tir a gollant,
>   Ond gwyllt Walia."

> "Their Lord they will worship,
> Their language they will keep,
> Their land they shall lose,
>   Except wild Wales."

This undying tenacity moved the admiration of the French historian, Thierry, which he eloquently expressed in the well-known passage, "These feeble remains of a great people had the glory of keeping possession of their last corner of territory, against the efforts of an enemy immensely superior in numbers and resources—often vanquished, but never subjugated, and bearing through the course of ages the unshaken conviction of a mysterious eternity reserved for their name and their language."

There are many who do not share the eloquent Frenchman's admiration, but regard this national tenacity as Welsh narrowness and obstinacy. It cannot be denied that there are limits within which the cultivation of national peculiarities should be retained. The national distinctions that lessen the usefulness of a nation in the world, and cramp its power of contributing to the universal weal of the human family, ought to be cast away. But the distinct national gifts that form the peculiar genius of a national character ought to be retained and cultivated, for they increase the sum of the moral and intellectual capital of mankind. The brothers in a family are often variously gifted, and have distinct gifts of character. It is not well for the family that the strong brother, exulting in his own gifts, should despise and attempt to crush the weaker, whose gifts, though of a different order, are no less real and no less necessary, in their degree, to the full life of the home. A man cannot change the nature he has received, although he can develop and cultivate it. The best of us must not expect our neighbours to transform themselves into our image, however desirable we may deem it. As in individuals, so in nationalities, there are typical distinctions which are imperishable, and which the will of man can no more change than he can add a cubit to his stature.

The Welsh are conscious of a distinct and strongly marked nationality. Any attempt to turn Welshmen into Englishmen by Act of Parliament, or by a line of civil or ecclesiastical administration, will be vain. But the Welsh are a loyal, sensible, practical people. They are impatient of arrogant dictation and patronizing condescension, but they are eager for progress, and ready to accept all reasonable counsels to aid them in pursuing it. They are perfectly prepared to cast aside, as soon as possible, all national peculiarities of which it is possible for them to divest themselves, if it can be shown that they can thereby become more useful and honourable subjects of the Queen and citizens of the world. But they feel that there are certain well-defined limits, within which it will be for their own happiness and for the advantage of the empire, that they should cultivate their own special gifts and live their own life.

It is well that upon this vexed question, so little understood by the English public, some authority more conclusive than the testimony of an individual should be cited. Such an authority is found in the "Report of the Committee appointed to inquire into the Condition of Intermediate and Higher Education in Wales," published in 1881. The Committee had for its chairman, in Lord Aberdare, a nobleman of known ability, of wide culture, of great social accomplishments, and singularly free (perhaps, some would say, excessively free) from any partiality for Welsh peculiarities. It also numbered among its members, in the late Canon Robinson, one of the ablest and most enlightened educationists of the day. As the members of the Committee traversed the whole of Wales, and examined witnesses from all sections of the population in every district concerning the religious, social, and intellectual condition of Wales, their conclusions are entitled to respect. Those who know well the inner life of Wales, will gratefully acknowledge that juster and wiser words have rarely been used upon the vexed subject of Welsh nationality than in the following passage of the valuable Report, to which, in the course of this article, it will be necessary to refer again.

"In any recommendations to be made with reference to intermediate and higher education in Wales, it appears to us that account should be taken of the particular circumstances and distinctive characteristics of the country, and that it should be considered how far these justify us in recommending the adoption of provisions for which there has hitherto been no actual precedent.

"1. The first thing to be noted is that Wales has a distinct nationality of its own. The fact that Welshmen are thoroughly loyal to the Government under which they live, that they are satisfied to possess the same institutions and be governed by the same laws as Englishmen, that there is no agitation amongst them for a separate political existence, though it tends to make their nationality less obtrusive and exacting, in no way destroys its reality.

"The spirit which elsewhere manifests itself in struggles against the central authority, and in protests against the supremacy of a dominant race, is in Wales content with maintaining the continuity of the national life, preserving the traditional sentiments of the race, and fostering those ideas and usages which are distinctive and characteristic of the nation.

"The sentiment of nationality cannot be ignored, and ought not, in our opinion, to be discouraged. Some of the witnesses who gave evidence before us expressed themselves strongly as to what they designated Welsh narrowness and provincialism, and seemed to be of opinion that whatever is specially characteristic of the people should be got rid of. To this end they contended that Welshmen should, as much as possible, be educated out of their own country, and that no encouragement should be given to institutions specially adapted to the national characteristic of Wales, or likely to perpetuate distinctively Welsh sentiments or ideas.

"That narrowness or provincialism, whether Welsh or English, should be corrected, and, as far as may be, replaced by breadth of view and comprehensiveness of thought, will probably be admitted without controversy; but this may be done without destroying the Welsh type of character, or converting the people of Wales into Englishmen. That system of education is most desirable for Wales which, while preserving the national type, improves and elevates it, and at the same time gives opportunity for the development of any literary tastes or intellectual aptitudes which may be characteristic of the nation.

"The existence, therefore, of a distinct Welsh nationality is, in our opinion, a reason for securing, within the limits of Wales itself, a system of intermediate and higher education in harmony with the distinctive peculiarities of the country."[1]

These wise words, written by a man of singular penetration, are inspired by a true knowledge of Wales, and represent the spirit that ought to guide the educational policy of the future. Hitherto a very different spirit has been dominant, and to its baneful influence the educational backwardness of the people and the decay of the Church are due. There is not a sentiment in the above passage which is not quite as applicable to the ecclesiastical policy necessary to the welfare of the Welsh Church, as to the educational policy by which the intellectual progress of the people is to be secured. Indeed, the Welsh Churchmen who

[1] Chap. iv. p. xlvi.

desire the progress of their country and the revival of the Church, and who have something more than a sham knowledge of Welsh, would desire no fuller or more forcible statement of their views than is offered by the closing words of the above passage, slightly paraphrased: "The existence, therefore, of a distinct Welsh nationality is, in our opinion, a reason for securing, within the limits of Wales itself, a system of ecclesiastical administration in harmony with the distinctive peculiarities of the country."

It is impossible to form true views concerning the inner life of Wales and the position of the Welsh Church without an accurate knowledge of the extent to which the Welsh language still prevails as the only organ by which the people can give effective expression to their ideas and feelings, and live their mental life. It is, therefore, highly necessary that the truth upon this point, which, for reasons well known to Welshmen, has been unhappily too long concealed in the high places of English life, should be really known.

Before unfolding the facts, it will be well to guard against the gross misinterpretation of their motives to which Welsh Churchmen who have desired to make known this truth for the good of the Church have been exposed. They have been accused of a Celtomaniac desire to exclude their countrymen from the knowledge of English, and to imprison them in the isolation of a language that cannot open to them the richest treasures of literature and science, or enable them to play their parts as citizens of the world. No accusation could be more unjust. The Welshmen of education, who have exposed the ruinous inefficiency of the dignitaries and clergy who have well-nigh destroyed the Church by their ignorance of the people and their language, desire the progress and highest good of their country. They recognize fully that ignorance of the English language is a grievous barrier to the progress of Welshmen, and gladly welcome every instrument by which that barrier can be removed. There are among them those who believe that Welshmen can continue permanently bilingual, and that English can become universal without causing the extinction of the older tongue. There are others who think that ultimately English must become the only language of the country, used not only in business and by the more educated classes, but also in the home life and worship of rich and poor. But all Welshmen are absolutely united in the conviction that the universal knowledge of English is essential to the welfare and progress of the people, and that, if it is impossible for the two languages to co-exist, Welsh must die and English take its place. It would be impossible to find any Welshman who does not share this conviction.

But it is more useful now to consider what is the present state of Wales than to speculate as to its distant future. It is important that the English people should know the whole truth as to the prevalence of the Welsh language in Wales, and its bearing upon the question of the Welsh Church.

The facts ought to be known and faced. Very

wrong impressions have long been general even among well-informed English people. The belief has been cherished that the Welsh language has rapidly receded, that the knowledge of that language is unnecessary for the exercise of social and religious influence over the people, and that English is understood by all. This belief is, unfortunately, unfounded. Its prevalence in England is due to the evidence of two classes of most unreliable witnesses. The tourist who passes, perhaps, rapidly through Wales along the well-beaten routes, travelling on coachroad or railroad, and sleeping at the hotels, finds that railway porters, coachmen, guides, and servants can speak English fluently; and if he spends a few weeks at Aberystwyth, Llandudno, or some other Welsh watering-place, he finds that in all the Welsh towns the lodging-house keeper, tradesmen, and servants speak his own language well. He returns to England with the full confidence that he knows the inner state of Wales, and reports that the Welsh language is dead, because he has everywhere found an understanding people who could receive his orders, and tell him the amount of his bill, and for a proper fee guide him upon a mountain. If he had left the hotels and lodging-houses and shops of the towns and entered the farm-houses and cottages in which the masses of the Welsh people live, he would have found that to the vast majority he was a foreigner, with whom they could not communicate except in broken sentences.

But there is another class who are still more responsible for the ignorance that prevails as to the lingual condition of Wales. Clergymen who have accepted Welsh preferment without any knowledge of the Welsh language, or with only that command of broken Welsh, known as "llediaith," acquired by an adult, which is practically worthless for influencing the people, and serves only, as was once observed, to enable the promotion-seeker to read himself in and to read his congregation out, are naturally desirous to persuade themselves and others that effective command of the Welsh language is not necessary for the highest service of the Welsh Church. Unconsciously they have misrepresented the facts, or at least have carefully suppressed them. This class have done the Welsh Church a deadly injury by misleading Church opinion in England concerning the Welsh Church. Many of them occupy high social and ecclesiastical position, although personally very powerless among the Welsh people; have the *entrée* into powerful circles in London, the ear of the ruling class in Church and State, and are able to poison the fountain of Church government in Wales. It cannot be supposed that they wilfully misrepresent facts. But the false position into which they have been raised tempts them to blind themselves to disagreeable facts, and they communicate their blindness to others. These facts can no longer be concealed. What are the facts as to the prevalence of the Welsh language among the people? To what extent is it the language of their home-life and of worship, of their habitual thoughts and affections, of their spiritual emotions and aspirations? How far is it necessary in

Wales that the religious teachers who are to influence the people should have a real command of the Welsh language? To compel clergymen to have Welsh services in parishes where they are not essential to the spiritual welfare of the parishioners is an error. But it is an error very seldom committed. The temptation to err in the opposite direction is most general. The fact is that in the four Welsh dioceses, Bangor, St. Asaph, Llandaff, and St. David's, Welsh prevails far more extensively than is generally believed among English Churchmen, misled by the testimony which has been described. Attempts have been made to prove that in the two southern dioceses, Llandaff and St. David's, the Welsh language has given place to English. But the facts are as yet not favourable to the efforts. It is true that in both dioceses there are considerable tracts in which English prevails. In the rural parishes and small towns of Monmouthshire, as well as in the large town of Newport, English is general. In the large town of Cardiff, and in some of the small country parishes in the Vale of Glamorgan, Welsh is not general. But in the populous hill districts of Glamorgan and Monmouth, where the real battle of the Church is to be fought, the vast majority of the people are Welsh-speaking. It is in the Rhondda Valley, Aberdare, Merthyr Tydvil, Dowlais, Rhymney, Sirhowy, Tredegar, Ebbw Vale, that a population numbered by hundreds of thousands is found. The masses in these districts are Welsh-speaking. But these Welsh-speaking parishes of the hills with their vast populations are few in number. The clergy in them are also few in number. The small rural parishes of Monmouthshire and the Vale of Glamorgan, a hundred of which would hardly contain a population equal to that of the two parishes of Aberdare and Merthyr Tydvil, vastly outnumber the populous parishes of the hills. In the counsels of the diocese the numerous clergy of these small English-speaking parishes outnumber and outvote the few clergy who are leading the forlorn hope of the Church among the alienated Welsh-speaking masses of the hills.

In the diocese of St. David's also, although English is very general in the towns in a part of Pembrokeshire, in Radnorshire, and considerable districts of Breconshire, a decided majority of the people are probably Welsh-speaking. The same can be said of the two northern dioceses. In Bangor, although in the towns and watering-places English is general, Welsh is the language of the masses, and Welsh services are required in all the parishes, with two or three very doubtful exceptions.

The English-speaking districts in St. Asaph are more extensive than in Bangor. In considerable districts of Montgomeryshire and Flintshire English is very general. But the most populous county of the diocese, Denbighshire, is mainly Welsh-speaking, and the old tongue still retains its hold up to that ancient line of division, Offa's Dyke.

To this day the parish of Llangollen on one side, with a population of six thousand, is mainly Welsh-speaking, and the adjoining parish on the other side mainly English.

These statements will be questioned by the unreliable witnesses already described. But there is one test by which the truth can be ascertained. The religious ministrations for which the people pay are offered to them in the language which they desire. If each of the Bishops in Wales will ascertain accurately what are the relative numbers of the Nonconformist chapels in which Welsh and English services are held, the facts so long concealed will be brought to light. It will probably be found that in each of the four dioceses, whatever may be the favourite language of its Church dignitaries, the majority of the people who wield political power and help to determine the fate of institutious worship in the Welsh language. Until this test is applied the truth will not be known. If it is not applied, it will be difficult to acquit those who neglect its use of a desire to conceal the facts that it would reveal.

In the mean time, perhaps, for those who are not blinded by self-interest, such authoritative testimony as the following passage in the Report of Lord Aberdare's Committee will suffice:—

"In close connection with the subject of Welsh nationality are the existence and prevalence of the Welsh language.

"The question of language is, and must be for a long time to come, a very important factor in estimating the condition, both social and educational, of the people of Wales. To those who are resident in Wales, the prevalence of the Welsh language is a matter of daily experience. According to calculations made after the census of 1871 by Mr. Ravenstein, in his work on the Celtic-speaking population of the British Isles, out of a population of 1,426,514 in Wales and Monmouthshire, no less than 1,006,100 habitually spoke Welsh. It has also been stated that of the Nonconformist bodies of Wales, 686,220, or, including children under ten years of age, 870,220 used the Welsh language in worship, as against 36,000 who worship in English.

"Twelve newspapers, with a weekly circulation of 74,500; eighteen magazines, with a circulation of 90,300; and two quarterly publications, with a circulation of 3000, are published in Wales. A large number of useful books, translations for the most part, are yearly published in Welsh. We were told by one witness, that in the year 1875 no less a sum than £100,000 was spent in Welsh literature of all kinds.

"The fact being thus established, the question will arise—What effect does this prevalence of the Welsh language produce upon the education of the Welsh child?"[1]

For the purpose at present in view it will only be necessary to paraphrase one sentence in the above passage, and to ask, "The fact being thus established, the question will arise—What effect does this prevalence of the Welsh language produce upon the state of the Welsh Church?" To that question an answer will hereafter be attempted.

[1] Report, p. xlvii.

This obstinate survival of the Welsh language, in spite of the apparently overpowering forces that have for many centuries been making for its extinction, seems to many a mystery. What is the secret? Why does the language survive? Some shallow observers attribute the fact to Welsh obstinacy and a stubborn unwillingness to learn English. No view could be more absolutely false. Educated Welshmen, who have lived all their days in Wales, and know their countrymen well, will testify that they have never known a single monoglot Welshman who would not give a great deal to be able to speak English.

Equally false and shallow is the assertion sometimes heard, that Welshman who know English pretend to be ignorant of it. The fact is, that pride in the knowledge of English is so universal that it has become a recognized form of vanity known as "Dic-shôn-Dafyddiaeth." It is true that as witnesses in courts of justice, or in the transaction of any business that is of vital importance to him, a Welshman who has a slight knowledge of English demands to be examined in Welsh. This demand is due partly to shyness and timidity, partly to legitimate caution and self-defence. A man naturally likes to wield the intellectual instrument which he understands. An Englishman, who knows enough to ask for his railway ticket and to order his dinner, if he were asked to give evidence upon which his life or interest depended, would decline to express himself in a language of which he has but a smattering. A Welshman is equally judicious.

But although the fact of the prevalence of Welsh has been established, there are sanguine people who hope that a very few years will suffice to enrol it among the dead languages. It becomes, therefore, an interesting question how long it is likely to retain a degree of vitality that will make it an influence of importance to the Welsh Church. No more authoritative answer can be given than in the following passage from the Report of Lord Aberdare's Committee :—

"It may be asked how far this state of things is likely to be permanent; and, in answer to this question, we feel bound to say that, in spite of the progress which, under the influence of the elementary schools, of railways, and other causes, the knowledge of English has made and is making, such is the attachment of the Welsh to their language and literature, so deeply interwoven are they with their daily life, their religious worship, and even their amusements, that in dealing with the subject of education, speculations as to the probable duration or disappearance of their native tongue are hardly of practical bearing. There is every appearance that the Welsh language will long be cherished by the large majority of the Welsh people, and that its influence upon the progress of their education, and upon them in competing with English-born students, will be for an indefinite time but little less in the future than it has been in the past."[1]

It is evident that the members of the Committee have arrived at the conclusion that the Welsh language

[1] Report, p. xlvii.

has before it, if not immortality, an indefinitely long life. There are now educated Welshmen knowing Wales as well as any, and much better than some, members of the Committee, who would hesitate to accept this conclusion, and incline to the belief that before the end of the next century the ancient language will have ceased to be an important living force. It is exceedingly difficult to decide whether its present vitality is due to the love of Welshmen for the language of their ancestors, or rather to their lack of opportunity for acquiring English. Much may be said for both views. It is undoubtedly true that even the most highly educated of genuinely educated Welsh-speaking men find in the old tongue an instrument subtly adapted to their nature, which summons up trains of ideas and stirs deep emotions that they cannot express in another language. There is a distinct life of Welsh thought and feeling that is untranslatable. But whether that life is of sufficient value to secure the permanence of the language may well be doubted. The Welshman is sentimental, but he is also generally a utilitarian. The language will not survive if the conviction becomes general that progress in life is to be obtained by sacrificing it.

It is true that Welshmen who settle in English towns retain the use of their language. Large communities of Welsh settlers in America, also, have numerous meeting-houses in which the ministrations are in Welsh; and a well-known Welsh weekly newspaper, *Y Drych*, exists with no inconsiderable circulation. But in the second and third generations the descendants become English-speaking. It may, therefore, be inferred that the language owes its vitality, not so much to the love for it inherent in the race, but to the power of early habit and the lack of opportunity.

On the other hand, there is much to restrain a prudent man from prophesying confidently the extinction of the Welsh tongue. Those who have spoken it in childhood, although unable to communicate the love of it to their descendants, cling to it with strange affection. A clergyman of the Welsh Church, in passing through one of the principal streets in Boston, Massachussetts, entered a large assembly room attached to a chapel, and was astonished to find a large number of Welsh-American citizens gathered together, after the manner of a Welsh Sunday school, to study the Bible in their native tongue. The teacher of the principal class, an old man, had been absent from Wales for more than forty years. The late Bishop Ollivant was wont to relate, in proof of the love of Welshmen for their language, that he had met a learned Welsh clergyman, resident nearly fifty years in England, who confided to him that in his private devotions he had never brought himself to use any language but Welsh.

There is another caution to be given. Confident predictions of the early extinction of the old language, made long ago, are as yet very far from fulfilment. On August 10, 1753, the chief Welsh bard of the eighteenth century, in a letter addressed from Walton, in Lancashire, to his friend Mr. Richard Morris, an ancestor of the author of the "Epic of Hades," records a conversation in which a young Welshman, named Owen, imprudently ventured upon prophecy. The bard writes—

"When we were set, the pleasure I expressed at seeing a countryman at this first interview turned the topic of the discourse upon Wales and the Welsh tongue. Mr. Owen, like an honest Welshman, owned that he was a native of Montgomeryshire, which pleased me well enough. But being asked by my patron—who, though an Englishman, has a few Welsh words which he is fond of—whether he could speak or read Welsh, I found the young urchin was shy to own either, though I was afterwards that same day convinced of the contrary. Then, when they alleged it was a dying language, not worth cultivating, and so on, which I stiffly denied, the wicked imp, with an air of complacency and satisfaction, said there was nothing in it worth reading, and that to his certain knowledge the English daily got ground of it, and he doubted not but in a hundred years it would be quite lost."

Upon this unfulfilled prediction, the biographer of Goronwy Owen, in 1876, commented in the following footnote :—

"A century and a quarter has elapsed since this prediction was delivered, and there is no sign of the dissolution of the language. It is spoken by more persons now than it was then. If we take into account the great increase in the population of the country, we might almost say that the number of the Welsh-speaking population has doubled. For, be it remembered, it is spoken by thousands in the large city of London, and in the towns of Liverpool, Chester, Manchester, and others. Nor is that all. If we cross the Atlantic Ocean, it is spoken by large communities on the continent of America. A century ago there was no newspaper, and scarcely a periodical of any kind, published in the Welsh language. Now the Welsh press teems with these publications. And what is stranger still, a Welsh newspaper has been published for years in America, and commands a large circulation. It is called *Y Drych*. As yet there are no signs of the decay of our Cymric tongue."

This impassioned Welshman, the late Rev. Robert Jones, Vicar of All Saints', Rotherhithe, evidently shared the belief in the immortality of the Welsh language, which seems to have also almost found acceptance from the soberer judgment of Lord Aberdare's Committee. But other observers, who think they can see deeper below the surface of appearances, are sceptical, and inclined to believe that the survival of the language is mainly due to the iniquitous efforts made to use the Church as an instrument for its destruction. As will be proved hereafter, the policy pursued has been to *drive* the Welsh into the adoption of English by despising and ignoring it in the high places of the Church. That policy has failed. It has *driven* the Welsh people out of the Church into the chapels, under the influence of intensely national Welsh-speaking teachers, and has prolonged the life of the language for many generations. The survival, attributed by many to the love of the

Welsh for their tongue, is more due to the hatred of its enemies—

> "Via prima salutis,
> Quod minimè reris, Graiâ pandetur ab urbe."

But although the Welsh people could not be driven by arrogant dictation and ecclesiastical oppression into the abandonment of their language, it by no means follows that they will not be *led* by sympathetic guides, and through the aid of increased educational opportunities, to that adoption of the English so essential to their highest happiness and progress.

There is another characteristic of the Welsh people, hardly less strongly marked than their nationality and language, namely, their fervent religious feeling. As among their kinsmen in Brittany and Cornwall, devotion to the exercises of religion is the leading feature of the Welsh people. An Englishman who successfully contested a Welsh county in 1880, in entering upon his electioneering campaign, asked his local adviser to tell him what were the two subjects that would chiefly interest the Welsh voters. The answer was, in the first place, "religion," and in the second place, "foreign policy."

It is well known that the proportion of the population who attend public worship on Sundays in Wales is very much larger than in other parts of the kingdom. This religious earnestness and enthusiasm is not a new characteristic of the Welsh people.

In 1188, the imposing pomp of Archbishop Baldwin's semi-military, semi-religious procession seems to have moved them through the sight almost as powerfully as the preaching of their modern orators affects them through the hearing. Dean Hook, in his "Life of Archbishop Baldwin," describes a somewhat amusing exhibition of religious earnestness in the following passage:—

"As they passed through villages or encamped on the river-side, they were heartily welcomed; for they came not as marauders, but as men abounding in alms-deeds. . . . So great was the enthusiasm excited, that on one occasion the Archbishop enrolled, as soldiers of the Cross, a number of persons who came to him in a state of nudity; their clothes having been secreted by their loving wives, unwilling to part from their gallant husbands."

In the early years of the eighteenth century, before the rise of Methodism, the same religious fervour that had marked their ancestors in the twelfth century was still found among the people of Wales. In his work, "A View of the State of Religion in the Diocese of St. David's, about the beginning of the eighteenth century, with some account of the causes of its decay, together with considerations of the reasonableness of augmenting the revenues of impropriate churches," etc., Dr. Erasmus Saunders has drawn a graphic picture of the religious life of the Welsh peasantry. His book was published in 1721, that is, fourteen years before Howell Harris, the founder of Welsh Methodism, began to preach, so that it enables us to realize the religious disposition of the people in pre-Methodist days. After dwelling upon the abuses in the Church, he writes—

"Insomuch that it may be justly wondered at that there are in some places any principles or observances of revealed religion still remaining.

"Nor, indeed, could it reasonably be expected in some places that there should be any, but for the extraordinary disposition to religion which, a learned historian observes, prevails among the people of this country: for whether it be owing to our solitude, or our poverty, or natural disposition, or to the extraordinary grace of God given to us, I know not; but so it is. There is, I believe, no part of the nation more inclined to be religious, and to be delighted with it, than the poor inhabitants of these mountains. They do not think it too much, when neither ways nor weather are inviting, over cold and bleak hills to travel three or four miles, or more, on foot, to attend the public prayers—and sometimes as many more, to hear a sermon; and they seldom grudge many times for several hours together, in their damp and cold churches, to wait the coming of their minister, who by occasional duties in his other curacies, or by other accidents, may be obliged to disappoint them and to be often variable in his hours of prayer. And then also, to supply in some measure the want of a more regular public service, there are many, even of the common people, who gladly make use of what little knowledge they have gained, and take the pains privately, by reading or discoursing, to instruct one another in their houses.

"And it is not uncommon to see servants and shepherds, as they have an opportunity, strive to do these good offices to each other. It is by this means that most or all of them do attain the knowledge of reading and writing in their native language, without which commendable industry it is not conceivable how many of them should understand or know anything of religion; for there being no Welsh schools, and but very rarely any English ones, except it be in market towns, they must consequently be altogether ignorant of letters, unless they make up their defect by the aforesaid kind offices towards one another. But this calamity is nowhere so very visible as in Cardiganshire, where I can't be informed of any the least endowment for as much as one charity school throughout that county.

"But to proceed to make their private instructions more agreeable and effectual, as they are naturally addicted to poetry, so some of the more skilful and knowing among them frequently compose a kind of Divine hymns or songs, which they call 'Halsingod' or 'Carolion,' which generally consist either of the doctrinal or historical parts of Scripture, or of the lives and worthy acts of some eminent saints, whose extraordinary piety and virtue they thereby endeavour to illustrate, and recommend to themselves and others. It is not to be expressed what a particular delight and pleasure the young people take to get these hymns by heart, and to sing them with a great deal of emulation of excelling each other. And this is a religious exercise they are used to, as well at home in their own houses as upon some public occasions; such as at their wakes, and solemn festivals, and funerals, and very frequently in their churches in the winter season, between All Saints and Candlemas, at which times, before and after Divine service upon Sundays or Holy Days, eight or ten will divide themselves to four or five of a side, and so forming themselves, as it were, into an imitation of our cathedral or collegiate choirs, one party first begins, and then, by way of alternate responses, the other repeats the same stanza, and so proceed till they have finished their 'Halsing,' and then conclude with a chorus."

Similar evidence is also forthcoming concerning the state of North Wales in the same period. In a large work lately published by Messrs. Blackie and Son, entitled "Cymru yn Hanesyddol, Parthedigol, a Bywgraphyddol," we have a concise and highly significant description of the religious condition of Anglesey, written in the year 1730 by John Evans, of Bala. His words were, "Yr oedd holl wlad Môn o un grefydd; nid oedd yno ddim pleidiau, ond pawb yn cyrchu i Eglwys ei blwyf yn o ddyfal, ac yr oeddynt yn rhagori yn hyn ar drigolion llawer o barthau Cymru. Byddai sôn mawr am bregeth, os dygwyddai hynny fod, gan mor anaml y byddai yr offeriaid yn pregethu." "All Anglesey was of one religion, and there were no sects, but every man attended his parish church with considerable regularity, and in this respect they surpassed the inhabitants of many parts of Wales. Great was the interest excited by the announcement of a sermon, if it happened to occur, so rarely were the clergy in the habit of preaching."

There are not wanting indications that regularity of attendance at the parish churches was not confined to the people of Anglesey. In some of the parishes of St. Asaph there are records to show that on Easter and other great festivals of the Church an extraordinary large proportion of the parishioners were wont to communicate.

The religious earnestness which found expression in the worship and Sacraments of the Church in earlier ages is still a marked characteristic of the Welsh people, and gives to the Nonconformist societies that vigorous life which enables them to maintain more than three thousand chapels, and to raise annually not much less than £300,000 for religious purposes. The island of Anglesey, so unitedly church-going, is to-day largely Nonconformist. But it still retains its religious earnestness, as may be inferred from the fact that it contributes to the Bible Society a larger sum in proportion to its population than any other county in the kingdom.

It is a cause for thankfulness that, although the religious unity of Wales has for a time been broken up, its religious earnestness survives. Unhappily the divisions are numerous. The 1,500,000 Welsh people of Wales and Monmouthshire are mainly divided into five religious bodies. The Church still retains a considerable proportion of the population, though a very decided minority. What the relative numbers of

Churchmen and Nonconformists are it is impossible to determine. But it must be freely admitted that the Church, although probably more powerful than any single Nonconformist body, is very largely outnumbered by the combined denominations. Of these denominations, the Calvinistic Methodists, Presbyterian in creed and government, are probably the largest and wealthiest body, and claim as adherents nearly a fourth of the entire population. The Congregationalists and Baptists are also powerful bodies. Wesleyan Methodism has not been successful in obtaining any strong hold upon the Welsh people, and has a far smaller number of adherents than the three other denominations. Religious disunion has great spiritual disadvantages. But it is difficult to exaggerate the activity and energy of the Welsh Nonconformist societies. In towns, villages, and rural districts alike, the chapel is the centre of the social and religious life of the people. There is hardly an evening in the week on which the doors are not opened. The " Cyfarfod Canu " (singing meeting), the " Cyfarfod Plant" (children's service), the " Seiat neu Gyfeillach " (that is, the esoteric meeting of chapel members, or some other meeting), is held throughout the week. The favourite meeting-place, where they can enjoy converse with their fellows, found by an Englishman of the upper class in their club, and of the humbler classes in the public-houses, is found by the majority of Welshmen in the chapel. In the towns, and in many of the wealthier country parishes, the chapels are often very handsome and costly buildings, admirably adapted to the purpose for which they are intended. The comfort of the preacher and hearer is successfully assured. In country villages, which have no suitable assembly rooms, the chapels are very frequently used for secular purposes, such as concerts, lectures, and political addresses.

The social state of Wales does not differ much in its outward aspects from districts of England, similar in physical conditions; but the direction of social influence is considerably affected by the language and the religious divisions of the country. The aristocracy of Wales, consisting of a few noblemen, native squires, and English settlers who have purchased estates or chosen residences in the more attractive parts of the country, is comparatively small. The upper middle class, consisting of the professional men and those who have been successful in business, is very similar to the same in England. The mass of the population consists class of the tradesmen, farmers, quarrymen, colliers, miners, sailors, and labourers. The feeling that exists between the different classes in Wales is generally good; but the difference of language and religious profession has the effect of lessening social sympathy and communion of thought. The aristocracy and the higher middle class are almost without exception attached to the Church, and have within the last forty years made very generous sacrifices for the restoration of the cathedrals and parish churches, and the erection of schools and new churches. That show of progress which the Church in Wales has been able to make has been mainly due to the liberality of many of the landowners and the wealthy English residents in Wales. A very large majority of the professional men, and a considerable proportion, though by no means a majority, of the tradesmen, adhere to the Church; but of the farmers and working classes a very large majority are Nonconformists. Of the less prosperous among the working classes, it is often found that many, unable to meet the heavy demands made upon them in the chapels, are glad to find a quiet refuge in their parish church, where their poverty will not expose them to the loss of consideration that accompanies inability to contribute to the "achos," the "cause." Thus in Wales, as in England, the Church is often attractive to the highest and the humblest class of society. But it must be admitted that a far larger proportion of the working classes are Nonconformists in Wales than in England.

On the other hand, the Church in Wales has by no means a monopoly of wealth and social influence. The leading Nonconformist societies comprise among them a very considerable number of very wealthy men, who have risen to riches and position by thrift and energy in commercial pursuits or mining enterprises, as shipowners, coal-masters, and merchants. It is this class, educating their sons in English schools, who have called into existence that limited number of English Nonconformist chapels in the towns of Wales, in which, according to Sir Hussey Vivian, 36,000 out of the entire number of 936,220 Nonconformist worshippers in Wales and Monmouthshire are found to worship.

The command of the Welsh language is almost entirely confined to the middle and working classes. There is not a single nobleman in Wales who can converse in the language; of the squires a few are able to talk to their tenants in unidiomatic broken sentences. But it would be difficult to find half a dozen squires in the whole of Wales who can write a Welsh letter or deliver a Welsh speech in such a manner as to win the interest rather than excite the ridicule of their audience. Among the native clergy, educated at Oxford and Cambridge, not a few have but a very imperfect command of the language of the masses. They are unable to express themselves with freedom and power in it, and nine out of ten are obliged to read their sermons instead of delivering the *extempore* sermons which the Welsh love of oratory so imperiously exacts. This inability to speak the Welsh language freely and effectively, which is found among the upper classes and in many of the native clergy, is due to their English education and the neglect of Welsh culture. It is impossible to speak Welsh well without very frequent practice. A Welshman who has known the language from childhood, if he spends a few months in England, finds that his power of speaking it with ease has been impaired, and is not to be recovered without practice.

Among the Nonconformists of Wales the native language is carefully cultivated. Their ministers and leading laymen read Welsh constantly, and speak it with elegance, fluency, and power. It has not yet become the fashion among them to despise the knowledge of the popular tongue, or to regard it as an endowment inconsistent with claims to social gentility.

It is difficult to estimate accurately the morality of a population. It has been asserted that the morality of Wales is by no means on a level with its high religious profession. Unchastity, drunkenness, and deceit are said to be very prevalent among a people who are exemplary in their attendance at religious worship and diligent in multiplying temples and teachers. These charges were recently urged with vigour in an article from the pen of a late ecclesiastic, who for many years occupied a high position in the Welsh Church. It cannot be doubted that he sincerely believed in the correctness of the estimate of Welsh morality, which he rather suggested than expressed. Those who knew him will not doubt that he was fully convinced that he was doing a good work in reducing what he regarded as the swelling of Welsh self-complacency. But it must be admitted that such serious charges against an entire nation ought hardly to have been made upon such evidence as was produced. The Welsh Nonconformists were adroitly summoned to give evidence against themselves; and, more strangely still, the witnesses who were summoned were not produced until they had died. The reviewer had given some attention more than thirty years ago to the Welsh language. He had acquired such knowledge of it as enabled him to read the Welsh magazines of the Nonconformist bodies. In these periodicals some of the Nonconformist ministers of the day wrote articles, in which gloomy views of the moral condition of their flocks were set forth for the meritorious purpose of inciting the careless and self-indulgent to a higher level of living. The language of these impassioned appeals to the conscience of their countrymen was not always measured and judicial. If posterity were to judge of the morality of the masses of the English people by quotations from temperance oratory and temperance literature, they would be led to form an estimate hardly justified by the facts. It is much to be regretted that, in order to illustrate the moral condition of the Welsh people in 1882, the reviewer should have been unable to obtain more reliable materials than the heated utterance and fervent ministerial remonstrances written in 1851. The quotations were calculated to mislead the English people as to the real state of Wales. The article of the reviewer, as a whole, produced a false impression upon the minds of the English reader who had no knowledge of the subject. It excited among the more sensitive classes of the Welsh people the same feeling that is provoked in England sometimes by those curious caricatures that appear in France from the pen of Frenchmen, who pose as authorities upon the mysteries of English political and social life. Impartial judges, who know Wales well, will testify that the morality of the Welsh people will bear a very favourable comparison with that of any district of the United Kingdom. There is no part of the kingdom in which life and property are safer. The prevalence of unchastity has been enormously exaggerated. Suits for divorce are exceedingly rare. Reliable statistics prove that bastardy, though too frequent, is far less prevalent than in many parts of England and Scotland. Among the working classes drunkenness is in Wales, as in England, a besetting sin. But that the conscience of the nation recognizes the obligations of sobriety is proved by the fact that the entire people of Wales with virtual unanimity asked for a Sunday Closing Bill to lessen the temptations to vice. Deceit and falsehood are freely attributed by a certain class of English tourists to the Welsh people. English travellers of the same spirit are wont in all parts of the world to exalt their own virtues by depreciating the people among whom they travel; but more generous and equitable judges form a more charitable estimate. Imperfect knowledge of the English language, and perhaps some consciousness of subjection, tend to create in the Welsh people a diffidence, a nervous timidity and cautious reserve, which are mistaken for insincerity and cunning. But those who are able to communicate freely with the people, and to learn their real thought and feelings, know that they are most frank, sincere, and warm-hearted.

The people have some right to complain that while their vices are exaggerated their virtues are forgotten. Their loyalty, obedience to the laws, peaceable industry, freedom from crime, religious earnestness, are sometimes lost sight of by writers, who, forgetting the statistics of English crime, immorality, and irreligion, dwell rather too much upon the infirmities found in the human nature of the Welsh as of every other people. Their very virtues have provoked this unjust criticism. Their devotion to religion is so great as to excite expectations of a spotless morality.

It can hardly have escaped thoughtful observers that the Welsh people are characterized by greater sadness of spirit than is found in England. The expression of the typical Welsh countenance is wanting in the brightness of joy and confidence. This may be due to natural temperament, and in some degree to the influence of a stern and gloomy theology. It is possible that the religious divisions, separating the people into opposite camps, and introducing little jealousies and rivalries, tend to quench the light that has its origin in the charity of a religiously united people. Whatever be the cause, sadness is a characteristic of Welsh life. All the favourite tunes sung in the great religious gatherings, and hummed in the farmhouse and the cottage, are in the minor key. In the words of an eloquent Welshman, "The sad minor key of our song is that of a grave people standing alone without sympathy."

It is probable that this short sentence contains the true explanation. Isolation and lack of sympathy are the burden that makes Wales sad. Both trials are due to the existence of a distinct language, and educational disadvantages. There is no part of the United Kingdom in which so large a proportion of the lower classes are devoted to intellectual pursuits. The newspapers of Wales, and its magazines, are almost entirely written by members of the humbler classes. There are thousands who practise for years the art of versification in the most elaborate metres. The number of verses of all kinds and essays written for the "Esteddfodan," and almost countless "Cyfarfodydd Llenyddol" (competitive literary meetings), is very large. Many of the "Beirdd" and "Llenorion" (bards and literary men) have great natural abilities. A working cooper, named Owen Williams, was the author of a Welsh encyclopædia in several volumes, which, if it had no other value, served to illustrate the intellectual activity and ambition of his class. He was gifted with a memory of extraordinary power, and had amassed a vast amount of ill-digested antiquarian lore. If he had been educated, he would have possibly been a renowned professor in some University. But all this intellectual activity, manifested in Wales, is to a great extent fruitless, owing to the isolation created by the language. Thousands of Welshmen are conscious of having intellectual powers, and of having exercised them; but their exercise has been almost as barren as ploughing the sand.

Hitherto the intellectual life of Wales has not only been crippled by the difficulties of language, but also by the want of educational opportunities. Lord Aberdare's Committee have revealed the destitution that has starved the intelligence of Wales, in the following pregnant passage: "In the Report of the Schools' Inquiry Commissioners estimates are given which indicate that about sixteen boys in every thousand of the population should be receiving education higher than elementary. Taking the population of Wales and

Monmouthshire to be about 1,570,000, and reducing the estimate, in consideration of the exceptional condition of Wales, from 16 to 10 per 1000, intermediate school accommodation should be provided for 15,700 boys, and that number ought to be in attendance. In contrast to this, our returns show accommodation in the public schools for less than 3000, and that accommodation to a great extent unsatisfactory. They also show an attendance of less than 1600."

There can be little doubt that the position of Welshmen has been greatly depressed by this grievous want of educational opportunities. It has often been remarked that Wales has not produced any number of distinguished men at all proportionate to the intellectual activity claimed by its people. Welsh students of brilliant distinction at the great Universities are rare. But it is not difficult to account for this failure. The reasons have been well stated in the paper read at the Swansea Church Congress, in 1879, on "The Higher and Intermediate Education in Wales," by the Rev. D. J. Davies, Rector of North Benfleet, late Fellow of Emmanuel College, Cambridge. "With regard to our educational endowments, official statistics show that the sum which is available for secondary instruction in Wales, is barely one-third of what it is in England, in proportion to population; and even in England educational resources, though of late years greatly augmented, are still acknowledged to be inadequate. What, then, must be the case in Wales, with a much poorer population? . . . It should be borne in mind that Welsh youths are heavily handicapped in the race for intellectual distinction. In many cases they have had to conquer the difficulties of what was to them a foreign tongue before they could fully profit by the instruction that was given them at school, while in most cases these difficulties have been enhanced by want of means."

By citing the comparative results attained in the elementary schools, which are as efficient in Wales as in England, Mr. Davies shows that in natural power the Welsh youths are certainly not inferior.

"Since then the children of the poor have everywhere been placed on a footing of educational equality, and Welsh children have shown themselves far superior to English children in ability to acquire knowledge. This, perhaps, is not the general impression, but it is a fact. In its two last reports, the Committee of Council on Education gives the proportions which the several sources of income of rate-supported schools bear to the total income for each of the four years, 1875–78. The chief sources of income of Board Schools are the rates and the Government grant, which varies with the proficiency of the children. Now, the average English child earned, in 1875, 15.4 per cent. of the total cost of its maintenance at school, while the average Welsh child gained 22.6 per cent. of the cost of its maintenance. In the following year, the percentages were 16 for England and 24.4 for Wales; in 1877, 18.3 for England and 29 for Wales; and in 1878, 19.6 for England and 31.2 for Wales. Thus it appears that as soon as Welsh and English children had the same advantages of education, the Welsh child soon outstripped its English brother, and is every year leaving him further and further behind. Of course, the greater the grant a child earns, the lighter the burden on the ratepayers. So we find that school rates were 12½ per cent. of the total cost of maintaining the schools less in Wales than in England; or, putting it in another way, an English ratepayer who pays £5 towards his school would have to pay only £4 7s. 6d. if all his geese were swans—if all his children were Welsh children! Is the inference unfair, if secondary education in Wales were also placed on the same footing as it is in England, that the children of our middle classes would exhibit a similar aptitude for the acquisition of knowledge, and in the course of time prove that the backwardness and obscurity with which we are sometimes reproached are rather to be attributed, not to want of mental ability, but to enforced ignorance for many generations?"

In England and in Scotland the Church has been the *Alma Mater* of higher education. Dr. Chalmers attributed the national prosperity of his countrymen to three causes: The ecclesiastical endowments of Scotland have been enjoyed by a native clergy; every parish has had its parochial school; the more gifted youths have been able to obtain the benefits of a high education in the three national Universities. These blessings are correlated. For ages they were denied to Wales. The starvation of her intellectual life, and the consequent depression of her people, have been mainly due to the fact that a higher clergy, ignorant of the language, and out of sympathy with the people, occupied ecclesiastical positions, the beneficent influence of which they were but very imperfectly able to exercise for the good of the national life. Within the last few months the Welsh people have given proof of their desire for higher education, and of their willingness to make sacrifices for its attainment. In a few weeks the people of North Wales contributed no less than £30,000 for the erection of a Welsh University College. Of this sum, the small island of Anglesey contributed within a few days more than £5000. The money did not all come from the wealthy. Farmers, small tradesmen, mechanics, labourers, servants, contributed freely, and gave in the aggregate more than £2500.

After thus reviewing the present social, religious, and intellectual condition of Wales, it will be well to consider briefly the governing forces by which its inner life for some generations has been, and at the present time still is, moulded.

Foremost among these forces is that of sacred oratory. The pulpit has for many generations been a great power in Wales. An eloquent preacher will always attract a large concourse. In the busiest hours of harvest-tide, hundreds of people have been often seen to leave the fields for two or three hours, in order to listen to the sermon of some famous itinerant preacher from a distant neighbourhood, who had sent before him the "cyhoeddiad"—the announcement of his intention to preach. The orator would probably travel for a month through a great part of Wales, preaching two or three times a day, as he moved on from parish to parish, and finding a cordial welcome and hospitality at the house of a farmer or village shopkeeper. This power of attracting was not confined to the Nonconformist preachers. The few really powerful native preachers in the Church—few, unfortunately, and far between—exercised the same influence. The announcement that Parry of Llywel, Jones of Vaynor, or Richards of Caerwys was to preach, would have sufficed, thirty years ago, to fill to overflow the largest parish church in any district of Wales.

But for more than a century the Nonconformist pulpit has been the home of Welsh oratory. The great preachers, Howell Harris, Rowlands of Llangeitho, Evans of New Inn, the Richardses of Tregaron, the Joneses of Llanllyfni, Christmas Evans, Williams of Wern, John Elias, and Henry Rees, have been the heroes of the Welsh people. They are as well-known names to Welshmen as Handel, Mozart, Beethoven, and Mendelssohn are to the musical people of the world.

The system of itinerating greatly multiplies the preaching power of the largest Welsh denomination, and enables the few really powerful preachers to extend their influence over the whole country. It is probable that there are very few members of the society who have not again and again had an opportunity of hearing the six leading preachers. They rarely preach on two successive Sundays in the same neighbourhood. Moreover, several times in the year the great open-air gathering, called the "Sassiwn," is held in different parts of Wales, and many thousands assemble to hear their most powerful ministers.

This system greatly lessens the labour of the preacher in the preparation of sermons. A small number of sermons, carefully written and committed to memory, serve as the ministerial equipment of a popular preacher for an entire year. Thus, while in the Church the clergyman Sunday after Sunday addresses the same congregation, the Methodist minister Sunday after Sunday preaches the same sermon. The habit of delivering none but carefully prepared, well-remembered sermons gives to the preacher fluency and impressiveness. The rank and file of Methodist preachers, men of very ordinary capacity, acquire the power of preaching with such skill as to win and retain the attention of a congregation. The leading preachers are masters of the art of popular oratory, and on special occasions are able to preach with much power. In past times the most influential of the Welsh preachers were in the habit of maintaining themselves by cultivating a farm or keeping a village shop. In the intervals of business they found time to read a good deal, and to prepare their sermons. This system, while it greatly increased and extended the preaching power of the Welsh Nonconformist ministers, made it impossible for them to discharge those pastoral duties that are expected from a clergyman.

But the Nonconformist congregations of Wales are by no means left destitute of pastoral attention. In many cases a minister is engaged to reside in a district for the purpose of visiting the sick and teaching the young during the week, while at liberty to itinerate on three out of four Sundays. In other districts where no such arrangement has been made, the pastoral work is often performed excellently by another body of men, whose influence in Walès is greater even than that of the preachers. Every chapel has its "blaenoriaid," the deacons of the congregation. These officers are elected by the congregation, not only to undertake the care of all monetary affairs, but also to exercise discipline, to take a leading part in prayer and exhortation, and to visit the sick and poor. They often discharge these duties with great ability and faithfulness. The "blaenoriaid" are a most influential body of men. It would be difficult to overestimate their religious, social, and political influence. They are invariably men of some power—the natural leaders of their fellow-men. The most active, energetic, and prosperous of the religious farmers and shopkeepers, who are able to combine temporal power with the influence of personal piety, are generally raised to office. But it is also true that often a poor artisan and labourer, if specially gifted in prayer or power of exhortation, is also chosen by virtue of his ability and piety. The position gives to a man power and consideration in his class, and is an object of ambition. It gives some worldly influence, sweetened by the consciousness that it also leads to heavenly promotion. There are in Wales probably not less than twenty-thousand "blaenoriaid"—the *élite* of the middle and working classes, who find in the Nonconformist system opportunities of doing religious work and exercising religious influence not so easily found in the Church.

It must also be observed that in the Welsh "blaenoriaid" and "diaconiaid" (elders and deacons) temporal and spiritual influences are united, and act and react upon each other. It is often the case that in the towns, villages, and country parishes, the energetic and strong-charactered tradesmen and farmers selected by their fellows to act as elders and deacons are also the largest employers of labour, and so wield the greatest pecuniary and social influence on the people. That influence naturally works in support of the religious system which they represent. While it is an advantage to the tradesmen to be prominent members of a large congregation, all of whom may be his customers, it is also a gain to the struggling mechanics and labourers to have a "brother" in the person of the rich shop-keeper or farmer who gives credit and employment. The posts of local honour, such as seats on boards of guardians, school boards, depend upon the suffrage of the people, and office in the popular chapel is the avenue for an ambitious man to reach these dignities. These temporal influences, acting upon and wielded by the chapel officials, are not, perhaps, used unfairly, but they are constantly in operation for the maintenance of the Nonconformist system, and are an obstacle to the Church's recovery of power.

There is another great force, at work silently, and constantly moulding the thoughts and feelings of the

Welsh-speaking million, in the native press and literature. Fifty years ago not a single weekly newspaper was published in the Welsh language. The founder of the Welsh weekly press was the veteran Dr. William Rees, known by his countrymen by the name of "Gwilym Hiraethog." He edited with much ability and vigour the *Amserau Cymru* (*Times* of Wales), and in its pages taught those principles of advanced Radicalism which the Welsh people have so generally imbibed. He has had many successors. The seed which he cast abroad has borne, for good or evil, an abundant harvest. The condition of the Welsh press was described in the following words by the Rev. D. Williams, in his paper on "The Welsh Church Press," at the Swansea Church Congress in 1879: "Our Welsh publications number twelve weekly, two quarterly, and eighteen monthly, with a published price varying from one penny to one shilling and sixpence. Out of this total the Nonconformists support two quarterlies, sixteen monthlies, and ten weeklies, entirely dependent on peasant writers and peasant readers, and, as might have been easily anticipated, have made the Welsh people a nation of political Dissenters."

It is probable that very few Englishmen realize the extent of the literature that is published in the Welsh language. Lord Aberdare's Committee, in their Report, state that they had received evidence " that in the year 1875 no less a sum than £100,000 was spent in Welsh literature of all kinds." In 1879, at the Swansea Church Congress, in the discussion on "The Welsh Church

Press," the following interesting description of the extent and nature of the Welsh literature that finds circulation was given, in his valuable paper, by the Rev. D. W. Thomas :—

"The Welsh is not like its sister Cornish, a language whose Dolly Pentreaths have passed away. It is not like its sisters Erse or Gaelic, a language with but little current literature; but it is a language with a good deal of literature, and the medium of worship to more than three quarters of a million of people, at the least computation, in the Principality alone. Its permanence or decadence, its beauty or ugliness, are no questions for the Church. Let railways, schools, commerce, the intermingling of races, accelerate its end; but the Church has to deal with it to-day as a living fact to be used for its own high and holy purposes. If the Church is the human instrumentality through which saving knowledge is to be conveyed to the souls of men, it must be done through the language which men understand best in each country, and not through that which they understand least. It would help us further to realize the importance of dealing with the Welsh language as a great factor in the religious life of Wales, and would also help to indicate lines of future action, if I point out one or two facts connected with the extent and nature of current Welsh literature. Reference has already been made to the weeklies and monthlies which exist, because of the demand for them, and not because publishers are more benevolent and patriotic than other people. I have looked over two catalogues belonging respectively to two large publishing firms in Wales, one located at Wrexham, the other at Denbigh. I am afraid I could not describe them as Church publishers. In the first catalogue I noticed, amidst several works on Biblical Exegesis, Homiletic Theology, Sunday School Aids, biographies of Nonconformist ministers, Hymnals, and particularly a volume of Essays by Dr. Edwards, of Bala, price 10s., on subjects which those unacquainted with Welsh books would suppose to be far above the comprehension of any possible Welsh readers. The subjects are (they may have an incongruous look, perhaps) the Works and Lives of Homer, Shakespeare, Milton, Coleridge, Morgan Lloyd, Gladstone, Goethe, Kant, Chalmers, Irving, Arnold, Hamilton, Mill; the periodicals of the Welsh; Logic; the poetry of Wales; 'The Evangelical Alliance;' 'The History of the Church in Geneva," etc. No one has better opportunities of knowing whether these articles, which (many of them) would not be out of place in an English quarterly, are suited to his fellow-countrymen, than Dr. Edwards, the leading minister of the largest Welsh Dissenting denomination. In the other catalogue, belonging to the Denbigh firm, I noticed a series on the elements of mechanics, the Myvyrian Archæology, an English and Welsh Dictionary, Butler's 'Analogy,' Paley's 'Horæ Paulinæ;' but the most striking book in the list is a Welsh Encyclopædia (the 'Gwyddionadur'), a work of unequal merit throughout, but partaking of the nature of Smith's 'Dictionary of the Bible,' and the 'Encyclopædia Metropolitana.' If time permitted I would quote extracts from the articles on 'St. Augustine' and 'Philosophy,' which would serve as specimens of the kind of writings which must be finding readers. The publisher says that the venture has cost him nearly £20,000, and that he hopes to be reimbursed in time. I confess that there was a time when, like most clergymen in Wales, I should not have believed there would be readers and buyers of such ambitious literature, but experience has taught me otherwise; and, by a just Nemesis, my incredulity has been overcome by a residence of twenty years in a purely monoglot Welsh parish. The copy I have of 'Philosophy' is a borrowed one, and that from a quarryman, who knows no English, and who is not unwilling to supplement his wages by a trifle for looking after my cow in his after-work hours. He is no exception to the ordinary class of subscribers; and only last week I saw attention called by a correspondent in the columns of the *Western Mail* to the published list of subscribers, which he says contains no less than ten from the small and remote parish of Blaenpennal, in Cardiganshire, which is occupied wholly by monoglot Welshmen of small means, but evidently not of small intelligence. Without referring to other catalogues, these two are sufficient to show that, besides newspapers and periodicals, a higher class of literature finds readers."

It is hardly necessary to observe that this large number of weekly journals and periodicals, and the considerable literature so generally read in Welsh houses, is exercising a powerful influence upon the religious and political opinion, and also upon the moral and intellectual character of the people.

There is another institution peculiar to Wales that exercises a considerable influence on its national life. From very early times the bards, literary men, and musicians of Wales have been wont to assemble in a kind of congress for competition in the presence of the multitude. This congress bears the name of "Eisteddfod," or "Session." The name ought, perhaps, to be limited to the principal gathering of the year, to which competitors from the whole of Wales are attracted by the value of the prizes, and which receives the name of the "National Eisteddfod." But the numerous local gatherings are also popularly called by the same name. The institution has a twofold character. It is a popular festival and an educational agency. As a festival of patriotic sentiment it appeals very strongly to the nature of Welshmen, recalling to their minds the romance, the poetry, and the music of their country, preserving the continuity of the national life, connecting the commonplace present with the remote past, and reminding Welshmen of to-day that they are the descendants of the Druids. The choral singing and the evening concerts, at which some of the leading *artistes* of the kingdom sing, are at once a delight and a source of improvement to the people. That the Eisteddfod is popular and a real power in Wales, may be inferred from the fact that at the great festival of the year sometimes £3000 or £4000 is received, mainly from the working classes, in payment for admission.

But the Eisteddfod is more than a popular festival. Within certain modest limits, in the days of educational destitution through which Wales has passed, it has been an educational agency. Prizes of considerable value are offered for poems, essays, musical compositions, and other efforts of a humbler kind. For many months in every year a number of Welsh youths are stimulated to study and intellectual effort by the desire of winning an Eisteddfod prize. The standard is not very high. The composition of many thousands of second-rate verses and countless very ordinary essays may not be very profitable, and it is to be hoped that, when the means of higher education are given to Wales, these energies may be devoted to some more fruitful fields. But the intellectual activity evoked by these primitive compilations has tended to enlighten and elevate the life of the people above the level of dull animalism. The native ability lying hid in many poor Welsh cottages has for centuries sorely lacked a patron. The social separation of classes caused by difference of race and language has prevented poor youths from finding a friend in the squire and clergyman. Too often both were unable to detect and slow to admire ability clothed in Welsh garb. The Eisteddfod has been an Alma Mater to many friendless youths. By the composition of a poem or essay, many a young Welshman of ability, born in the humblest position, has been first able to make his merits known, and to rise out of his obscurity into local usefulness and eminence.

Not a few of the ablest Nonconformist ministers and

Welsh journalists have risen from among the Eisteddfod prizemen ; some of the ablest and most influential of the native clergy, who have done most to preserve the hold that the Church still retains upon the Welsh-speaking people, such as Walter Davies (Gwallter Mechain), John Blackwell (Alun), Evan Evans (Ieuan Glan Geirionydd), Morris Williams (Nicander), are indebted for aid to the Eisteddfod. It has been supposed by English people that the Eisteddfod is an instrument for the glorification of the Welsh language and the exclusion of English. No idea could be more baseless. The proceedings are conducted in the English language to a considerable extent. This Welsh national gathering has, like similar institutions among other nations, certain features that present ludicrous aspects. Like the Lord Mayor's Show ceremony, it appears to many mere useless mummery. But as the Londoners find in the city pageant a link that connects the citizenship of to-day with the municipal life of distant centuries, so the Welshman, in addition to advantages of a more solid value, finds in his Eisteddfod a nursery of healthy patriotic sentiment and of legitimate pride in the history and traditions of his ancient race.

We have now reviewed the peculiar national life, religious divisions, and social conditions of Wales, and have considered the forces that are most powerfully influencing the Welsh people of to-day. It becomes necessary to inquire into the causes of the Church's weakness in Wales. Why has the Church, that has inherited the lineage of the ancient Bishops and saints of Britain, and the religious endowments of the country, lost her hold of the majority of the Welsh people, so attached to their old traditions and institutions? The general alienation of the people dates from the eighteenth century. That alienation has been gradually increasing for a hundred and fifty years, and its progress can hardly be said to have ceased. It is very essential to the recovery of the Church that the causes of her decay should be understood.

The causes may be divided into two kinds—
1. Those that are common to England and Wales.
2. Those that are peculiar to Wales.

The chief of the causes common to England and Wales was the poverty caused by lay impropriations and pluralities. In his work upon the diocese of St. David's, published in 1721, Dr. Erasmus Saunders dwelt at length upon this evil, and its fatal effect in depriving parishioners of the regular and effective ministrations of a duly maintained clergy. In his able paper, read at the Swansea Church Congress, Canon Bevan stated, "Crushing poverty and the disorganization consequent thereon were, in Dr. Saunders' view, at the bottom of all the evils that then afflicted the Church in Wales." After a careful perusal of Dr. Saunders' work, we are unable to agree with Canon Bevan's estimate of his view. It is true that Dr. Saunders exposed the spoliation to which the Church had been subjected, and dwelt upon all the evils that followed her impoverishment. But it is quite evident that Dr. Saunders looked upon another abuse, to which we shall presently allude, as the primary cause of her ruin. We are equally unable to accept Canon Bevan's dictum as to the present difficulty of the Church in Wales. He stated at Swansea, "Poverty is still the besetting infirmity of the Church in Wales. Poverty is still the main cause of her existing inefficiency."

It is quite true that poverty does cripple the progress of the Church. But it is not true that poverty is the "main cause of her existing inefficiency," and "at the bottom of all the evils." To those who know the Welsh people it must be obvious that the poverty of the Church is not so much a cause as an effect. The systems that supplanted the Church, and occupied the ground which she had once held, won their victories without the aid of any endowments whatever. The Church comparatively poor gave way before societies absolutely penniless. Those societies at present raise annually not less than £300,000 for religious purposes in Wales. It is obvious that, if the Church had retained her hold of the affections of the people, this large income would have been offered upon her altar, and have enabled her to accomplish her mission without lack of resources. The poverty of the Welsh Church, therefore, is due to the alienation of the affections of the Welsh people, and the radical cause of her decay must be found in the influences that produced that alienation.

It may also be added that the spoliation of ecclesiastical revenues, so far as it was more general in Wales than in England, must be traced to an influence peculiar to the position of the country. That spoliation, especially in the southern counties, was most thorough. In his essay on "The Causes which have produced Dissent from the Established Church in Wales," Arthur James Johnes, in 1831, writes the following words: "It is impossible for the mind of man to conceive a more appalling picture of devastation than is presented by a mere muster-roll of the names of the present possessors of Church property in many of the South Wales counties. Opposite to the most valuable part of the endowments of the most valuable benefices, we shall generally find the name of some English nobleman or gentleman, resident in London, in Devonshire, in the most distant parts of the kingdom; and again, in juxtaposition with the paltry pittances left to the clergy, we shall continually meet with the name of some reverend pluralist, living equally remote—the incumbent, it may be, of a rich benefice in Northamptonshire, or residing free from all parochial duties in London! Would that this were an imaginary picture; but alas! it is but a too literal description of the Church, as it exists in Radnorshire and Cardiganshire, the two poorest counties in South Wales."

The poverty of the Church in the two counties named is undeniable, and, according to Canon Bevan's view, the weakness of the Church in them ought to be exceptional. But in Cardiganshire, where a native clergy have always officiated, the Church is stronger than in some districts whose richer endowments have attracted the presence of strangers.

In many districts of England poverty has afflicted

the Church. In the new groups of population called into existence by mining and manufacturing enterprise, there has been a great want of resources to provide churches and ministrations. In different forms, therefore, poverty has been a cause of depression common to the Church in England and in Wales.

Another cause of Church weakness common to England and Wales was the general religious apathy and spiritual deadness that prevailed among clergy and laity. There can be no doubt that Wales suffered her full share from this cause. The spiritual tone of the men who enjoyed the revenues, while unable or unwilling to do the duties of the Church in Wales, must have had a deadening influence upon the people. But there were some lights in the darkness. Before the end of the seventeenth century Thomas Gouge and his associates had made a noble effort to spread religious knowledge among the Welsh people. In 1709 Griffith Jones began that ministerial career in which, by means of circulating schools, he taught 150,000 of his countrymen to read the Scriptures in their own language. His influence upon Wales has been profound and permanent. His Catechetical Manual upon the Creed, the Lord's Prayer, and the Ten Commandments is one of the very best that exists, either in Welsh or English. From it the Calvinistic Methodists have drawn all that is best in the teaching of their denominational manual, the "Hyfforddwr." Griffith Jones, who did more, probably, for the religious life of Wales than any other man in the eighteenth century, lived and died in the communion of the Church, but never received any high dignity or emolument in recognition of his magnificent services. In the "Welsh Piety" for 1741, p. 29, a letter is extant in which he complains that the Bishops of Wales did not countenance his labour. But he was loved and respected by the common people, who crowded to hear him preach. Dr. Erasmus Saunders, in a passage already quoted, has described the eagerness with which the Welsh peasantry sought religious instruction, and the delight with which they engaged in psalmody and worship. It is, therefore, clear that religious apathy and deadness did not exist in an exceptional degree in Wales. Before the rise of Howell Harris and Rowlands, the founders of Methodism, there was one religious leader in the Church of extraordinary influence, and the masses of the people manifested, in the words of Saunders, written in 1721, an "extraordinary disposition to religion."

It cannot, therefore, be said that religious apathy existed in Wales to a greater extent than in England. But Nonconformity has obtained an ascendancy in Wales far greater than it has reached in any district of England.

It is, therefore, necessary to look for the secret of its vigour in some cause peculiar to the country.

That cause will be found in the influence of race. It is natural that a dominant race should endeavour to seize every vantage-ground. The higher offices of the Church, carrying with them temporal power and social influence, have always been an object of ambition.

The rulers of the State at one time, and the social leaders of a diocese at another time, have naturally sought to strengthen their position by placing their adherents and kinsmen in the high places of the Church. Promotion in obedience to worldly motives has always had a deadening effect. But when such promotion involved, as in Wales, the intrusion, among a deeply religious, sensitive people, of ecclesiastics unsympathetic and ignorant of their language, the deadly effect was greatly increased. This evil has existed from the twelfth century, and has not yet entirely disappeared. In 1196 the Welsh princes, in a petition to the Pope, used the following strong language: "The Archbishops of Canterbury, as if it were a matter of course, send among us English Bishops, ignorant alike of both our customs and language, and who can neither preach the Word of God to the people, nor receive their confessions except through interpreters. These Bishops, arriving from England, love neither ourselves nor our country; but, on the contrary, vex and persecute us with a hatred rooted and national; they seek not the good of our souls, but only desire to rule over us, and not to benefit us."

That this anti-national policy was deliberately adopted, is proved by a few extracts from the documents collected by Spelman and Wilkins, and edited by Arthur West Haddan. The mind of Richard I. is expressed in the following words: "Rex nullum Walensem, præsertim autem-illum, qui principes Walliæ sanguine contingeret, episcopum in Walliâ habere volebat." The Archiepiscopal mind in the reign of King John is described in these words of the chapter of St. David's: "Prædictus Archiepiscopus cum regis officialibus nobis extraneum aliquem, linguæ nostræ et morum patriæ prorsus ignarum, contra electionem nostram et privilegia nostra violentiâ intrusione præficere volebat."

"The contest," wrote Mr. Haddan, "between Chapter, Crown, and Pope for the right of nomination to bishoprics—a contest complicated in Wales by questions of race and of English domination, ... the freedom and self-government accorded to the National Church of almost all dates, and diminished gradually as Henry III. and Edward I. brought English law to bear upon the subject, *pari passu* with their gradual and attempted Anglicizing of Wales, and *the commencement of that bane of the Welsh Church*, the imposing upon it of a clergy that could not speak Welsh, and the treating its sees as mere pieces of preferment,—all these are surely subjects which have a living interest, and belong to questions of which the moving forces are active in the present day."

The Tudor dynasty, being of Welsh origin, adopted a wiser and a juster course. Elizabeth adopted the policy of a Welsh Episcopate; and of sixteen Bishops appointed in her reign, thirteen were Welsh. The same policy gave to the Welsh people that noble version of the Scriptures, from the pen of Bishop Morgan, published in 1588. That policy, undoubtedly, secured the reception of the reformed faith in Wales. For had the Scriptures been withheld from the Welsh as they were from the Irish, there can be little doubt that Wales would have been to this day no less ultramontane than Ireland and Brittany. But after the close of the Tudor dynasty, the old anti-national policy was gradually revived, until at last, from 1700 to 1870, the Bishops of Wales were almost exclusively Englishmen. In every generation this fatal policy called forth "protests" from those who loved the Church. In 1721, the third section of Dr. Erasmus Saunders' work, to which allusion has already been made, headed, "Wherein are considered the injuries occasioned to religion by pastors that neglect the use of our language, by non-residence," etc., contains the following passages:—

"This is a part very disagreeable, and what I wish my subject would permit me to overlook and pass by; and so to prevent the angry resentments which (I am sensible) the telling of unacceptable truths must expect to meet with. But since I have gone so far, it will, I think, be necessary to proceed a little further, and to point out the causes that mostly seem to have contributed to the desolations I have been describing; and this I shall endeavour to do, without regard to any other view or interest but that of truth."

This passage, and what follows, is quite inconsistent with Canon Bevan's opinion that poverty was, in Dr. Saunders' view, at the bottom of all the evils that afflicted the Church in Wales. Dr. Saunders proceeds to add—

"First, then, if it was not an opinion that did not seem very well to comport and bear with the sense and practice of many learned and eminent men, I could not forbear thinking that the disposing of Welsh preferments, I mean those especially that are attended with the cure of souls, to such as are wholly ignorant of that language, to be a practice that has contributed not a little to the decay and desolation of our religion. . . . What benefits are the people to expect, as to knowledge or information, from the ministry of such, who can neither preach nor pray so as to be understood by them? . . . Again, it was upon the same principle (as I am informed) that the present worthy and learned Bishop of Carlisle, though there were many motives to induce him to it, did yet decline accepting of a bishopric in Wales, namely, because he was a stranger to the language, and that he therefore conscientiously feared he should not be able to be so useful to his diocese, nor so capable of edifying and instructing them, as he thought himself obliged to be. But all are not of his opinion; some have greater courage, and undoubtedly don't want their reasons."

The protest against this unjust policy, uttered in such strong language by Dr. Erasmus Saunders in 1721, was renewed fifty years later on a memorable occasion. In the year 1766, Dr. Bowles, an Englishman, utterly ignorant of the Welsh language, was presented by the Bishop of Bangor to the living of Trefdraeth, in Anglesey, a parish which was then, and is still, entirely Welsh-speaking. The patriotic Welsh baronet, Sir Watkin Williams Wynn, and the Cymrodorion Society, assisted the churchwardens in bringing an action to prove the illegality of the presentation. The action was tried before the Worshipful G. Hay, LL.D., Dean of the Arches, and a full report of the depositions, arguments, and judgment is extant in the British Museum, bearing on its title-page the significant motto, "Cwn mudion ydynt, heb fedru cyfarth" (Esay)—"They are dumb dogs that cannot bark" (Isaiah). Some of the evidence was most painful. But inasmuch as the evil which it exposes has not yet entirely disappeared, it will be well to reproduce some passages. It is perfectly well known among Welshmen that no man, who has only acquired Welsh as an adult, has ever been able to master the pronunciation so as to be able to address a Welsh audience without producing some jar on their ears. The late Mr. George Borrow, an accomplished linguist, who claimed to understand twenty-eight languages, acquired a thorough knowledge of Welsh, and was deeply read in its literature, but he could never speak it with any approach to the correct accent, though he lived some time in Wales, and endeavoured to converse daily with the peasantry. He was in the habit of saying that it was the most difficult language in the west of Europe. Poor Dr. Bowles seems to have been but an indifferent linguist, if we may judge from the evidence of Richard Williams, of Tre-ddafydd, Trefdraeth, who deposed "That the first Sunday he (Dr. Bowles) officiated in the said church, as rector of the said rectory, he read or performed Divine service in the English language, and brought one Robert Edwards, of Llandegfan, with him, to give the necessary answers in the different parts of the service, as the greatest part of the inhabitants and parishioners who composed the congregation that Sunday, of whom the deponent was one, did not, as he verily believes, understand a single word that was said; ... that he soon afterwards, on a Sunday, preached a sermon in the said parish church in the English language, when the deponent was present, the text to which sermon the said Thomas Bowles attempted to give out in the Welsh language, but both the sermon in the English and the text in the Welsh language were totally unintelligible to the whole congregation; ... that he afterwards attempted to administer the Sacrament to such of the parishioners as chose to attend; that a great number of them attended accordingly, among whom was the deponent, but the said Thomas Bowles could not then make himself understood to any of the communicants, and so ridiculous was the attempt, that many of them burst out into loud laughter, while others were holding their hands before their mouths, to prevent the like irregularities on so solemn an occasion."

Dr. Bowles' morality seems to have been quite as defective as his Welsh pronunciation. In order to prove his ability to pronounce Welsh intelligibly, he produced a certificate, showing that he had satisfactorily performed Divine service in that language, and signed by his own son-in-law and by two Welsh parishioners. In court one of the witnesses, John Thomas, of Tanylan, deposed that the signature of the two parishioners were not honestly obtained. "He verily believes the said signatures to the said certificates were, so far as relates to Hugh Williams and Richard Williams, obtained by fraud and imposition; that Richard Williams signed the same without being at all acquainted with the contents, and that Dr. Bowles obtained Hugh Williams's signature by a stratagem, in the manner following, as the said Hugh Williams informed the said respondent. The said Hugh Williams is by trade a shoemaker, and Dr. Bowles went to him to bespeak a pair of shoes, at which time he asked the said Hugh Williams what his name was, and producing a sheet of white paper, without any writing upon it whatever, desired the said Hugh Williams to write his name upon it, in order that he might know his name properly in case he should want it; that the said Hugh Williams accordingly wrote his name upon such sheet of paper and delivered it to Dr. Bowles, and that the said Hugh Williams was afterwards informed that he had signed a certificate of Dr. Bowles' having performed Divine service in the Welsh language, which alarmed him very much, and knowing he had not signed any paper for Dr. Bowles except as before mentioned, he, the said Hugh Williams, went before a justice of the peace, and made an affidavit of the whole transaction, and such certificate has been the general talk of the whole parish ever since."

Concerning this unworthy artifice, significant of the moral condition of men who seek ecclesiastical promotion on false pretences, the judge of the court expressed himself in these severe words—

"Dr. Bowles appears before me in a very unfavourable light, on account of the manner of obtaining this certificate, which almost destroys the very end for which it was produced."

It has been alleged by some that the appointment of Englishmen to the Welsh sees, and of clergy ignorant of the language to Welsh parishes, were simply errors in judgment and acts of carelessness, not measures dictated by a deliberate policy. But this theory is inconsistent with the language of the advocate employed to defend Dr. Bowles' position, and to justify the presentation of the Bishop. It must be supposed that he had received instructions, and that his argument expressed the views of his clients. His reasoning, therefore, is interesting. He said, in the course of his speech—

"Wales is a conquered country. It is proper to introduce the English language, and it is the duty of the Bishops to endeavour to promote the English in order to introduce the language. . . . It is the most effectual way to bring about so desirable a change. The confusion of languages at the Tower of Babel was revealed to us as a curse from heaven."

These words clearly indicate that such appointments were made in pursuance of a deliberate policy. The advocate for the churchwardens, whose words are prophetic of the utter failure that has attended that policy in the last hundred and ten years, made the following sensible reply—

"We may admit that it would be to the advantage of the country if the Welsh language was entirely abolished, and only one language to be used in every part of the kingdom. But this is not the method of doing it, neither will it attain that end."

The verdict of the court justified the action of the churchwardens. It did not deprive Dr. Bowles, but it guarded Welsh parishes against the repetition of such appointments. The judge ruled—

"It is proper that the Bishops in Wales should take such order for the cure of souls, as to appoint pastors that are acquainted with the language of the country. It is the primitive law of the Church, and it is law at this time."

Iniquitous appointments, such as that of Dr. Bowles, have not been unknown or, indeed, unfrequent in the last hundred years. But if the churchwardens of Trefdraeth had not brought their action, such abuses would have been more frequent. The parishes were protected by the decision. But the dioceses unfortunately derived no such benefit from the case. It must be confessed with sorrow that men have been advanced to the highest position in the Welsh Church who have not shrunk from officiating in Welsh in such a manner as to excite the ridicule rather than to edify the souls of their hearers, and who must be pronounced guilty of having, whether consciously or unconsciously, in the words of the advocate for the Trefdraeth churchwardens, "burlesqued Divine service, and profaned the ordinances."

From the twelfth century to the present time there have not been wanting in any generation some intrepid Welshmen to protest against the unjust policy that has destroyed the spiritual efficiency of the Church in their country. But the most powerful protest against the system, and the most exhaustive statement of the evils that have arisen from it that has ever been made, is contained in the able and learned essay from the pen of the late Arthur James Johnes, "one of Her Majesty's Judges of the County Court of Record," first published in 1832, and republished by him in his old age, in 1870. It is a work that ought to be read by all who desire to understand the inner life of Wales, and the present position of the Welsh Church. As a highly educated Welsh layman, a zealous Churchman, and an able lawyer, Judge Johnes was peculiarly qualified to state the case fully and powerfully, and to marshal the evidence against the system which he so mercilessly condemned. A Welsh clergyman, writing upon the subject, exposes himself to the poisoned arrows of those who seek to defend an iniquity by imputing to its assailants selfish motives. The testimony of a layman is not open to such imputations. It is, therefore, well that the strong language employed by Mr. Johnes in 1832, and deliberately repeated in 1870, should be known to the English public, who are so often misinformed by interested witnesses upon this question. From the second chapter of his essay, headed "The unpopularity of the Episcopal clergy ascribable to two causes: 1. Their want of sympathy with the feelings and tastes of the people. 2. Their neglect of the language of the people. Both these causes themselves the effects of an English hierarchy," we take the following extracts :—

"The unpopularity of the Church in Wales has a deeper cause than is generally imagined. There are certain differences in the characters of nations that resist all attempts at perfect assimilation. . . . In accounting for this spread of Dissent in Wales, in my humble opinion, too much stress has generally been laid on the neglect of the Welsh language, and too little on the peculiarities of the Welsh character. I cannot help thinking that if the Cambro-British dialect could be annihilated in a day, the want of sympathy between the clergy and their flocks would still continue to alienate the hearts of the people from the Establishment. . . . It is with the greatest reluctance that I feel myself bound to state a conviction that may at first sight seem to savour of an ungracious national jealousy; yet, after the most anxious and careful consideration of the subject, I feel that I owe it to truth to state my persuasion that the crying abuse of the Church in Wales, and the fundamental cause of all the defects peculiar to the Church in that country, is the system of conferring her bishoprics on Englishmen. . . . No one would protest more strongly than I should against a puerile clamour at an Englishman holding a high office in Wales, merely because he was an Englishman; my objection is founded purely on the broad Protestant principles of the Church of England. . . . If the principle was emancipation from a slavery to mere superstitious sounds, and its object to give religion once more to the hearts and language of the people, I cannot perceive any real distinction between the present ecclesiastical government of Wales and a recurrence to the worst practices of popery. . . .

"What are we to say of the mode in which the rite of Confirmation was administered in Wales? It cannot, in this case, be said that the responsibility rests with the parochial clergy, and attaches but in a slight degree to the Bishop; for in this instance a duty arises attaching primarily, solely, and exclusively to the Bishop—a duty which cannot be performed in any other language than that of the nation to whom it is administered, without a complete mockery of the very nature of the ordinance, and of every principle of the Church of England. Yet it is thus administered! . . .

"An English Bishop, in discharging the duties of a Welsh see, labours under every possible embarrassment. To distribute patronage so as best to provide for the religious wants of the community, requires a knowledge of the peculiar talents of the clergy and of the various local exigencies of a diocese. Now, an English Bishop in Wales has in this respect everything to learn. From his ignorance of the language, he must judge of circumstances at second hand; from his want of sympathy with the temperament of the people, he cannot rightly appreciate even the information he may receive. . . . Hence the Bishops in Wales generally abandon after a time that line of policy which at first appeared indisputable; and thus it is that, often with the best intentions on their part, their conduct is a series of vacillations. . . .

"When the mainspring is not right, the whole

machinery must necessarily go wrong. I do not, of course, mean to affirm that the English spirit of the Welsh Bishops operates as a positive discouragement to preaching and instruction in the Welsh language; but it withdraws from these practices that encouragement which it is the object of their office to afford. Even should they feel desirous of rewarding merit of this kind, they cannot do it satisfactorily, as they cannot detect or appreciate it; much less can they prevent the more worldly and narrow-minded part of the inferior clergy from entertaining the notion that a neglect of their native language is likely to recommend them to the favour of their English diocesan.

"But perhaps in no respect are the evils of the system more apparent than in their ill effect on the higher ranks in Wales. The clergy ought to be, and generally are, the link of intelligence between the aristocracy and the lower and middle ranks; but in Wales, the clergy being all either strangers or men of humble rank, this link is broken, and what is the consequence? Why, that the higher classes, though in other respects often highly gifted and well disposed, will frequently be found ignorant of all that is going on in their own country, of the very rudiments of her literature, and even of her language! It is deeply to be regretted that the aristocracy of Wales should have allowed their Church thus to grow up into a prescriptive abuse; it has been the means of weakening that attachment which the people once felt to them and their fathers."

But it will be said, by those who have no knowledge

of the inner state of the Welsh Church, that the long-lived abuse which has alienated the Welsh people and weakened the Church has ceased to exist, inasmuch as the present Bishops in Wales have some knowledge of the Welsh language. It is true that in 1870 Mr. Gladstone reversed this anti-national policy by the appointment of a Welshman to the see of St. Asaph, and that two natives of Wales have since been appointed to Welsh sees. But the abuse, that has been at last condemned and removed, has left behind it evils that still exist, " testa diu," etc.

The neglect of the Welsh language and national jealousy of Welsh preaching and literature, which were inevitably produced by the example and influence of the English Episcopate, has left consequences that will not disappear in one generation. The tone and spirit of the old *régime* still survives in a large number of the clergy. Welsh preaching, speaking, and writing are still considered vulgar, and left by the superior clergy to the Nonconformists. The inferior clergy naturally imitate the mental habits of their superiors. Consequently the agencies that mould the life of the Welsh-speaking million of Wales are too often neglected by the Church, and the higher clergy are content to be apostles to the genteel.

An examination of the professional qualifications and performances of the leading clergy of Wales will confirm this statement. There are twenty-eight leading dignitaries in the four Welsh dioceses, in each of which, as has been shown, a majority of the population, if

Sir Hussey Vivian's testimony is correct, must be supposed to worship in the Welsh language. Of the twenty-eight dignitaries, there are thirteen who cannot be said to have any command of the Welsh language. Of the thirteen, ten are absolutely ignorant of it, and three, being only able to read or recite it with very great difficulty, and a most imperfect accent, are quite unable to converse in it. Out of the remaining fifteen, not more than four have any power as Welsh preachers and not more than three have ever attempted to contribute to the religious or secular literature of Wales. The result of this state of things is that those forces which have been described as most potent in influencing the Welsh people of to-day are not wielded by the Church.

1. The gift of oratory, to which the Welsh people are perhaps more subject than any other section of her Majesty's subjects, has not yet been cultivated by any considerable number of the clergy. Seeing that the places of dignity are attained by men utterly devoid of Welsh oratorical power, the younger clergy have been tempted to think that broken Welsh and faltering utterance are at least not incompatible with the highest promotion. The practical result may easily be imagined.

2. The peculiar influence that belongs to Bardism and the Eisteddfod, which, if duly guided, might have been made powerful for good, has been lost to the Church by the unpatriotic spirit dominant in its high places. It is remembered with bitterness throughout Wales that clergymen who were also eminent as bards,

such as Walter Davies (Gwallter Mechain), Evan Evans (Ieuan Glan Geirionydd) and others, who might have done the Church immense service, were treated by the Bishops of the day with long-continued neglect.

Another evil common to the Church in England and Wales has been greatly aggravated in the Principality by the separation of the higher clergy and of the squires from the middle and working classes, through ignorance of the language and want of social sympathy. The Welsh people have, in the Nonconformist societies, been accustomed to self-government. The more intelligent farmer and tradesman, if a Nonconformist, takes an active part in the government of the chapel. At the great meetings he is brought into association with his fellows of similar position throughout the denomination, and his desire for activity and his love of society are at once gratified. The Church layman in Wales is doomed to inaction and isolation. The autocracy of the Bishop in the diocese and the autocracy of the clergyman in the parish leave very little room for the activity of laymen. They may be consulted, but they have no recognized place or functions in Church work except as churchwardens. If the Bishop, before making an appointment to a benefice, visited the parish and met the principal parishioners and landowners in consultation, it would be a step towards the limitation of Episcopal autocracy and the ecclesiastical enfranchisement of the laity. It could be done voluntarily without legislation. In past times a Bishop ignorant of the language and of the people could not have ventured to draw near to a laity with whom he would have been unable to deal with the authority that is given by superior knowledge and sympathy. He was obliged to entrench himself in the solitary dignity of an unapproachable autocracy, in order to conceal his real weakness as an overseer of souls whom he could not understand. Native Bishops, masters of the language and in sympathy with the people, can venture to lay aside autocracy, and to take the laity into their counsels, so as to gain for their Episcopate the strength which it cannot have without the support and concurrence of the laymen of the diocese.

In parishes, clergymen unable to guide their flocks could not venture to take the laymen of their parishes into consultation. But every parish priest, who knows the language and feelings of his people, would find strength by voluntarily forming a parochial council to consider all parochial matters, and to aid him in ensuring the progress of the Church.

These measures would gradually attract into the Church that admirable and influential class of men who now find work as "blaenoriaid" and "diaconiaid" in the chapels, by giving them a sphere for the exercise of their religious zeal and energy, and a field for the attainment of social power. In the past, inefficient and unsympathetic Bishops and clergy, unable to attract to their aid a laity whom they did not understand, weakened the Church by sending into Nonconformity the pillars that would have been its most powerful supporters among the population.

But it is when we regard the condition of the Welsh press and literature that the ruin of Church influence, wrought by an Episcopate and clergy negligent of the Welsh language, becomes most apparent. The terrible losses inflicted upon the Church by the want of a friendly and by the attacks of a hostile press are vigorously set forth by the Rev. D. Williams, in his paper read at the Swansea Church Congress.

"The Church cannot exist, as a living body demanding recognition, appreciation, and reverence at the hands of the people, without a powerful and adequate representation in the press. It is upon the press we must depend to reach the masses. There are scores of Welsh parishes where Dissent could not coexist with the kindness, ability, and devotion of the clergy, only for the dissemination of the distinctive doctrines of secularism and disestablishment by means of the Dissenting press. The good work of the clergy is more than counterbalanced by the Dissenting newspapers. The press of Saturday is more than a match for the pulpit of Sunday. They read the Dissenting publications, and will not come to church. There is not a chapel throughout the length and breadth of the land without its newspaper correspondent and distributor, and to the enormous power they exercise many a clergyman can bear abundant testimony. . . . Now, what has the Church Welsh press produced in books or pamphlets, in literature, in theology, in physics, by way of travels, commentaries, manuals, etc., for the enlightenment of the Welsh nation? What has come from our grammar schools, colleges, cathedrals, and Episcopal palaces? There is only one sad, monotonous, melancholy cry, 'Nothing, nothing!'"

Mr. Williams, in language which may appear to some to be irreverently plain-spoken, gives his view of the cause to which the weakness, or rather the non-existence, of a Welsh Church press and literature is due.

"I unhesitatingly aver, without fear of contradiction, that the true cause does not lie in the apathetic ignorance of the Welsh mind, or in the want of appreciation of true talent, or in the absence of literary culture in the Church. It lies at the door of the Welsh Bishops and the dignified clergy, who have for generations sneered at the Welsh language and the Welsh press. This cause lies deep in the history of the Welsh Church. . . . It is supposed to be a genteel thing in Episcopal palaces to throw cold water on literary efforts and tendencies. . . . The decadence of Church literature in Wales is directly traceable to an unsympathetic Episcopate."

This clergyman may be thought to have given way to strong feeling, and under the influence of national sentiment to have exaggerated the shortcomings of the Welsh Church's rulers. It will, therefore, be well to cite the testimony of an able Welsh layman, selected by the late Bishop of Llandaff as the most competent in his diocese to speak with authority concerning the Welsh press. Mr. Titus Lewis, F.S.A., an able and energetic man of business, well known throughout South Wales, which his commercial avocation compels him to traverse frequently from year to year, and therefore thoroughly qualified by personal observation to speak of the religious and social life of the country, used the following language in a paper read at Swansea on the same occasion :—

"Let us, then, even if the avowal bring shame with it, acknowledge that the press, the most powerful engine, under God, to propagate her principles and to defend her rights, has in a great measure been neglected by the Welsh Church. It is not to the point that this failure to turn such an engine, now an enemy on the whole, into an ally, may have been brought about by the apathy of Churchmen. It matters not that the clergy, whose lead the laity follow, may have made no effort to circulate among their flocks those Church periodicals already existing. It may be true, as I have heard asserted, that there are scores of parishes in South Wales and Monmouthshire in which not a single Church periodical is ever seen. The fact remains that the press, as an exponent of Church views, has no hold on the Welsh people. On the contrary, it is said that the people of Wales, far from deriving their knowledge of the religious world from Church sources, are ripe for disestablishment. If it be true, the reason is obvious ; they are being educated by the Dissenting press, and the Church sits still, and, on the whole, makes no effort to let her children hear both sides of the question. While this is the state of things, it is worse than useless to talk of organization and co-operation.

"These terms imply material to organize and co-operate on. While the Nonconformists have their organization complete, with a staff of agents in every parish and village to distribute their periodicals, of the Church it has been said, 'The only reward a man will have for defending her in Wales, will be a pauper's funeral, and a costly tomb.' ... These are bitter truths, and you may think, from what I have already said, my attitude, instead of being that of a faithful Welsh Churchman, is one of Dissenting partisanship. But, as I have said, we must face the bitter ere we can create the sweet. Now, it is essential to reform in this matter that the people be appealed to in the vernacular. Englishmen say, 'Why, railroads have so far Anglicized the country that it is a rare thing to meet a native who does not speak and read English, and therefore the high-toned religious press of England is at his disposal.' This is the argument which presents young Englishmen to Welsh livings, provided they possess such a qualification as a smattering of Rowlands' Welsh Grammar and an indulgent examining chaplain may secure to them, when a thorough hearty conversation of five minutes' duration would thoroughly unmask their radical ignorance. This is the policy which has thrust on us men, clever enough indeed to learn our tongue, but never to feel it, or for the people who speak it. Our tongue cannot be learned by a stranger; 'its fire burns only in the native breast.'"

These testimonies, of a representative Welsh clergyman and of a representative Welsh Church layman, selected to speak for their class, will enable the English public to understand why that instrument, which during the last thirty years has been most powerfully influencing the Welsh-speaking people, has not been wielded in support of the Church, but virtually handed over to those who have left her. It is to be hoped that Mr. Williams's warning and appeal uttered on the same occasion will not be in vain. "The same blind and suicidal policy is now pursued by our Church dignitaries towards the Welsh press as was pursued by their ancestors towards the preaching of Daniel Rowlands of Llangeitho, and Charles of Bala. It was not genteel then to preach to the masses; it is not genteel now to write to the Welsh press. But if a fatal mistake is acknowledged on all hands to have been committed in the past as to Welsh preaching, in God's Name let us not repeat it in our day towards the press."

Native Bishops, understanding the language and people, able to appreciate literary ability in Welsh clergymen and laymen, will have no difficulty in gradually creating a Welsh Church press and literature that will extend her influence among the masses. They will realize the importance of the work, and take counsel with each other, and summon to their aid from the four dioceses the clergymen and laymen most capable of aiding, by advice, literary service, and pecuniary resources, in removing a dangerous source of weakness, and supplying that instrument of strength, the need of which has been so vigorously and vehemently set forth in the above extracts.

It may well be asked why the clergy and Churchmen of Wales have not raised louder protests against the system of appointments that has produced results so disastrous. The answer is not difficult to find. In Wales it has been true in a peculiar sense that "Ecclesia est in Episcopo." A very large proportion of all the benefices and all the cathedral stalls are in the gift of the Bishops. Many of the Welsh clergy are poor men, and those who are not poor have the natural desire to win their share of professional success. Poverty and professional failure would have been the inevitable lot of any clergyman who, in the last hundred and eighty years, had ventured to protest against the misgovernment of the Bishops, who, although not masters of the language or affections of the people, had the chief command of all their ecclesiastical endowments and dignities. The squires, being themselves ignorant of the language, were unable to realize the evil. The masses of the Welsh-speaking people made their protest by seceding from the worship of the Church of their fathers. Up to 1867, under a restricted suffrage, political power in Wales was largely in the hands of the non-Welsh-speaking landowners, whose tenants formed the county electorate, and voted as they were told. At the general election of 1868 political power passed into other hands; many of the former representatives, both Whig and Tory, who were not in sympathy with the people, gave place to men who, though owning little land, could command popular sympathies. The expression of Welsh national feeling by the previously unenfranchised classes in 1868 was so decided, that the election has been humorously called the "Revolt of the Welsh." The old landowners of Wales are themselves, upon the whole, generous and benevolent, and enjoy a large measure of popular good will. Their loss of political influence is mainly due to the unpopularity of the Bishops and higher clergy, with whom they were associated in the popular mind, and from whom they derived their social tone and their habit of ignoring the Welsh language. It is noteworthy that the enfranchisement of the Welsh masses in 1868 was almost immediately followed by the elevation to the Episcopal Bench, on the nomination of the great Liberal statesman, whose ear has never been deaf to the cry for liberty and justice, of the first Welshman mitred in a hundred and fifty years.

It has, then, been honestly admitted that the Welsh Church is in an anomalous position, as asserted by Mr. Dillwyn in his notice of motion, inasmuch as a majority of the Welsh people have ceased to worship habitually in her sanctuaries, although they have by no means altogether deserted them. But that anomaly is due to no causes inherent in the position of the Established Church, but to abuses which have been partially removed, and against the recurrence of which the Welsh people have in their own hands effective safeguards. A system of Episcopal appointments, anti-national and unjust, made in obedience to the dictates of a false policy that has proved a failure, and in defiance of the wishes of the then unenfranchised Welsh masses, has produced the Church's depression and created the anomaly that exists. But for the future the Welsh people will have the virtual power of appointing the prelates that will occupy their sees. No Premier, under the present political condition, will ever have any other object in view, when appointing to the Welsh sees, than to give legitimate satisfaction to the people of the Welsh dioceses.

But it can excite no surprise that a system of ecclesiastical misgovernment so glaring, and obstinately maintained until it was destroyed by the emancipated popular voice, should have left upon the mind of the Welsh people a painful impression, and created a profound prejudice against a Church presented to them in so odious a light. Many of the Welsh people are unable to think of the Church except as "Yr Eglwys Wladol," a State Church using religion as an instrument for fulfilling the purposes of a short-sighted statecraft. The Liberation Society at one time found eager hearers and warm adherents in Wales. A cry for the disestablishment and disendowment of the Welsh Church was heard in 1870, and found expression in Mr. Watkin Williams's motion on the floor of the House of Commons.

But there is some reason to think that, since that date, Welshmen, who are a thoughtful and cautious race, have learnt to look at the matter more calmly; to remember not only the past abuses in the Church, but also its future possibilities of usefulness, and to ask themselves whether it would be wise to avenge an old wrong wrought by strangers at the expense of inflicting upon their country a lasting injury. The arguments against the destructive Liberationist policy commend themselves to the sober-minded, thoughtful, and unprejudiced men, who can emancipate themselves from that narrowness of view from which neither Churchmen nor Nonconformists are always free. The Liberationist arguments, on the other hand, are plausible, and appeal at once to such natural, but not very noble, passions as social jealousy, pecuniary cupidity, and the love of novelty. But there are also nobler motives and aspirations working on the same side, such as the love of fair play, and the hope of greater religious unity. Many honest Welshmen firmly believe that disestablishment and disendowment would put an end to a social inequality of an arbitrary kind now existing between the clergy and Nonconformist ministers, and to the apparent injustice that now obliges a Nonconformist farmer to pay tithe-rent charge for the support of clergy whose ministrations he does not often seek; that the voluntary system would suffice to maintain a sufficient and well-qualified body of religious teachers; that ministerial discipline and efficiency would be more easily maintained; that all religious denominations in Wales would be drawn into more harmonious relations; and that the tithe-rent charges, by which the clergy are now maintained, might be more usefully devoted to the payment of the education rate or some other object of secular utility.

In considering the attractions of the Liberationist programme, it will be well for Welshmen to realize as clearly as may be the losses that will also be inseparable from any gains that may accompany its realization. One serious loss will be the partial destruction of the only really ancient institution that belongs to the Welsh nation. The Church which it is proposed to destroy existed before the Saxon invasion. Its ancient churches are mostly dedicated to the saints who adorned the earliest ages of British Christianity, and connect the Welshmen of to-day with ancestors who were Christian Churchmen while the Anglo-Saxons were still in the darkness of heathenism. Around their walls countless generations of their forefathers are sleeping. To destroy the ancient parish churches of Wales will be to break the objective link that connects the Wales of to-day with that antiquity of which it is so justly proud.

Now, it is inevitable that, if the endowments of the Church are secularized, a very large number of the churches in country districts must fall into ruins. A still larger number will be virtually lost to the Welsh people, and be handed over to the exclusive use of the English-speaking upper class, who, having wealth, will be the chief supporters of the few clergy that will remain. Thus the Welsh people will suffer grievous loss, and the Welsh Church a sad degradation. The people will lose their ancient Church, and that Church will be degraded into a little Church of the lairds.

The clergy are at present bound to minister to all classes alike, in sickness and in health, if they choose to avail themselves of their services. If they are not always eloquent popular preachers, they are generally philanthropic men of high character, always ready to visit the sick, to relieve the poor, to console the sorrowful, and to perform those occasional offices, baptism, marriage, and burial. Throughout Wales the Nonconformists still continue to avail themselves largely of the services of the clergy on such occasions. There are scores of Welsh parishes, inhabited by a majority of Nonconformists, in which the services of the parish clergyman are still almost invariably required at the burial of the dead. The devoted earnest Welsh clergyman, in the quiet sequestered country parish or lovely mountain vale, living the life of an unpretending student and an unambitious philanthropist, eschewing controversy and bickerings, patiently teaching the doctrines and administering the Sacraments of the Church, giving the example of a high-toned innocent life, is still a powerful agent of Christianity and civilization, whose value perhaps will never be fully realized until it has been forfeited for ever. Although, in consequence of forces already described, all the results, literary and social, that might have been expected have not come forth from it, the Welsh parsonage is still a centre of enlightenment and gentle beneficent influence. The parishioners who do not profess to be his disciples are not uninfluenced by the daily presence of the clergyman.

At the same time, it can hardly be doubted that the services of the Church have an indirect influence upon the faith of the Nonconformist societies. The creeds and formularies afford a doctrinal standard which tends to repress the wild exuberant novelties that crop up in the countless sects and disfigure the religious life of America, where such restraining influence is less uniformly present. The truth of this view is strongly supported by the fact that in Wales the Church and Nonconformity are often found to exercise a beneficial influence upon each other. It has been observed, by those who know the country well, that Nonconformity is more spiritually healthy and vigorous in districts where the Church is active, than where her influence is virtually non-existent. In the hills of Glamorgan the Church is feebly represented. The population has outgrown her resources. Nonconformity has an unchallenged predominance. What is the result? The Nonconformist denominations have conferred inestimable benefits upon the masses, who must have otherwise been left in a state of heathenism. But their own inner life has suffered from the absence of the Church's modifying influence. It is notorious that discipline is more lax, the standard of morality lower, and the tone of some of the preachers less satisfactory among the Nonconformist bodies in the great mining districts, where the Church is so weak, than in any other parts of Wales. It is from these districts that Mormonism drew its Welsh recruits, the number of which Lord Aberdare, at the Swansea Church Congress, dwelt upon as a proof that the Welsh are addicted to religious extremes. The Mormon perverts of the South Wales mining districts are now witnesses to the spiritual loss entailed upon districts which are spiritually bereft of the Church's sobering influence, working jointly with the energy and freedom of Nonconformist enthusiasm.

There is another attraction offered by the Liberationist programme to the natural thrift of Welsh tithe-payers. The Nonconformist farmers are led to believe that they now pay out of their own resources for the maintenance of the Church to which they do not conform, and that disendowment will relieve them of that burden. But it is obvious that the farmers and peasants of Wales will not gain anything, but lose much, by the alienation of the Church's resources. It is often suggested that the tithes might well be devoted to the payment of the education rate that now presses heavily, or to the removal of some other burden. The education rate, and all public burdens of the same kind, are burdens that press ultimately, not on the cultivators, but on the owners of the soil. The landowner who finds that his tenant no longer pays £5 a year in School Board rate, will not hesitate in arriving at the conclusion that the farm is by that sum more valuable than it was, and will raise the rent accordingly. Thus the tithes, to whatever public purpose they may be applied, must inevitably add to the wealth, not of the masses, but of the landowning ratepayers, or of the wealthier tax-paying classes. The landowners of Wales, who are the real though not often the direct tithe-payers, deprecate the disendowment by which they would pecuniarily profit, because they well know that no personal or social blessings would in the long run accompany their advantage.

The church, the parsonage, the clergyman, now exist for the parishioners, rich and poor. They are in an especial sense the patrimony of the poor, which they have inherited from the religious zeal of their Christian ancestry. To disendow the Church will be to deprive the poor parishioners of their patrimony in order to lighten the burdens of the rich, and to give to landowners wealth which they neither want nor desire.

The spoliation of the Church will also be the alienation from many parishes of some portion of the wealth expended within their limits. The clergyman is the only landowner who is always resident, and who expends his rent-charge among those who till the soil upon which it is paid. When the Church tithes are alienated from religious purposes, and find their way, as they ultimately must do, into the coffers of landowners, who are frequently non-residents, as to large portions of their property, the parish will find that it has lessened by some hundreds a year the amount of money expended within its boundaries.

But these material and sublunary considerations, that tell against the destructive policy of the Liberationists, might well be disregarded if moral and spiritual advantages could be secured by it. All must allow that it is essential to the welfare of Wales, as of every other country, that its people should have among them a highly educated, duly qualified body of religious teachers. The labourer is worthy of his hire. A highly educated ministry cannot be secured, under the economical laws that God has ordained, unless an adequate maintenance is offered to them. Self-sacrificing martyrs and heroes will arise and give themselves to the service of their fellow-men. But the world has been so ordered that the people, who set so low a value upon religious teaching that they will not provide adequate maintenance for religious teachers, will be left destitute of the spiritual privileges that they despise. A peasant ministry is a very useful element in the religious organization of a country, but other elements are necessary. The religious tone of a country suffers, and religion loses power, if its representatives are insufficiently educated, or engaged in menial and worldly occupations. The Aristotelian maxim—

οὔτε γεώργον οὔτε βάναυσον ἱερέα καταστάτεον, ὕπο γὰρ τῶν πολιτῶν πρέπει τιμᾶσθαι τοὺς Θεούς (" Pol.," lib. vii. i. 9)—

is still true, and reverence for Divine Majesty will undoubtedly be impaired in this country if ever the ministrations of religion are left entirely to the voluntary efforts of the farmer or artisan.

Now, it is assumed by the advocate of disendowment that because the Welsh Nonconformists have built a very large number of chapels, and contribute noble sums annually to religious purposes, the voluntary system will suffice to secure an educated and duly maintained ministry. But the facts are not favourable to this assumption. The Nonconformist ministers of Wales as a body are very popular, and among them are some men of considerable acquirements and great eloquence. But it cannot be denied that the remuneration received by them is entirely inadequate. The average ministerial income of the Welsh Nonconformist minister is probably not more than £60 per annum. The number who receive more than £200 is exceedingly small. There are many who do not receive more than a few pounds. A really able and eloquent man has been known to ride thirty miles in order to officiate at a chapel, and to have half-a-crown offered to him as the hire of which he was worthy. It is hardly necessary to add that ministers so miserably paid are in most cases obliged to combine their ministerial labour with some more lucrative calling. Not a few of the most powerful preachers have been shopkeepers and farmers, who, attending to their business during the week, travelled on Saturday to deliver sermons in some distant neighbourhood, which were delivered in other districts again and again in the course of the year. The itinerant system, as it relieves the preacher from the necessity of preparing fresh sermons for every Sunday, leaves him at liberty to till the soil or to sell his wares during the week. The results attained by the system in the past have been wonderful. But it has lived its day, and is doomed ere long to diappear. The Calvinistic Methodists, amongst whom it chiefly prevailed, are endeavouring to substitute for it the resident pastorate of men entirely devoted to the ministry. But only the wealthiest congregations are able to maintain a "bugail," or pastor. The poor people in the congregations of thickly populated country districts, who perhaps more than any others need the continual help of ministerial guides, are unable to secure the privilege. It is in such districts that the loss of the pastoral care of the parochial clergyman would be severely felt in the course of time by many who prefer the preaching in the chapel.

The voluntary system of the Nonconformist bodies, with its freedom and elasticity, and the ready avenues to success and influence that it offers to men endowed with popular gifts, is admirably suited to develop preaching power, and to secure a number of attractive pulpit orators. But it is not adapted to provide for the permanent spiritual needs of a population, by maintaining through the country an adequate number of qualified pastors, ever at hand and able, if not to dazzle on the Sunday, to guide, console, instruct, and advise their parishioners in their daily life.

The Nonconformist ministers have often great secular advantages over the clergy. The eloquent preacher, who in the course of a year probably preaches on the Sundays in all the principal chapels of his country, wins for himself fame and exercises great influence over his fellow-men. At the same time, he not unfrequently becomes a rich man in the successful pursuit of his week-day business. He thus combines ecclesiastical status and no small social influence and spiritual authority with a very fair degree of worldly wealth. Thus it happens that not a few of the Methodist preachers die in possession of riches which a fairly beneficed clergyman could never hope to acquire. A voluntary system which produces these results is admirably fitted to supplement, but not to supplant, that parochial system which extends to the whole country the benefits of regular and equable religious ministrations.

There is another consideration which ought not to escape the attention of patriotic Welshmen. Wales is about to enjoy the long-denied blessings of higher education. A large number of its gifted youth will acquire knowledge and be fitted for an intellectual career. There are very few openings for the energies of educated and studious Welshmen in their own country. The legal and medical professions are crowded. There is no career more worthy of a noble ambition than that which makes a man the guide of his brethren in life, the consoler in sorrow, and their enlightener in the darkness of coming dissolution. The ministry of their ancient Church ought to afford to the noblest youths of Wales a happy and honourable calling. Hitherto the Heaven-born teachers of Wales have been excluded by educational disadvantages and ecclesiastical abuses from their own place in the sanctuaries of their country. A better day is dawning. If Welshmen disendow their Church, instead of reforming and reviving it, they will deprive their most gifted countrymen in the future of a career suited to their genius—a career in which they can confer inestimable blessings upon their country.

The manse of the minister has been in every generation the nursery of some of Scotland's noblest sons, foremost in intellect and moral power. The Welsh parsonage might be equally prolific of intellectual power and moral virtue in Wales, if it had enjoyed that blessing which was one of the three providential mercies to which Dr. Chalmers attributed the greatness of Scotland, viz. ecclesiastical endowments enjoyed by a native clergy. But, even under the disadvantages that have existed, the Welsh parsonage has not seldom been the birthplace of the most eminent Welshmen in every generation.

It is well known that in Wales, as in Scotland and England, not a few men of natural gifts have risen, through the ministry of the Church, out of obscurity into high and honourable positions. To disendow the Church is to close one of the few avenues by which the intellect and moral force of men born in poverty can attain their due rank among men. In the words which a great statesman put into the mouth of an ardent young reformer, "The estate of the Church is the estate of the people, so long as the Church is governed on its real principles. The Church is the medium by which the despised and degraded classes assert the native equality of man, and vindicate the rights and power of intellect. It made, in the darkest hour of Norman rule, the son of a Saxon pedlar Primate of England, and placed Nicholas Breakspear, a Hertfordshire peasant, on the throne of the Cæsars." It will be the wisdom of patriotic Welshmen not to destroy their ancient Church, but to see that she "is governed on its real principles."

The most honourable motive alleged by the Liberationists of Wales, as instigating them to seek the disestablishment and disendowment of the Welsh Church, is the desire of restoring some degree of religious harmony to a people now distracted by divisions. This is an object worthy of a noble ambition, and its attainment would repay very great sacrifices. It is easy to exaggerate, but easy also to underrate, the evils of religious disunion. It has very disastrous effects, and greatly lessens the sum total of human happiness in the country where it prevails. There is no deep gulf of separation and no serious animosity between the Churchmen and Dissenters of Wales. But still there is everywhere and always present a heavy atmosphere, clouded by the consciousness of antagonism, and charged with some degree of controversial bitterness that every now and then breaks out into showers of abuse. There is a strong feeling of jealous rivalry between the various Nonconformist bodies. They build chapels that are hardly needed in order to supplant each other, or at least to guard against being outstripped. There is much strain and financial exhaustion in consequence.

In many neighbourhoods the various bodies, in this race of rival chapel-building, are much in the same position as the Continental nations that are exhausting themselves in the maintenance of bloated armaments. But the antagonism between the Church and the Nonconformist bodies is keener. On account of the Church's supposed position, all the sects, though not otherwise united, will sometimes combine against her influence. These jealousies, rivalries, and petty animosities poison the social atmosphere. In every local election, when members have to be chosen for school boards, boards of health, boards of guardians, burial boards, and town councils, too frequently the contest is degraded by sectarian spirit, and both Churchmen and Nonconformists are guilty of asking concerning a candidate, not whether he is best qualified for a public duty, but whether he attends church or chapel. The local newspapers, again, are sometimes filled with the utterances of this wretched sectarian bitterness. In the pulpit, also, though not very frequently, violent denunciations are sometimes heard. There is everywhere a spirit of controversy, that to some extent sours that milk of human kindness which naturally flows very abundantly in the genial population of Wales. In every district there is some degree of social estrangement. Instead of being a united body, the community is divided into two camps, that watch each other with jealous, restless, sleepless rivalry.

These evils have an unfavourable effect upon character, and are injurious to the human spirit. Happiness is lessened by them. No evil comes except as the result of a violated law. Religious unity is a law. Disunion never fails to bring with it pains and losses. The responsibility for disunion is heavy. Wherever that responsibility lies, those who are burdened by it are bound to do all they can to remove it from themselves, by fulfilling on their part the law of unity.

Before there can be any hope of religious reunion in Wales, it will be necessary that Churchmen and Nonconformists should lay aside many prejudices and traditions of antagonism, and recognize the real forces that exist on both sides. Any reunion that is to be realized must be secured, not by the destruction of vital forces, but by bringing them into harmonious operation. When Nonconformists realize that the Church has within her a Divine principle and power, the loss of which would entail impoverishment, if not ultimate deadness, upon the nation; and when Churchmen, on their part, admit that there are forces in Nonconformity working for the good of the national weal, the restriction and fettering of which by an iron uniformity would be a grievous spiritual injury, it may be possible to recreate by degrees a practical harmony that will give to Wales the unspeakable blessings that will flow from unity of spirit.

The real contest during the last hundred and fifty years has been not between Churchmen and Nonconformists, but rather between Uniformists and Non-uniformists. The masses, who have separated themselves in some degree from the Church, have not been induced to do so by disbelief of her doctrines, but by the insufficiency of her ministrations. In the eighteenth century the most powerful and popular ecclesiastic in Wales, if power be estimated by influence over souls, and not by command of outward rank and endowments, was Griffith Jones, who wrote concerning the motives that led to Nonconformity as follows: "I must also do justice to the Dissenters in Wales, and will appeal for the truth of it to all competent judges, and to all those themselves who separate from us (except only such who have hardly any more charity for those they differ from than the Church of Rome), that it was not any scruple of conscience about the principles or orders of the Established Church that gave occasion to scare one in ten of the Dissenters in this country to separate from us at first, whatever objections they may afterwards imbibe against conforming. No, Sir! they generally dissent at first for no other reason than for want of plain, practical, pressing, and zealous preaching, in a language and dialect they are able to understand ; and freedom of friendly access to advise about their spiritual state."

This account of the origin of Welsh Dissent is true of its continuance. The causes that gave it birth still continue to feed it. The want of powerful preaching and of spiritual association is the great weakness of the Church. It is necessary to acknowledge this weakness, and to realize that to some extent it is inherent in the Church's system. The good preachers of the Church are restricted mainly to their own parishes. Their influence is limited. The good preachers of Nonconformity circulate continually, and have consequently a wider field of influence. The Church can never satisfy all the spiritual needs of Wales, by the ministrations of her stationary parochial clergy.

But there can be no religious unity except through the Church. She is clearly the only possible centre of unity in Wales. The great question is—How can the unity that the Church alone can give be reconciled with the freedom and power that are found in Nonconformity?

Perhaps the best means of recovering religious unity will be by realizing the causes that led to its being for a time lost. In order to preserve unity, no conditions should be imposed except those that are essentially necessary. Every unnecessary restriction upon liberty endangers unity. The Act of Uniformity, which was intended to secure for the nation the blessings of religious unity, was framed to perpetuate Common Prayer, the due administrations of the Sacraments, and frequent preaching of the Gospel. Its authors tried to do too much. They restricted liberty of prophesying and of praying far beyond the point that was essential to unity. Dissent in Wales has been a revolt against the system that restricted the freedom of preaching. The liberty of preaching is a spiritual right that orthodox Nonconformity cannot, will not, and ought not to sacrifice.

But the Church, on her part, has committed to her a mission that she must fulfil. The unity of the spiritual kingdom is a truth to which she must testify. That unity can only be preserved by order. The functions of the central government must be restricted to those who have authority to discharge them, in order to save a nation from anarchy. Those central functions should be as few as possible, in order that liberty may not be restricted. But liberty cannot exist without order, and order is, in the long run, destroyed by the want of liberty.

The administration of the Holy Communion, in all ages of the Church, has been restricted to those officers who have been authorized to perform that function on behalf of the congregation. The Holy Communion, therefore, is the true centre of unity. Those who can recite conscientiously the articles of the Nicene Creed are, as far as their belief goes, able to conform to the one condition necessary to the unity of the Church.

For two generations in Wales, the Calvinistic Methodists were very generally in the habit of communicating in the parish churches. It was not until 1811 that the denomination ceased to regard the ministrations of the clergy, authorized by the Apostolical Commission, as essential to the due celebration of the Sacrament of Unity. It is difficult not to look back with regret to the early days of Welsh Methodism, and with an earnest wish that the state of things that terminated in 1811 might be restored.

There must be in all the orthodox Nonconformist bodies thousands of earnest souls who yearn for unity, and would rejoice to partake once more of that one communion which would bring them into direct spiritual fellowship with their fathers in the ages that are gone. There are thousands of earnest Churchmen who would rejoice to be free to avail themselves occasionally of the privilege of hearing the more powerful preachers of the Nonconformist bodies. It would be well if Nonconformists could come to their parish churches three times in the year to receive the Sacrament of unity. It would also be well if, in parishes where feeble preaching is starving the souls of the parishioners, the Church-people were at liberty to hear sermons in the meeting-house.

But this practical reunion cannot be brought about by any formal agreement. The Nonconformist denominations have their chapels, their organization, and vested interests. These must remain. The Church cannot absorb them. She cannot do the work which is done by them without great changes in her system.

On the other hand, there seems no prospect whatever of any unity among the Nonconformist bodies. They cannot supersede the Church. The restoration of unity is hopeless, unless Nonconformists can gradually be brought to see the duty of communicating in the parish churches, and Churchmen to recognize heartily the liberty of prophesying as a right that belongs to the Nonconformists.

It cannot be doubted that the vast majority of the Welsh Nonconformists are, in their acceptance of the central truth of the Incarnation, more orthodox than a large number of men who worship and even minister in the Church. It is sad that those who are one in faith should not be one in communion. If all the orthodox Nonconformists in the parishes, worshipping in their own synagogues and hearing their own prophets at other times, came up to the Jerusalem of the parish church three times a year to receive the Holy Communion, it cannot be doubted that the Divine Spirit of unity would drive out of the land the wretched jealousies, rivalries, and social divisions that now mar its life.

There is much in the tendencies of the present age to make such a reconciliation possible. The religious Liberalism, if it has endangered the hold of some ancient truths that must not be sacrificed, has also banished many prejudices and much narrow ignorant bigotry that made reunion more difficult than it now is.

The Bishops and clergy of the Church were very willing to enter into relations with the Salvation Army, as long as it seemed possible that its operations would be restricted to evangelizing the masses. It is, surely, far more desirable to keep in view, as an object of true ecclesiastical wisdom, the desirability of re-establishing communion with those great orthodox Nonconformist bodies who have done and are doing so much to Christianize millions of the people of this country.

If relations of sympathy could be informally renewed between the Church and the denominations, the passage from the Nonconformist preaching ministry into the priesthood of the Church ought to be made easy. There are many men who know that their gift is that of the preacher. They would lose influence if they became parish priests. The wealthiest benefice would not tempt a great preacher to settle down in one limited sphere as a parochial minister. In early life especially the ministry of preaching would be more attractive to such men, who would not be happy if unable to exercise their gift and to wield that widespread influence which a leading Nonconformist teacher acquires in every district of Wales. But there are among the Nonconformist ministers many who feel, especially as they advance in life, that the quiet labours of the priesthood would be more in accordance with their taste, and that they would be glad to retire from the excitement of great assemblies into the calm of pastoral work.

If such a unity of spirit, with liberty of multiform operations, could be restored in Wales, the power of Christianity would be enormously increased. The denominations would lose none of their spiritual energy, the Church none of its spiritual stability. All earnest men, now separated by sectarian jealousies, would be able to consult and work together for the common good. Social life would be far happier. The grace of unity would be diffused on the whole body, from the head even to the skirts of the garment. For this end Churchmen must recognize the liberty of prophesying, and Nonconformists must recognize the Sacrament of unity.

WHY ARE THE WELSH PEOPLE ALIENATED FROM THE CHURCH?[1]

INTRODUCTION.

HAVING been requested more than nine months ago by the Welsh Churchmen of Liverpool to preach at their annual festival in St. David's Church in Welsh, and also to deliver a sermon at a special English service, in the hope of exciting on their behalf the generous sympathy of their English fellow-Churchmen, the author deemed it a not unfitting occasion for briefly reviewing the past and present relations of the Church to the Welsh-speaking population of Wales. The views which he has formed concerning the cause that has mainly provoked the alienation from the Church of three-fourths of the religious people of Wales, were fully set forth nine years ago in a letter, entitled "The Church of the Cymry," addressed to the Right Hon. W. Ewart Gladstone, a statesman who knows and loves the Welsh people. Those views may be thought by some to be

[1] Preached in St. David's (Welsh) Church, Liverpool, at a special English service, attended by the Worshipful the Mayor and the Corporation, on Sunday, May 25, 1879.

Why are the Welsh People alienated, etc.? 289

erroneous, but the author can claim the credit of having held them with consistency. Longer and wider experience has only served to confirm in him the conviction that the serious decay of the Welsh Church, since 1700, has been mainly due to the fact that the clergy in its chief places have ignored the maxims of that Apostolical spirit, which constrains the true ministers of Christ to adapt their ministrations to the spiritual needs of every nationality.

He is firmly convinced that the correctness of his conclusions will be questioned by no one who is qualified, by *a knowledge of the Welsh language and of the inner life of Wales*, to form a judgment. The author is aware that this sermon contains admissions that may be painful to Churchmen, but believes that the truth should be known. He ventures to express a strong hope that an accurate return may soon be published in each of the four dioceses of Wales, showing the number of congregations, and of the worshippers in them, *both conforming and non-conforming, that worship in the Welsh language*, in order that the ignorance of the lingual and religious condition of Wales, which so extensively prevails, may be dispelled by reliable information. He is sanguine that, when light shall have been thrown upon the real state of the Welsh Church, efficacious remedies may yet be found for a sickness which is not beyond the hope of gradual recovery.

"I am made all things to all men, that I might by all means save some. And this I do for the Gospel's sake, that I might be partaker thereof with you."—1 COR. ix. 22, 23.

IN this chapter St. Paul reveals the spirit of his own ministry. The leading characteristic which he claims for it is unselfishness. He tells the Corinthians that the ministerial office, by the very nature of things, has rights. One of those rights he declares to be that of maintenance: "Even so hath the Lord ordained that they which preach the Gospel should live of the Gospel."

By a providential law, in the economy of God, all who do true work have a right to eat, or, in other words, all who enrich society have a right to share its riches.

Now, it is obvious that, although the minister of religion is not directly occupied either in the production or distribution of wealth, his work goes down to the very root of material prosperity, and fosters the growth of social riches, though more indirectly, not less really than does the energy of agriculturist, manufacturer, or merchant. It is easy to illustrate this truth.

The wealth of this great town, in which we are assembled, is known in all the world. What is the root of that prosperity? Is it due entirely to your noble river, and your position on the shores of the highway of nations? No; the Mersey flowed, and the paths of ocean were as wide, in the days when naked savages fed their flocks in the wild forests, and looked abroad over the waste of waters on which the great leviathans of your commerce are floating to-day. Natural advantages—climate, position, soil, mineral resources—are all God's gifts for the wealth of society. But there is one force without which these are vain. That force is the spirit of man. If truth, integrity, industry, and purity were wanting, no outward gifts could save a people from material decay. The virtues of a community are the first of the forces that create its wealth.

It is the function of the minister of religion to call into play the spiritual motives that produce the virtues of a community, and thereby give to it wealth, honour, peace, and happiness. Happy is the people who have moral power; their garners will be full, affording all manner of store: there will be no complaining in their streets; "Yea, happy is that people whose God is the Lord."

It follows, as St. Paul teaches in this chapter, that the minister of religion, being a promoter of wealth, has as good a right to share it as the cultivator who produces or the soldier who guards it.

But while asserting this right as a general principle, St. Paul tells us that for special reasons he thought well not to avail himself of it. It was his lot, not to labour among Christians enlightened in an organized Church, but rather to organize Churches by bringing men out of darkness into the light of those Divine truths upon which the wealth of society is based. As a stranger he went forth to various nations to teach truths that were new to them. He had to gain a hearing from them, and, if possible, to win their confidence and sympathy. For that end it was all-important that they should know him to be disinterested. It is obvious that in our own day a missionary, who sought to maintain himself at the expense of his hearers in a heathen country, would labour under disadvantages as one who came seeking his own gain. A missionary of Christ, the King of sacrifice, if he does not show the credentials of disinterestedness, is powerless. He must be able to say to those whom he would save, "We would not be chargeable to any of you." Among the ignorant and uninstructed, no ministry that seeks payment from them can succeed in winning influence.

But if in the moral weakness of an infant Church an *unpaid* ministry was essential, at all times, in all places, and among all men every ministry that will be spiritually powerful must be *unselfish*. If it could be shown that the Christian ministry afforded worldly advantages beyond other callings, so that an able man could make more money as a clergyman than he could by devoting the same talents and industry to the work of a physician, a lawyer, or a merchant, it would be disastrous to his spiritual power. In this country, however, in our days, it will, I think, be acknowledged that the power of the Christian ministry is not generally exposed to these dangers.

But to minister without payment is not the only form of ministerial unselfishness. Indeed, a man may minister without pecuniary reward, and yet be moved by very selfish aims. Therefore, in the text, the Apostle holds before the Christian ministry of all ages the example of unselfishness in a much higher and nobler form.

Pecuniary disinterestedness is a great power, but living sympathy is infinitely greater.

The truth declared in these words, to which I wish to direct your attention, is that in order to save souls in the Church of God a ministry infinitely sympathetic is essential.

Let us consider—

I. The ruling motive of the Apostolic ministry as declared in the words, "For the Gospel's sake, that I might be joint partaker of it."

II. The consequent course of action and its aim: "I am made all things to all men, that I might by all means save some."

I. The informing motive that gave to the Apostolic ministry its impulse and shaped its course is declared in the words, "This I do for the Gospel's sake." Now let us try to realize how the central truth of the Gospel bears upon those duties of the Apostolic ministry of which St. Paul speaks. How does the Gospel make every true Christian ministry self-denying and sympathetic? In order to understand this, we must have a clear view of the living power of the Gospel. We know that the Gospel means glad tidings. But what are the tidings? And why do they gladden the being of man when he receives them?

These are questions which a thoughtful and inquiring

human soul must solve before it can find peace. We cannot answer the question, "What is the Gospel?" unless we can answer that other inquiry, "What is man?" For the Gospel is that revelation of truth that tells us the nature and destiny of man, and enables us to find our full human life and to attain the inheritance of wealth and dignity that belongs to it. It is revealed that man was created to be partaker of the Divine life, to bear God's image, to be changed into the same image from glory to glory through all the stages of growth in spiritual enlightenment and power. Therefore the great question for the soul is this: "What is the image, or, as we should say, the character of God?" The answer to that question of humanity is the Gospel. Such is the teaching of the Apostle as summarized by him in this Epistle: "I came to you . . . declaring unto you the testimony of God. For I determined not to know anything among you, save Jesus Christ, and Him crucified."

The career of Jesus Christ is the revelation or testimony of God. In his Epistle St. John tells us that "God is love," and that "he that dwelleth in love dwelleth in God." But when St. John sums up the power of the Gospel in the brief formula, "God is love," his teaching is identical with that of St. Paul, when he comprehends all in the words "Jesus Christ, and Him crucified;" for the crucifixion of Jesus Christ, the Divine Man omnipotent, is the one infinite expression of the Divine love. To act, therefore, as the Apostle professes to act, under the power of the Gospel, is to live under the guidance of the Divine Spirit of Christ, in obedience to the promptings of eternal love.

That power which in the New Testament is called, sometimes "love" and sometimes "charity," is the spring that quickens all moral life. Wherever there is goodness, even in a heathen, it has its origin in the omnipresent infinite love. But as there are many who breathe the air of physical life and are strong, and yet are unable to explain the chemical elements that form it, so are there many in the east and in the west, in the north and in the south, who personally act upon the principle of love, while unable to name its constituent elements or to define its relation to other spiritual forces. There is a Light that lighteth every man that cometh into the world, and the world knoweth it not. To know Jesus Christ is to know that mystery, and to receive that power which makes us sons of God.

The Life, Death, Resurrection, and Ascension of Jesus Christ unfold to the human spirit the mystery of Divine love. Can we define the nature of that love? We can only try to understand it by gazing for ever at the career of Jesus.

The feature that first strikes us in that career is power —the miracles, the storm calmed, the sea subdued, the bread multiplied, the sick healed, the dead raised. In life, power is the attribute that first attracts and awes the natural man—material, intellectual, social power. The career of Jesus reveals to us One endued with infinite power over nature, over men, over the wealth of the universe. The fact that Jesus had all power implies that power is good; that man is justified in striving to subdue nature, to grow in intellectual energy, and to add to his material wealth in that social struggle and competition that are going on around us in the world's life. The energy and business of the world are simply the travail that God hath given to the sons of man to be exercised therewith, the effort that man is impelled to make in search of that power which is an attribute of Jesus.

But the revelation of power in Christ is not the Gospel, so the attainment of power by man is not his salvation. The moral value of power depends upon the motives by which it is directed. Power is good or evil, as it is used for base or noble ends. The muscular force of a giant may be used to save life or to murder; so the power of intellect, of rank, of riches, or any other power, may be used for evil as well as for good. Power may fly to and fro as a fallen angel, spreading gloom and misery as it expands its wings, or may reign as an angel of light and blessedness.

In Jesus Christ we see perfect power directed by the perfect motive. What is that motive? It is the principle called love and charity, and the highest attribute in the nature of God. It is the eternal motive that, as it were, impels God to give life and blessedness out of His own fulness to the greatest possible number of creatures. In His eternal existence God is giving Himself, pouring forth the wealth of His own Being in order to give life to those whom He has called out of nothingness.

So in Jesus Christ human nature, while wielding the

power of Godhead, sacrificed its vital energies in the flow of redeeming blood, in order to give to the world moral and spiritual life. The great lesson of the Cross is, that to use power unselfishly, for the good of others, is to live in the life of God.

But the natural man will say, "These are no glad tidings. There is no gladness in checking personal inclinations, in enduring pain, in crucifying the flesh and its impulses."

It is quite true that they who follow Christ afar off, and see Him on the Cross and go no further, miss the gladness of Christianity. Had the career of Jesus ended in the self-renunciation of the Cross, His mission would not have brought glad tidings. But the Cross was only a short though bitter passage leading on to the Resurrection, the Ascension, and the endless life of triumphant glory. Hence the manifestation of Jesus Christ in all its fulness gives to man infinite gladness, through the assurance it brings that pain, suffering, and self-sacrifice lead to the eternal elevation of the human being.

It is obvious that this principle of Divine love working in the nature of man has an infinite power both negative and active. He who loves God with all the energies of his being, and his fellow-man as himself, and has learnt to devote himself to the good of others and the glory or manifestation of God, has in him the spirit which destroys all vice and creates all virtue. Love, both negatively and positively, is, in St. Paul's words, "the fulfilling of the Law."

Every human vice and sin has its origin in the power of personal selfishness that isolates the man from the corporate life of humanity. The man who has crucified his self-will is free from the bondage of sin. Why does the sensualist yield to the temptations that debase his being? Because he has not learnt to sacrifice selfish passion. Why does the dishonest man defraud society? Because he has not been inspired by that spirit of the Cross which teaches man to sacrifice himself for the good of others, and to lose his lower life that he may find the higher life risen out of its grave.

But this principle is not merely negative; it not only restrains from vice, but impels to virtue. It not only creates the pale holiness of the hermit who has tamed the passions and renounced the world, but it also fosters the noblest activities of robust virtue in all its social modern forms. The untiring philanthropist, the ardent prophet of religious truth, the brave soldier and sailor, the generous honourable merchant, the large-minded and large-hearted statesman, the good energetic honest citizen whatever be his calling,—all, whether knowing it or not, draw their virtues from that inexhaustible fountain opened upon the Cross; for instead of living the life of selfish indulgence and shutting up the energies of his life-blood in himself, each of them, as the ordinary phrase so simply and yet so deeply expresses it, "devotes himself." Hence, the more completely a man is able to go out of himself, to forget his lower self, to pour out himself, and to throw himself in a stream of thought and will into his true life-work, which God shows to all who inquire aright for their calling, so much does he become a nobler, happier, and more exalted man. This life of self-devotion was the life of St. Paul, as he tells us in another Epistle: "I am crucified with Christ: nevertheless I live."

So in this passage, after saying that the Gospel was the ruling principle of his life, he declares that he strives to be not merely a teacher of its doctrines, but also a sharer of its power. It is possible for a man to be a teacher of the truths and a minister of the rites of religion without being a partaker of its life. That is the fate which St. Paul strove to escape by practising self-devotion as well as preaching it. "I keep under my body, and bring it into subjection: lest that by any means, when I have preached to others, I myself should be a castaway."

The significance of the Apostle's expression, "partaker thereof," is very full and deep. It is not difficult to illustrate the meaning of that Greek compound which he used. It is a word that would represent partnership. Now, if I were to ask some ardent youth beginning his career in this great emporium of commerce, "What is your animating motive? To what do you look forward? You work hard; you practise self-denial, from early morn till dewy eve: 'through dusky lane and wrangling mart' you devote yourself to business, and if you lie awake in the watches of the night, your mind is full of your vocation. Why do you find pleasure in giving up yourself so absorbedly to it?"

—he would probably answer, "The glory of commerce has fired the imagination of the thoughts of my heart. This great mercantile city in which I serve is as Tyre, one of the queens of the ocean—has a high name and boundless resources; from every clime her ships bring earth's products to enrich human society; and they spread their wings before every breeze to bear to distant nations goods that add to the beauty and comfort of life. The vision of some future commercial glories has fired my soul. I am to-day but a humble worker in the life of this great community; but some day I hope to become myself a partaker of the honour and wealth of successful commerce."

Such is the Apostle's thought. "The Church of Christ, of which on earth I am a minister, is an eternal city of splendour and wealth, into which the kings of the earth do bring their honour and glory; in which the merchantmen seeking goodly pearls are ever at work in the fields and marts of eternity; in which the unsearchable riches of Christ are found. I intend not to be a mere mechanical agent of its blessings to other, but to be myself a full partaker of its glory and its weal."

Such ought to be the spirit and language of the Church's Apostolic ministry in every age and land. We are called not only to preach the truths of the Cross, but to live them; not only to be ministers of the Gospel, but also partakers.

II. Let us pass on to consider the practical effects of this principle upon St. Paul's ministry.

It impelled him to adapt himself to all kinds of men.

What enabled him to practise that self-adaptation? His large knowledge of human nature, joined to his intense unselfishness that impelled him to influence other for their good, as he expresses it—" that I might by all means save some."

His one aim among men was to win influence for good. Now we see how a man acts when he desires to influence another. When we seek to obtain anything from a man, we try to know him thoroughly; we consult his wishes and study his tastes. We take care not to run counter to his ideas, and respect even his prejudices. We try to look at things from his point of view, and to win his confidence by sympathy. Thus men act when they would gain from another some earthly advantage. Thus St. Paul acted when he wished to gain his fellow-men. He did not want their money, but he wanted their hearts. He wanted them to entrust their lives to him, to be moulded by the Divine truths which he had to teach; his own words were, "I seek not yours, but you."

Acting upon this spirit, he tells us that, in dealing with the Jews, he did not run against their national ideas, but looked upon life from their point of view—dwelt upon the truths that he held in common with them, and spoke as one who knew and loved their Law and their prophets; when addressing Greeks, who had received no Divine written Law, he appealed to natural reason, and enforced his teaching by reference to their national poets and philosophers; and when face to face with peasants like the islanders of Malta, who were intellectually weak, he used words and figures suited to their capacities. " To the Jews," he says, " I became as a Jew, that I might gain the Jews; to them that are under the Law, as under the Law, that I might gain them that are under the Law; to them that are without Law, as without Law (being not without Law to God, but under the Law to Christ), that I might gain them that are without Law. To the weak became I as weak, that I might gain the weak."

The man who has this power of insight into men of various natures, and can understand them and sympathize with them, is the man who will have the widest influence. He is like the trained diplomatist, at home in all lands, speaking the tongues of many races, knowing the customs of many peoples, the etiquette of many courts, and able to win the ear and the confidence of men everywhere.

What gives that power of sympathetic self-adaptation? It is light tempered by love, knowledge of human nature imparted by the spirit of unselfishness. The selfish man thinks so much of himself, that he considers it only due that all men should enter into *his* feelings and study *his* tastes, and not he *theirs*. The hard, proud, vain, conceited, narrow-minded man wants that subtle power of sympathy, that delicate tact, by which soul touches soul, and feels as it feels, in the moment of contact. When he deals with men of different associations to his own, he is like a man handling an instrument that he cannot play. Under his rough hand it gives forth no harmonious sounds; and he, in his narrow self-complacency, thinks that there is no music in it, because he knows not how to draw it forth.

St. Paul tells us that he had acquired the power of all-embracing sympathy; and he says that it was the teaching of the Gospel, the Divine Spirit of love, destroying selfishness, that had given it to him.

Now, I need not remind you that few barriers separate men from each other more than a distinction of nationality. We know, by familiar experience of the composite population of these islands, the subtle but imperishable differences by which nationality distinguishes men. The physical frame, countenance, temper, language, and even, when language has ceased to be different, pronunciation, tone of voice, rhythm, and accent,—all these proclaim the difference of race. Englishmen, Irishmen, Scotchmen, Welshmen, even when they speak the same language, are yet different in countenance, in voice, and accent.

As in the outward man, so undoubtedly in the inward man, there are distinctions arising from nationality that are indelible. St. Paul, in his sermon at Athens, speaks of these distinctions of nationality as ordained by God. He declares that all men are of one blood, that the principle of life is identical in them all, but that they are separated into nations, for whom God "hath determined the times before appointed, and the bounds of their habitation."[1]

In Jesus Christ's human nature every national temperament is represented. He knows the language of all

[1] Acts xvii. 26.

human souls, and can feel with every human heart. "He knew what was in man"—not merely in the Jewish or the Greek man, but in "man." Therefore, as the Head of human nature and the countryman of all men, He is called "the Son of Man." In Him, Greek, Jew, Barbarian, Scythian, find their country and their home.

This Divine cosmopolitanism of the God-Man, inspiring a sympathy of humanity as wide as the world, is also given by the Holy Spirit to the Church. In the city of God, no preference is to be given to any man on account of his nationality. On the Day of Pentecost the Church spoke all languages, so as to reach all hearts: "Parthians, and Medes, and Elamites, and the dwellers in Mesopotamia, and in Judæa, and Cappadocia, in Pontus, and Asia, Phrygia, and Pamphylia, in Egypt, and in the parts of Libya about Cyrene, and strangers of Rome, Jews and proselytes, Cretes and Arabians, we do hear them speak in our tongues the wonderful works of God." It is also revealed that the Church of the redeemed will embrace in itself the features of all nationalities in the "multitude, which no man could number, of all nations, and kindreds, and people, and tongues."

This Divine Spirit of Pentecost, that constrains the Church to adapt her ministrations to the peculiar needs of every people, must be present in her government before the saving power of eternal love will operate in her Apostolic ministry. This truth is so obvious that in those fields of her action, where the eyes are not blinded by the film of prejudice and the cataract of self-interest, it is recognized by all.

In the fields of her foreign missions, the Church of England adapts herself, as rapidly as she can, to the peculiar needs of the various nationalities, to whom she offers the saving influence of Christianity. In Africa, in India, and in all the mission field, it is acknowledged that a native ministry must be created before the masses of the people can be won. The Hindoo and the negro alike must hear the words of eternal truth in their own tongue, from the lips of men to whom God has given the stamp of the same national features, and the emotions of the same national temperament, before they can be moved to acknowledge the wonderful works of God, and to partake of the salvation in Christ. In order to save them, the Apostolic ministry must become "all things to all men."

To-day we are all thinking of an ancient race, that peopled this island thousands of years ago, before its wonderful march of human progress had well begun; who have seen and survived as a distinct people all the changes that have passed over it; who were here, speaking the same language as to-day, when Julius Cæsar landed his conquering legions on its shores; when your bold, strong, freedom-loving ancestors left their homes in the depths of the wild forests of Germany and Scandinavia; when the chivalrous Norman, strong in energy and organization, came and made a realm and reigned. That ancient British race has the strongly marked features of an indestructible nationality,

x

some of which are likely to survive till the last day has dawned in earth's history. They have a distinct national language, the power and beauty of which are denied by none except those who are ignorant of it. The language is still spoken, as we have lately been reminded on the authority of a great statistician,[1] by 1,006,100 souls, that is, by nearly five-sixths of the people of Wales. It is the language in which three-fourths of them still worship God.[2] In this great town one denomination alone has more than twenty chapels and preaching stations, and numbers no less than 13,000 Welsh-speaking communicants.[3] In London, Birmingham, Wolverhampton, Shrewsbury, Chester, Manchester, Barrow-in-Furness, Middlesborough, and all the great centres of British industry, where Welshmen congregate, as good quiet citizens, to do honest work, the old language of the ancient Britons is heard, and, from fervent congregations, the pious strains of Williams of Pantycelyn are wafted towards the eternal throne, upon the wings of the plaintive minor tones of religious Wales. The temperament of the people is even a more

[1] Mr. E. G. Ravenstein, F.R.G.S, "On the Geographical Distribution of the Celtic-speaking Population of the British Isles."

[2] "The Calvinistic Methodists, the Congregationalists, the Baptists, and the Wesleyans in Wales numbered in their ranks 686,220 persons, exclusive of children under the age of ten, and of that number only 36,000 worshipped in the English language. There was also a large circulation of Welsh newspapers and magazines and of Welsh translations of English books in Wales."—Speech by Mr. Hussey Vivian in the House of Commons, July 1, 1879.

[3] The Welsh Calvinistic Methodists in Liverpool, since 1826, have expended £130,000 in providing religious ministrations for the Welsh settlers in the town.

distinctive and, possibly, a more lasting characteristic of their nationality than their language. National temperament is difficult to define. But who does not feel its power, when in its presence, although it eludes description?

The Welsh people have national traditions, reaching back into the dim past peopled by the shades of the Arthurian heroes. Their warm, eager, emotional, quick temperament is known to all. Their shrinking sensitiveness, which is so easily wounded by a slight, that it appears to the stranger to savour of morbid, proud, touchiness, will not escape the close observer.

But most strongly marked of all their national features, is their powerful religious sentiment. It appears in all their literature, and is stamped upon their social life. In America, where Welsh-speaking settlers are said to be almost as numerous as those whom they have left behind, they cling to their language and their religion. The first public building that rises, in a new Welsh village in America, as in the mining districts of Wales, is the simple house of prayer.

In every age of their history the Welsh people have been moved, amid the struggles and disappointments of this fading transitory life, by deep, eager, melancholy yearnings after the Infinite and Eternal Good—"*Y môr didrai o Hedd*,"—the ebbless ocean of peace, as one of their favourite hymn-writers has called it.

This characteristic of their nationality is as fresh to-day as it was two thousand years ago. If any of my hearers has ever listened to the outpourings of these religious aspirations, as they surge forth, at one of their open-air meetings, from ten thousand voices, swelling into vast heaving tides of solemn song, in the deep roll of their favourite tunes, *Eifionydd, Diniweidrwydd, Hyder, Dymuniad,* at the moment when the strong wind of some native prophet's fervent eloquence has swept over their souls in rhythmic gusts, stirring to their inmost recesses all the deeps of mystic emotion in their being, he can hardly fail to have been borne back in thought to the woodland shrines of their forefathers; and, in the gleams of severe joy breaking through clouds and darkness, at once lighting up and melting the melancholy features which, by long mental gazing at the hard, gloomy, loveless image into which ultra-Calvinism changes the glory of the Loving God, have themselves been changed, from sadness to sadness, into the same image of leaden gloom, he must have recognized the spiritual successors of those natural sunbeams[1] that pierced the shadows of the Druidical groves, streaming as smiles from "the Face of the Sun"[2]—in the words of their ancient motto—and as glances from "the Eye of Light," to relieve the sombre enthusiasm of an ever-devout, God-seeking race.

The temperament of this ancient nationality is distinct and unquenchable.

[1] "Yn ngwyneb Haul a Llygad goleuni."

[2] "Solis nosse deos et cæli numina vobis,
Aut solis nescire datum. Nemora alta remotis
Incolitis lucis."

(Lucan, "Pharsal.," i. 452-454.)

Let us briefly review the history of the Church's dealings towards it. In ancient days, ere your Saxon forefathers had yet become Christians, the Church gained the Britons by becoming British. The records of those old days are scanty and unreliable. But the most ancient parish churches of Wales bring down to us the names of the early British saints, who in their day led its religious life. From the dawn of Christianity down to the twelfth century, the British people seem to have been religiously united under an Apostolic ministry, that was of their own race and spoke their own tongue.

But the days of Welsh independence passed away; and at once we trace, in her religious and ecclesiastical affairs, the influence of the temporal power of the dominant race. The temptation to avail itself of its superior force to dictate, in religious matters, to a weaker race that may be united with it, will always beset a dominant people. At the same time, a nation is, perhaps, peculiarly slow to receive spiritual influence from a people that exercises over it temporal supremacy. It may have been on this account that, in the order of Divine Providence, the chosen race, which has exercised supreme spiritual dominion over the chief races of men, was, politically, among the feeblest of the nations.

The English race is a strong, dominant race. But the English Church has failed to exercise spiritual sway over other races. In the British Isles, the Irish, Scotch, Welsh, and Cornish races have to a great extent thrown off her authority. Why is this? Can it be that the English Church has sometimes been inelastic, hard, wanting in sympathy, and has failed to become "all things to all men"? History will hardly give a negative answer. The Norman kings used their power to shape not only the political but also the ecclesiastical destinies of the Welsh people. I cannot dwell upon the details of the history to-day, but its substance may be given in a few words. Ecclesiastics were sent into Wales who had not the Apostolical spirit and could not do Apostolical work. They came, not to make themselves all things to their flocks, but to make their flocks all things to them. The high-handed intrusion of Chancellor Bernard, in 1116, into the see of St. David, the expulsion of Bishop Peter de Leia from St. David's, and of Harvey from Bangor, by popular violence, and, notably, the long struggle of Giraldus Cambrensis, were incidents that marked the course of a policy which ruined the Church in Wales for more than two centuries. The ministry that had not the Apostolical spirit, that could not speak the language, adapt itself to the spiritual needs, or estimate the sympathies of the people, was powerless to save them. So far had Christianity, as taught by these unsympathetic guides, lost its hold over the Welsh people in that age, that an attempt was made to revive the Druidical theosophy as the national religion.[1] But the unjust policy long prevailed. Ambitious

---

[1] "In primis hoc volunt persuadere, non interire animas, sed ab aliis post mortem transire ad alios; atque hoc maxime ad virtutem excitari putant, metu mortis neglecto."—Cæsar, "De Bello Gall.," lib. vi. 14.

ecclesiastics, who had the ear of the court, were able to persuade the temporal rulers that it was desirable to permit them to rise upon the ruins of the Church in Wales.

The injustice has left its mark upon the current of Welsh history. In 1196, Llewelyn, Prince of Gwynedd, Gwenwynwyn, and Madoc, Princes of Powys; Gruffydd, Maelgwyn, Rhys, and Meredydd, sons of Rhys, Prince of South Wales, addressed a petition to Pope Innocent III. for deliverance from the wrong. "The Archbishop of Canterbury," they said, "as a matter of course sends us English Bishops, ignorant of the manners and language of our land, who cannot preach the Word of God to the people . . . they seek not the welfare of souls; their ambition is to rule over us, and not to benefit us."

At the beginning of the fifteenth century the national impatience of the people found a more violent expression. The national chieftain, Owain Glyndwr, in 1402 burnt the cathedral at Bangor; the cathedral, Episcopal palace, and canons' houses at St. Asaph; and destroyed the castle of the Bishop of Llandaff, and the house of his Archdeacon, as a protest against the presence in Wales of pastors who came in the garb of Apostles, but were devoid of the spirit that seeks to adapt religion to the needs of the people. Four years later Dafydd Daron,[1] Dean of Bangor, was outlawed by

---

[1] Dafydd Daron was the original of Shakespeare's "Archdeacon," in whose house Hotspur, Worcester, Mortimer, and Glendower met to discuss their division of the kingdom. *Vide* "Henry IV.," Part I., act iii. sc. 1.

the English king for the part which he took in the national rising.

At length, in the providence of God, a Welsh dynasty, springing from the loins of Owain Tudor, the Anglesey squire of Plas Penmynydd, rose to the throne of Britain. In their days ecclesiastical justice was done to Wales. From 1547 to 1700, the followers of the Apostles in Wales were Apostles indeed. They became to the Welsh people as Welsh. The most illustrious of them, William Morgan,[1] gave to his countrymen their noble version of Holy Scripture—subsequently revised by Bishop Parry and Dr. John Davies—the words of which have formed the life of millions of Welsh souls, and will, in eternity, form a note in the concert of tongues when the white-robed multitude are gathered before the throne of God. In those days, led by the example

[1] Wales is, to ordinary Englishmen, a *terra incognita*. The ignorance of Welsh Church history that prevails is only equalled by the ignorance of the social and religious features of the inner life of Wales, as it exists to-day. Let one example of the former suffice. Bishop Morgan translated the whole of the Bible into the Welsh language, finishing the task in 1588. The version is a noble one. That translation was a great work, and surely ought to have won for him a place in the roll of ecclesiastical worthies. But so learned an English Churchman as Dean Hook seems never to have heard of him. In his Ecclesiastical Biography, which occasionally records the doings of obscure English divines, not a line is devoted to recording the name or work of so great a Welshman. The leading bard of Wales, a very learned clergyman, died a few years ago. His career at Oxford was distinguished, and he rendered so many literary services to his Church and country that his widow has received a literary pension from the Premier. An English prelate, occupying at the time a Welsh see, on being asked to contribute to a fund raised for the erection of a monument in honour of this distinguished native clergyman, replied that he was not aware that he had ever rendered any literary services. It seems that some fate still keeps " Penitus toto divisos orbe Britannos."

of their chief pastors, the laymen of Wales did their part in the work of the Church. William Salesbury, Rowland Heylin, and Sir Thomas Middleton, strove to promote the religious enlightenment of their countrymen; and the immortal parish priest and sacred poet, Rhys Prichard, gave to them, in their own tongue, that religious volume of didactic song, entitled "The Candle of the Cymry," which for centuries has been read in the homes of Wales, and has exercised an influence, inferior only to that of Holy Scripture and the Book of Common Prayer, in guiding Welsh souls through the darkness of earth. In that period the Church sought to save the Welsh people by agencies fitted to influence the Welsh nationality. The result was that her power in Wales was undisputed. In the troubled times of the Civil War and the Commonwealth, when political discord and religious divisions were rife in England, Wales remained undisturbed, undivided, and unmoved, under the guidance of her native Apostolic ministry. How fiercely Royalist and Anti-Puritan, notwithstanding the efforts of Wroth, Penry, and a few others, was the popular feeling of Wales in those days, may be realized by any reader of the poems of the farmer-poet, Hugh Morris, of Pontymeibion, in the Vale of Ceiriog, who was a popular bard of his age. In 1715, with the exception of thirty-five separatists' congregations, the entire people of Wales adhered to the Church.

But after that date, for more than a hundred and fifty years, the rulers of the state, in pursuit of a worldly policy, sent into Wales chief pastors ignorant of its language and traditions, and aliens in sympathy, to the people. During that long period, the followers of the Apostles came into Wales, not to accomplish the spiritual work of saving souls, but as Government agents, to destroy the language and quench the national spirit. The fruits of this policy are known to you. The thirty-five meeting-houses of 1715 have become, in 1879, nearly three thousand. As long as the Apostolic spirit was set at nought, the Church in Wales withered, and from year to year her desolation increased, until well-nigh three-fourths of the people left her sanctuaries, to seek a saving power in forms of worship which, however imperfect some of us may judge them, appeared to them to be undefiled by worldly motives and unmarred by the accent of the self-seeker.[1]

[1] English Churchmen, not knowing how extensively the Welsh language still prevails in Wales, and how strong is the national feeling, are sometimes unable to sympathize with the objection made to the systematic introduction of strangers into all the chief places of the Welsh Church. They denounce that demand, which seeks ministerial efficiency, ecclesiastical justice, and an Apostolical ministry, as if it were a narrow cry of "Wales for the Welsh!"

A more careful study of their own Church history would enable them to take a truer and a more sympathetic view. When the feeblest of the Plantagenets chose to surround himself with Poictevins, Gascons, Provençals, Italians, and Savoyards, the English people did not bear it very patiently. When the Pope tried to pension his favourites upon English endowments, the Roman court was detested in England. "He sought," writes Dean Hook, "through these iniquitous and unconstitutional means, to pension non-resident foreigners, who, when they retired, did not, as a general rule, return to their English benefices; or who, if they resided for a time in England, only did so to further some anti-English scheme of policy. . . . The indignation of every true-hearted Englishman was aroused. . . . The English and the Roman courts were thus both obnoxious, for

alienated from the Church?

It is, perhaps, well for Wales that this policy prevailed-in the eighteenth and not in the sixteenth century. There can be little doubt that the reception of the truths of the Reformed Church by the Welsh-speaking Celts was due to the sympathetic rule of the great Tudor queen, that gave them native pastors and the Scriptures and Liturgy in their own language. In Ireland, at that critical period, a different policy was followed. English prelates, English Bible and Liturgy, were forced upon the Irish-speaking people. The ministry of the Church did not adapt itself to the Irish nationality. At times fitful efforts were made; laymen like Audley Mervin, and clergymen like Nicholas Brown, Rector of Donacary, Dromore, and Rossory, and Walter

the same reason—both tried to compel England to submit to be governed by foreigners. The foreigners invaded both Church and State."

The remonstrances which have been uttered by patriotic Welsh Churchmen who have grieved to see three-fourths of their countrymen alienated from the Church have their parallels in English Church history. With a change of two or three words, the protest addressed by the English Archbishop and his council to the king in 1234, against the promotion of Peter des Roches and Peter de Rivaulx, might have been addressed by Welsh Churchmen to their ecclesiastical rulers on many occasions: " Lord King, we tell you, in the name of God, that the council you receive, and act upon—that, namely, of Peter, Bishop of Winchester, and of Peter de Rivaulx—is not only not wise or safe, but is ungenerous as regards the realm of England, and dangerous to yourself. These men hate and despise the English nation, and when the English assert their rights they call them traitors. They estrange you from your people, and alienate the affections of the people from their king."

If Englishmen will bear in mind that in that age the population of England was not very much larger than that of Wales is to-day, they will perceive that the analogy between the two situations is not unworthy of their attention. *Vide* " Lives of the Archbishops of Canterbury," vol. iii. pp. 167–170.

Atkins, Vicar of Middleton,[1] early in the eighteenth century, tried to gain the Irish people by approaching them through the Irish language. But these were rare exceptions. The treatment dealt to the Irish people was as that afterwards given to the Welsh. In 1725 Jonathan Swift, the ablest Irishman of his day, wrote to the Lord-Lieutenant these words—that might have been written by any Welshman who loved his country—"The misfortune of having Bishops perpetually from England, as it must needs quench the spirit of emulation amongst us to excel in learning and the study of divinity, so it produces another great discouragement, that those prelates usually draw after them colonies of sons, nephews, cousins, or old college companions to whom they bestow the best preferments in their gifts. . . . I believe your Excellency will agree, that there is not another kingdom in Europe where the natives, even those descended from the conquerors, have been treated as if they were almost unqualified for any employment either in Church or State."

[1] Of the Rev. Walter Atkins' work it is recorded, "He proceeded to perform the offices of religion for the natives in their own tongue. . . . He buried the dead according to the Liturgy of the Church; and gave thereby so much satisfaction to the living, that they participated in the service with great devotion, and joined audibly with their voices in the Lord's Prayer, and the previous responses; and on occasion of a burial in the churchyard, one of them was heard to say, that 'if they could have that service always, they would no more go to Mass.' In process of time his ministerial labours became so acceptable to the natives, that they of their own accord sent for him, from all parts of his parish, to baptize their children, to solemnize matrimony, to church their women, to visit their sick, and to bury their dead." *Vide* Mant's "History of the Church of Ireland," vol. ii. pp. 165-168.

alienated from the Church?

The result was that the Irish people were repelled from the reformed religion, which came to them vested in an anti-national garb,[1] and speaking the language of conquest, and under the guidance of native teachers became the most unswerving subjects that the Papacy can boast in Europe.[2] Had the same policy been pur-

---

[1] (1) "There are upwards of 800,000 persons in Ireland who speak Irish, one-fourth of the number being under twenty years of age. (2) There are upwards of 100,000 who cannot speak any language but Irish; and the minds of those persons can at present be reached only through the medium of the *one* language which they understand, whilst the larger number, above named, *are more easily approached by reason of their attachment to it as the national language.* (3) There are various efforts being now made to teach the people to read the Irish language. . . . (5) The literature generally circulated among the people by *other agencies* is partly Roman Catholic, and partly disloyal and seditious." *Vide* Report (for this year) of Irish Society for Promoting the Scriptural Education and Religious Instruction of the Irish-speaking population, chiefly through the medium of their own language. That the present rulers of the Irish Church are at last alive to the long-forgotten necessity of becoming to the Irish as Irish, may be gathered from the following extracts: "If patriotism can supply such a motive-power for the stimulating of zeal and the preservation of unity amongst Churchmen, how unspeakably important will be the assertion of our nationality in our efforts to enlist the sympathies of those who do not belong to our Communion, and who now, alas, stand aloof! Oh! what a position may not our Church take up, no longer . . . as the so-called 'Church of the English foreigner,' but as the representative of the ancient Church of St. Patrick, Irish to her very core, and thus possessing claims upon Irish nationality! . . . The method in which it is sought to communicate the knowledge of these truths is, as you doubtless are aware, through that medium which is most likely to win for them a ready welcome —even that familiar mother-tongue which is associated in the hearts of so many of our Irish poor with their dearest sympathies."—Sermon by the Most Reverend Lord Plunket, Bishop of Meath, on St. Patrick's Day, March, 1878.

[2] The language of Swift concerning these abuses in the Church of Ireland is almost identical with that used by an able layman concerning the treatment meted out to the Welsh Church. "On putting to a gentleman,"

sued in Wales at the same period, it is almost certain that the same results would have followed—that the Welsh, like their kinsmen in Brittany, would have been fervent votaries of Romanism, and all Wales as that little valley in Breconshire, the people of which are said to have adhered to the Roman Church through all the changes that have passed around them. But the policy which arrayed all the forces of nationality[1] against

he writes, "upon whose accuracy I can rely, the following question, 'What proportion of the collective income of the Welsh Church is held by Englishmen?' I received the following answer: 'Four bishoprics, a great portion of the deaneries, prebends, and sinecure rectories, and many, if not most, of the canonries.' During the reign of the house of Tudor and Stewart several Welshmen were mitred" (forty-three between 1558 and 1715), "but not one since the accession of the house of Brunswick. The consequence was that the prelates brought into their respective dioceses their sons, nephews and cousins to the ninth degree of consanguinity; the next consequence was a change of service (on the borders) from Welsh to English; and a third and important consequence was the desertion of the Church. Dissenting places of worship were erected in every direction." Writing of the attempts made by English incumbents to qualify themselves for holding Welsh preferments, he adds, "His uncouth attempts to officiate in his church in a tongue unintelligible to himself can be felt by his congregation as nothing better than a profanation of the worship of God. . . . The strangers, as a makeshift, underwent a lecture or two in the Welsh language *in order to be able to read in*. But the voice of the strangers, instead of collecting a flock, scattered the sheep." *Vide* essay by Judge Johnes on "The Causes of Dissent in Wales," p. 65. Published in 1832, and reprinted in 1870, by Houlston and Sons, 65, Paternoster Row; and John Pryse, Llanidloes.

[1] In a speech delivered in the House of Commons in opposition to Mr. Watkin Williams' motion for the disestablishment of the Welsh Church, the Right Hon. W. Ewart Gladstone, then Prime Minister, used these words: "It has been no question of National Establishments that has led to the growth of Welsh Dissent. In my opinion it is due to the cruelly anti-national policy that was pursued. So long as the national sympathies were cultivated, the Church of Wales was acceptable to the

alienated from the Church?

the Church was not adopted in Wales until the eighteenth century. At that period its effect was to make the Welsh people not Romanist, but Nonconformist.

Why was it then adopted? Was there no Welsh clergyman in that age fitted to be the chief pastor of his countrymen? It was adopted, as in Ireland, for purely political purposes. The greatest Welshman of the century was a clergyman. Griffith Jones, the founder of the circulating schools, and educator of his countrymen, who taught by his system 158,237 souls to read God's Word—the author of the most admirable Catechetical Manuals of scriptural instruction existing in the language, and still used throughout Wales—the man who, above all others, influenced his country for good, lived and died the rector of the little rural parishes of Llandowror and Llandilo-Abercowin, on an income of £226 per annum. He lived in no palace and enjoyed no dignity, but he was the chief pastor of the souls of his countrymen. In his day he raised his voice against the grievous wrong by which the Church in Wales was being ruined. Speaking of it, he said, " It is not my present business to inquire who this is owing to ; but be they who they will, and how little soever they lay it to heart for the present, they will hereafter find themselves answerable to a grievous charge." For these brave, manly words he was probably accused of seeking his own advancement. But a man

people of Wales. . . . It is a fact of some interest that the people of Wales were the stoutest Churchmen in the country as long as the Church was administered in a spirit of sympathy, and in accordance with the national feeling."

who knows that he speaks words of truth and justice, and denounces nothing but wrong, can afford to disregard the sneers and false imputations aimed at him, especially when they come from men who are content to sit in blind self-complacency amid the ruins of a Church which they have desolated, as long as they can find any[1] polished fragment to afford them an elevated

[1] The only section of society in Wales that gave its approval to the system of appointing to the chief places in the Church men ignorant of the language of the people, were the non-Welsh-speaking gentry, and the non-Welsh-speaking clergy, many of whom were too like the mercenaries in the garrison of a foreign conqueror. The former, non-resident during a great part of the year, and devoted to field sports and secular business, were not the best judges of the religious needs of the people. The small section of anti-national, unpatriotic, non-Welsh-speaking clergy, introduced by the English Bishops, were naturally in favour of a system which kept them in countenance and concealed from themselves the anomaly of their own position. What Dean Hook says of Henry III.'s anti-national patronage in England might have been said for generations of the Bishop in a Welsh diocese: "He became more and more alienated from the national party, though occasionally his better nature prevailed. His chosen companions were the Poictevins, Gascons, Provençals, Italians, and Savoyards. Their refined tastes harmonized with his own. By them he was flattered and caressed." These gentlemen, without flocks, and without influence among the Welsh people, but placed in leading positions by their patron, assumed the authority of leading clergy, and ventured to give their views freely to Englishmen about the religious state of Wales, of which they had but the most superficial knowledge. Ignorant of the language, the literature, and the religious ideas of the people, they were not leading, but *misleading*, clergy. Their opinions of tithes and church buildings would have been entitled to weight; but of Welsh thought, feeling, and character, they were but sorry exponents. That any clergyman should venture to discourse upon the Welsh Church, while ignorant of the language and literature of the Welsh people, is certainly a great proof of his own courage, and of his confidence in the patience of his hearers. English Churchmen, who desire to know the real religious state of Wales, ought to be on their guard against the misleading testimony of clergymen enjoying Welsh preferments, but ignorant of Welsh language and life. What value would be attributed to

seat. He has a shelter in the Divine pavilion of conscience from the strife of tongues, and replies to the gainsayer, "I believed, therefore have I spoken."

In Ireland and in Wales alike, the lesson has been taught by God, that the ministry which refuses to adapt itself to national peculiarities, and provokes the forces of nationality into antagonism, will lose all power of gaining and saving the souls whom it professes to seek.

In Ireland the warning was too long disregarded, and easy self-complacent ecclesiastics enjoyed their comfortable preferments, until the forces of that nationality, which they had despised, arose and demanded, with power, that the crosier, which had been transformed into the rod of the oppressor, should no longer be gilded by the religious endowments of the nation.

Those who believe that the national life should be sanctified by a national recognition of religion, will do well to bear in mind the significance of the warning.[1]

the judgment of an Englishman resident in France, but ignorant of French, if he ventured to pose as an authority upon the problems and difficulties of the French Church in its dealings with the French masses?

[1] It will be a serious source of weakness to the Establishment, if the ablest and most high-spirited of the native Welsh-speaking clergy, who alone among Churchmen have any influence over the Welsh masses, and who have hitherto borne the brunt of Church Defence in Wales, are forced to the painful conclusion that disestablishment offers the only way of liberation from a system of high-handed anti-national appointments which have alienated their countrymen by wounding their patriotism, as well as by offering them, in high places, ministrations which they cannot understand. There are unselfish Welsh clergymen—whatever motives may be sometimes attributed to them by the mercenaries of mercenaries—whose "hearts' desire and prayer to God for" Wales is that she may be restored to the Church, and who, *in order to secure that end*, would gladly sacrifice, if necessary, glebe, house, and benefice. It is significant that Glamorgan-

It is impossible to ignore the serious alienation of the Welsh people from the Church. It is sad for a Churchman to reflect that for a hundred and fifty years the dignified clergy of the Church have given to them hardly any literature in their own tongue. The literature of Wales, though much of it is fugitive and perishable, cannot be despised, for it influences a million of souls.[1] More than a dozen semi-religious weekly journals, a still larger number of monthly periodicals, go forth to shape the minds of the native population. No small number of books of a more lasting character are published in the language, year by year. Of this literature, five-sixths are produced by those who do not conform to the Church.[2] For generations the dignified clergy of Wales were above the work of enlightening the people whose religious endowments they enjoyed. Can it excite surprise

shire, the most important county in Wales, returns to Parliament six members who, without exception, vote for Nonconformist measures, and gives to the Liberation Society its Parliamentary leader. It is also ominous that the rector of the most important parish in South Wales has publicly declared himself in favour of disestablishment, on the ground that it affords the only hope of winning back the alienated Welsh people.

[1] "Of all the Celtic-speaking races in the United Kingdom, the Welsh were the most important, and in the maintenance of their own language they showed by far the greatest amount of vitality."—*Pall Mall Gazette* on Ravenstein's Paper, 1879.

[2] Within the last fifty years an English dignitary in a diocese, which was at the time almost exclusively Welsh-speaking, expressed an opinion that it was not necessary to provide religious ministration for the Welsh people in their own language. The Church, he said, was for the upper classes, while the conventicle was the proper place for the Welsh-speaking masses. He was not alone in his opinion. The idea that the Church is not to be the Church of the Welsh, but practically the Church of England in Wales, is still prevalent and influential among some of the anti-national clergy.

that the Welsh people have, to some extent, been alienated from a Church that offered them such a ministry? No; the cause for wonder is that, deep in their hearts, there still survives a love for the Church of their fathers.

If it is permitted to the departed spirits to behold the scenes of their former career on earth, the long line of anti-national pastors, under whose influence the Welsh people were driven from the sanctuaries of their ancestors, have had to look down upon churches emptied, a land saddened, and an affectionate people soured and embittered by the divisions that arose out of their ambition for the chief places of a temple in which they could not effectually minister, and for the short-lived advantages, that must now seem to them as dross, while they hear the reproachful voice of the Eternal Spirit of love and sympathy saying, "Where is the flock that was given thee, thy beautiful flock?" "My sheep wandered through all the mountains, and upon every high hill: yea, My flock was scattered. . . . Neither did My shepherds search for My flock, but the shepherds fed themselves, and fed not My flock. . . . I will require My flock at their hand, and cause them to cease from feeding the flock; neither shall they feed themselves any more."

Although the ignorance that prevails in England concerning the inner national life of Wales[1] is a darkness

---

[1] Welsh Churchmen have had reason to complain that the English press, including, with one or two honourable exceptions, the Church papers, have steadfastly denied them the opportunity of stating Welsh

that seems to be impenetrable, it is not unknown that Dissent is dominant in all its counties.

The Welsh people are divided in their worship. I would not exaggerate the evils of division, or forget who really caused them. But all will acknowledge that the Saviour desires that His people should be united. Spiritual concord is the mother of numerous blessings. To-day the life of Wales, though in many respects prosperous and peaceful, is dwarfed by sectarian littleness, soured by petty distractions, and paralyzed in its social and intellectual progress, because the classes are separated in sympathy by divided worship. It is not difficult to understand how this result has arisen. The chief pastors of the Church mould its life. The cathedral city is the capital of the diocese, and sets its fashion of thought and feeling. As the prelate is, so will the clergy be, and as the clergy are, so will be the people who accept their influence. For a hundred and fifty years the prelates of Wales were hostile to the nationality of the people. The clergy and leading Church laity imitated the tone of their ecclesiastical leaders, despised the Welsh language, derided Welsh traditions, and while learning the languages of Greece and Rome, of France and Italy, in order to accomplish their social efficiency, lived in ignorance of the living language of the people amongst whom they dwelt, and whose social leaders God had appointed them to be.

They were indignant because the humble peasantry

facts, and making known to the English public the real state of the Welsh Church. English editors have more than once, of late, tempted Welshmen to exclaim—Where is the boasted English love of fair play?

had not learnt their language, forgetting that to learn a language is not easy, and that they themselves had not shown an example of triumphing over the difficulty, although duty, interest, and honour alike called them to do it; for their ignorance of the language of the people deprived them of political, social, and moral influence.[1] They abdicated the leadership that God had given them, and it fell into the hands of humbler men, who, speaking the language of the masses, held the key that opened their hearts, and won an influence that gold cannot buy, and pride cannot command.[2]

[1] No intelligent man, who knows the country, can doubt that a real command of the Welsh tongue adds greatly to the social and political influence of its possessors in Wales. In 1868, when the extension of the suffrage gave freer expression to the Welsh masses, one result of the change was to increase very considerably the number of Welsh-speaking members in the House of Commons. It is certain that, in seeking the suffrages of a Welsh constituency, a Welsh-speaking candidate would, *cateris paribus*, have an easy victory over any opponent not so qualified.

[2] It has been observed that the Welsh are sensitive almost to touchiness. To ignore such a characteristic is not wise on the part of those who would win them to the Church. Yet it is well known that an English prelate, within the last fifty years, applied to a large body of his poorer native clergy the opprobrious epithet "cart-horses." The insult has never been forgotten. He should have remembered that the Bishop is the "Father in God" of his clergy, and that, if they are deficient, their deficiencies may well be partly attributed to the spiritual fatherhood of him who called them into ministerial being. It will excite no surprise that he was unable to appreciate Welsh ability. The ablest Welsh scholar in his diocese, author of a Biblical commentary, the chief Welsh poet of his day, some of whose hymns are among the best in the language, was permitted to die in a small perpetual curacy that hardly afforded his maintenance, while English clergymen, relatives of the Bishop, were transplanted from distant districts into the richest benefices of the diocese. The poor Welsh may well say, "Our soul is filled with the scornful reproof of the wealthy, and with the despitefulness of the proud."

It was grievous that, by losing the power of popular sympathy, the social leaders forfeited the power of influencing the people for their good. It is true that the people have done much for themselves; but it is equally true that they have been greatly injured and retarded by the want of patriotic and enlightened social guides. The opportunities offered to the youth of Wales for obtaining higher education have been, and are still, grievously deficient. It is said that the average Welsh boy has only one-third of the educational endowments that are offered to the average English boy, to enable him to make the early steps in the path of enlightenment. Why has the key of knowledge been thus withheld from the Welsh people? It is the mission of the chief clergy of a country, especially a poor country like mountainous Wales, to animate others, and to labour themselves in the noble work of developing its intellectual and spiritual energies. The pastors of the people who do not find and develop the natural gifts of heart and mind lying hid, as rich treasures, in the obscurity of poor, friendless, but talented youth, are but sorry promoters of a country's moral weal.[1] In Wales these natural riches of intelligence and spirit are abundant. In their primitive national competitions they glitter through the rubbish that encircles them, as gold and

---

[1] "The estate of the Church is the estate of the people, so long as the Church is governed on its real principles. The Church is the medium by which the despised and degraded classes assert the native equality of man, and vindicate the rights and power of intellect. It made, in the darkest hour of Norman rule, the son of a Saxon pedlar Primate of England, and placed Nicholas Breakspear, a Hertfordshire peasant, on the throne of the Cæsars."—Coningsby.

alienated from the Church? 327

silver, embedded in the rocks of difficulty, unsought, untrained, undeveloped. Sympathetic chief pastors would have seen these treasures, and have developed them by a system of higher education. As it is, they have been too often lost to the Church, and employed in antagonism to her, while her prelates have not seldom been laying their hands on men who, in a haphazard system of clerical supply, offered themselves, without fitness for the priest's office, for the sake of the piece of bread.[1]

It is true that the College of St. David's was founded a little more than fifty years ago. But for that foundation little credit is due to those who were the rulers of the Welsh Church. Writing of its creation, an able Welsh Church layman has used these severe words: "If ever there was a time when disinterestedness was called for on the part of the rulers of the Welsh Church, it was then. But how did they emulate the good example that had been set them? Did they sacrifice

---

[1] This reproach no longer exists. Nearly ten years ago the Bishop of Bangor invited the other Bishops of Wales, and leading laymen of their dioceses, to attend a conference at Llanidloes, for the purpose of forming a scheme to promote the education of gifted Welsh youths for the ministry of the Church. This work has since been vigorously carried on in the diocese of Bangor, and at this time nearly twenty young men are being educated at a cost of nearly £1000 per annum, contributed by the liberal laity of the diocese in voluntary subscriptions. These students are sent to the English Universities, and are at the same time, by the cultivation of their native language, and by experience of ministerial work, prepared to minister efficiently both to the small English and large Welsh-speaking classes of the diocese. [It may be mentioned that the Paper which gave the first impetus and form to the scheme referred to in this note, is published in this volume (see p. 360).—Ed.]

a sinecure rectory, a prebend, or any of those superfluous revenues, which are professedly intended to provide learning, though, in general, they are far otherwise employed? Alas! no. The college was endowed with a cluster of poor livings in the county of Cardigan, which were in some instances so completely stripped of their scanty revenues, that the parishioners were left without funds to support a resident minister!"[1]

[1] *Vide* Judge Johnes' Essay, p. 115.—Since the first edition of this sermon was issued, the writer has been informed that the above statement, made by Judge Johnes in 1832, and unchallenged for forty-seven years, is not accurate. The livings with which the college was permanently endowed were sinecure rectories in South Wales (one of them only being in Cardiganshire) previously held by the Crown, but transferred, through the influence of Bishop Burgess, to the support of the new institution in which he was much interested. Judge Johnes' mistake seems to have arisen from the fact that at the time when he wrote, in 1832, the principal or some of the professors were permitted to hold some of the livings in Cardiganshire for the augmentation of their own income rather than the benefit of the parishioners. Dr. Burgess is entitled to credit for his well-meaning and unselfish labours in establishing St. David's College. He was a kind and generous man, and being himself the son of a Hampshire grocer, and having risen to a high position through those educational advantages which are so far more liberally offered to poor and talented youths in England than in Wales, he sympathized with the humbler classes in their struggles for education. But, in common with the other non-Welsh-speaking Bishops of Wales, he was unable to restrain his zeal for the extinction of a language which he did not understand. His want of sympathy with their national feelings excited the susceptibilities of some of the most estimable of his clergy, as may be seen from the following passage in the biography of the Rev. Eliezer Williams, Vicar of Lampeter (p. 75): "As to one point in the management of these schools (circulating Welsh Charity Schools), the Bishop and my father were again unfortunately at issue. His lordship felt anxious, as was certainly very natural, that the schools should be organized on a plan that would tend to the ultimate extinction of a language of which he himself was ignorant; while my father, being, as we have already seen, thoroughly acquainted with the circumstances and habits of the flock under his care, knew by experience

It is well known that Dr. Chalmers attributed the intellectual and moral advancement of Scotland to three blessings, viz.—

1. Ecclesiastical endowments devoted exclusively to the maintenance of a native clergy.[1]

2. Parochial schools to educate the natural intelligence of the people.

3. National colleges, in which the ablest of the Scotch youth could obtain higher education.

These blessings have not fallen to the lot of Wales.[2]

that the people were not able to receive religious instruction in any other tongue, and that to persist in such a scheme would drive away the Church members that yet remained." Bishop Burgess's memory has found a zealous, if not a temperate eulogist, in the Rev. F. Jayne, the recently appointed Principal of St. David's College. Mr. Jayne is a man of scholarly acquirements, experienced in collegiate tuition, can speak with authority on subjects in his own sphere, and will doubtless do good service in Wales. But he would have been more able to estimate correctly the official difficulties of a non-Welsh-speaking Bishop in Wales, if he had himself possessed a knowledge of the Welsh language, and of the inner life of the Welsh people.

[1] It has often been observed that the condition into which the attitude of the anti-national and non-Welsh-speaking clergy tends to reduce the Church in Wales is that of the Episcopal Church of Scotland, a "little Church of the lairds." As long as a few squires with their servants and a few genteel English residents accept their ministrations, they are content to see the main stream of Welsh life flowing far from them, and entirely ignoring their presence in the country. They should remember that this state of things cannot be permanent, and that Welsh religious endowments must ultimately be devoted to the service of the Welsh people.

[2] The educational benefactors of Wales have almost without exception been patriotic natives, e.g. Hugh Prys, Leoline Jenkins, and Meyrick, the founders and benefactors of the Welsh College at Oxford; and Archbishop Williams, who created exhibitions at Westminster School and at St. John's College, Cambridge, in aid of poor Welsh scholars. David Hughes, the founder of Beaumaris Grammar School; Geoffrey Glynne, of Friars' School, Bangor; Godfrey Goodman, of Ruthin Grammar School; Edward

Eighty years have hardly passed away since one prelate, in a Welsh diocese, absorbed for himself and family more than half its revenue, and ran a career which, in many points, may not inaptly be compared to that of Verres in Sicily.

At the present time Wales, scantily endowed already, is threatened with the further loss of no small portion of the educational revenues provided for her sons, in other days, by the patriot Welshmen Hugh Prys, Leoline Jenkins, and Meyrick. For the purpose, as it is alleged, of conferring some indirect and impalpable advantages upon the Welsh people, it is proposed to deprive them of their special interest in several thousands of the annual revenue of the Welsh College at Oxford.[1]

Richards, of Ystradmeurig; Thomas Phillips, of Llandovery; Leoline Jenkins, of Cowbridge, were all native Welshmen. The long line of English prelates and dignitaries, who during a hundred and fifty years must have drawn from Wales several millions of money, have not, I believe, left behind them a single educational institution created by their bounty. Dean Hook, in contrasting the benefactions of native English Bishops with the unsympathetic greed of the foreign ecclesiastics intruded by Henry III. and the Pope, observes, "When the persons so employed were Englishmen, they admitted the claim made upon them for local purposes, and felt a peculiar attachment to the town or village from which they derived their surname. When they retired from public life, they returned to their respective dioceses, and by their munificence very frequently became public benefactors. . . . The chroniclers and poets of the period had a constant theme of invective in the swarms of Gascons, Poictevins, Savoyards, and Provençals, who, like locusts, arrived only to devour; and took flight, only when they saw no further prospect of satisfying their greed." For "chroniclers and poets" read "bards, preachers, and ballad-writers" like Twm o'r Nant, and the analogy between Wales in the eighteenth and England in the thirteenth century will be complete.

[1] The decay of the Welsh College at Oxford has been a consequence of the decay of the Church in Wales. The grammar schools have been

It is simply a repetition of the old plausible anti-national, unsympathetic policy which has sought to transform badly endowed, and, being under the influence of an unpopular clergy, have failed during the last hundred and seventy years to attract the youth of the middle and lower middle classes so generally alienated from the Church. The college has, therefore, drawn its recruits, not from the entire people of Wales, but from that minority which has adhered to the Church. The most vigorous intellects and independent spirits, as might have been expected under an anti-national Church *régime*, in Wales have not seldom been Nonconformist. The college might be revived and made a source of inestimable blessings to Wales, if the Meyrick Trust Fund could be devoted mainly to the encouragement of intermediate education, and the maintenance in the grammar schools of poor scholars of natural ability. The minimum expenditure of a student has been estimated by the new English principal at £120. This sum excludes a large number of Welsh youths. It would seem desirable to adapt the college, as the national college of Wales, to the social condition of its people, by reducing the rate of expenditure to a much lower figure, and enlarging its accommodation. It seems strange that the governing body of a college, having a net corporate income of £10,000 per annum, cannot provide education at an even cheaper rate than the unendowed Keble College, where young men of a much wealthier class than the average Welsh student are educated for less than £100 per annum. But for the first time in its history the Welsh college is under the influence of an English principal, who, notwithstanding his many high qualities, lacks sympathetic insight into the peculiar needs of Wales, and ignores its national rights. It is no secret that, in approaching the Oxford University Commission, now sitting, the principal and fellows have used language implying that the Welsh endowments of the college should no longer be necessarily confined to the education of Welshmen. They generously ask the commissioners to give them power in dealing with the scholarships "so long as they shall deem it expedient for the interests of education in the Principality of Wales to declare a certain number not exceeding two-thirds to be Welsh scholarships"! They make the same generous proposal with regard to the fellowships! The plain English of this proposal is that all the Welsh endowments are to be alienated from Wales whenever the principal and fellows, desiring more genteel pupils, shall think it expedient. Assuming that the commissioners will, as a matter of course, deprive Wales of her rights, they magnanimously ask that they, as the executioners of the decree, may have power to spare some portion of them *so long as they shall deem*

Wales by ignoring its national rights, and has resulted in the shame of its authors and the injury of the country. Let us hope that the social leaders of Wales will defend their countrymen against this threatened wrong, which is grievous, though it comes veiled in the phrases of a pretentious reform. Had the people of Scotland been threatened by such an injustice, its leaders would ere this have raised a cry that could not have been disregarded.[1]

it expedient. It is difficult to believe that the commissioners will sanction such a scheme, or permit endowments, intended to be the aids of poor Welsh students, to become the prizes of wealthy English youths, expensively trained at the English public schools. It will be another attempt to cure a patient, fainting from loss of blood, by blood-letting.

[1] Since the first edition of this sermon was issued, the writer's views have been confirmed by the authoritative testimony of a great statesman, whose residence in Wales has enabled him to form a correct estimate of its ecclesiastical misgovernment, and of the evils which have flowed from it. Speaking in the House of Commons on Tuesday, July 1, 1879, in support of Mr. Hussey Vivian's motion concerning the deficiency of higher education in Wales, the Right Hon. W. Ewart Gladstone expressed himself in the following eloquent and generous language: "It was rarely that Wales urged any local claim on the notice of Parliament. The noble lord had most fairly compared the case of Wales with that of Scotland and Ireland. But, although Wales had in many respects less of a historical and political existence than Scotland, she had in many respects also a more strongly marked nationality. Wales had a population of about a million and a half; Scotland, a population of three and a half millions, and Ireland a population of about five and a half millions. But in the population of a million and a half in Wales there was a greater number who spoke and clung to the national language than in the nine millions who inhabited Scotland and Ireland. As to the Church, the National Church of Scotland did immense service in fostering the national intelligence. The case was the same in Wales until the unhappy system of proscribing the Welsh tongue was established. Now the Welsh as a nation were a nation of Nonconformists. Two hundred years ago they were, strictly speaking, a nation of Churchmen. The old Puritanism, which was so powerful in

Why do I dwell upon these wrongs and weaknesses of Wales? Because I believe them to be mainly due to the violation of that Apostolical principle declared in the text, and the want of a ministry in living sympathy with the people to whom they were sent.

Had the Church in Wales retained the national sympathy, a patriotic clergy would have led the people many parts of England, took no root whatever in Wales. After the Revolution, English Bishops were appointed. Every living was given to Englishmen; the dregs were left to the people of Wales. The people of Wales were driven out of connection with that great national institution which in time would have afforded means for the cultivation of the national intelligence, so that Parliament and the British Government had not only done nothing for Wales, they had not only withheld from Wales the aid that had been given, especially during the present century, to Scotland and Ireland, with more or less liberality, according to the views they maintained, but they positively drove the people of Wales out of the enjoyment of the only institution which offered any means of fostering and educating the national mind. Now, he contended that *the condition and history of Wales invested it with a claim that could not be much longer overlooked. It was not the fault of the people of Wales that they did not find their way to the enjoyment of higher education in the same proportion as the people in the other divisions of the United Kingdom. They had shown quite as great a disposition to profit by the advantages of education, whenever they had access to it, as had been shown by the people of Scotland. The Welsh cherished among themselves a literature of their own, institutions of their own. They kept alive their national traditions; and the warmth of feeling which they entertained on this subject, the affectionate manner in which they clung to those recollections, must command respect. There are many who thought the Welsh language was a calamity, and that the sooner it was got rid of the better. It was not the abstract question they had to consider—whether one tongue in the whole of the United Kingdom was desirable or not. Where you had a large population warmly and closely attached to this tongue, and where that tongue had become the emblem of the traditions they had received from their fathers, that attachment should be respected; and no measure should be taken by Parliament under the supposition that they were to be weaned from their own language."

onward in the march of progress, would have impelled them to acquire the English language[1] without forgetting their own, and would have preserved for them the priceless blessings of religious unity and social concord.

To-day I plead before you on behalf of the Welsh Church in this town. It has struggles and difficulties and debt. Is its weakness attributable to any lack of zeal or ability in those who have immediate charge of its work? No. The weakness of the Church among the Welsh settlers in England—and that it is weak no one, who knows that there are more than a hundred Nonconformist congregations, great and small, worshipping in Welsh in the towns of England, and only four belonging to the Church, can deny—is a consequence of the general debility that has overtaken its entire system in Wales, as the result of those abuses upon which I have dwelt. For a hundred and fifty years Welshmen were taught to regard the Church as hostile to their nationality and alien to their hearts. They bring those feelings with them when they settle in your

[1] No educated Welshman desires that his countrymen should continue in ignorance of the English language. He knows that the knowledge of it is essential to their social and material advancement. He regrets the anti-national policy that has been pursued, because it has *retarded* the progress of the English language in Wales. Since 1700, the masses of the population have been under the influence of native preachers, of whom a majority, though often very able and intelligent men, have had no command of the English tongue. As the teacher is, so will the taught be. The anti-national policy, which was designed to kill the Welsh language, has created Nonconformity, and Nonconformity has had the practical effect of excluding the English language! In this case the wisdom of this world has proved to be also worldly foolishness.

great towns. Therefore the Church has a hard struggle to win their confidence.

It is true that the evil anti-national policy has been reversed (although there are some who still cling to the superstition that the ministrations of clergy whom the people will not hear, and cannot understand, have in some mysterious way an elevating effect upon their nature), and better days have dawned upon the Church in Wales. But the wrongs of a hundred and fifty years cannot be undone in a generation. Although the Church is to-day gradually adapting herself to the people, and becoming to the Welsh as Welsh, some generations must pass before she can exert the saving influence that will induce the whole people to accept her as their spiritual mother.

In the day of her weakness I appeal to you, the generous citizens of this great town, to aid this little Welsh Church of St. David, struggling under a debt of nearly £100. The citizens of Liverpool are known to be wealthy and liberal. You are not narrow in your sympathies. You see among you men of all races, and can sympathize with all. The presence of the chief magistrate and the powerful municipality of this great community—equal in wealth to some ancient states that have left their mark on history—is a testimony that Welsh Churchmen have your good will. I have tried to excite your interest and sympathy by unfolding to you that tale of wrong by which the higher spirit of Wales has suffered loss.

Will you show your sympathy with the weak by

giving to my countrymen here that aid which they sorely need? The crumbs that fall from the table of the merchant princes of this great town would enable this little Welsh congregation to do its work and to go on its way with joy. Let me entreat you to help them with that princely liberality for which many of you are famous, knowing that "the liberal soul shall be made fat."

THE PAST AND PRESENT POSITION OF THE CHURCH IN WALES.[1]

THE wording of this subject is significant. Till the twelfth century, the Church was the Church of Wales. Then Norman force, filling Welsh sees with strangers, maintaining Harvey at Bangor by arms, subjecting St. David's to Canterbury, banishing Gruffydd, rejecting Giraldus Cambrensis for Peter de Leia, provoking the appeal of the Welsh princes to the Pope, changed the Church *of* Wales into the Church *in* Wales. The native Church seems to have been free from Roman influence. The oldest parish churches are rarely dedicated to the Virgin. The churches of St. Mary (Llanfair) are found under the shadows of the fortresses built by the Normans. In Wales Mariolatry was a Norman import. In the thirteenth century the bards, impatient of an anti-national clergy, tried to supplant the Church by theosophical Druidism. In 1402 Glyndwr burnt the cathedral at Bangor, the cathedral,

[1] An address delivered at the Church Congress, Swansea, October 9, 1879; with Appendix.

palace, and canons' houses at St. Asaph, and the Bishop's castle and Archdeacon's house at Llandaff.

Eighty-three years later, a Welsh dynasty, indebted to the Welsh soldiers of Bosworth, ushered in happier days for Wales. In 1588 Bishop Morgan gave her his version of the Bible, and Archdeacon Prys a metrical psalter. In the seventeenth century, the Welsh Church, tried by the blasts of Republican Puritanism, was not moved; for she was then, not a sickly exotic, but the Church of the people. Native clergy ministered, scholars like John Davies wrote for her, and Rhys Prichard sang sacred songs still cherished in the homes of Wales. Then the popular cry was "Church and King!" In 1715 there were but thirty-five Nonconformist chapels in Wales.

At that date the Government, resenting Jacobite sympathies, began to import ecclesiastics ignorant of the language and manners of the people. The fountain-heads of her ministry then froze in worldliness. In dark days Gruffydd Jones taught 150,212 souls to read the Welsh Bible. With intelligence came spiritual thirst. A ministry frozen at the fountain could not satisfy it.

Then Howell Harris and Daniel Rowlands the preachers, Peter Williams the commentator, and Williams of Pantycelyn, the poet of Methodism, opened new wells in the wilderness. In 1800 the thirty-five chapels of 1715 had become well-nigh a thousand. Methodism, long exposed to the outrages of mobs and to the frowns of authority, grew; for its roots were nourished by the waters that forced their way outward, when men had choked their true channels in the Church. In 1879 it has 1134 congregations, 116,016 communicants, 275,406 hearers, and raises £164,073 5s. 4d. a year. The Welsh Congregationalists have 983 chapels, more than 180,000 adherents, and raise more than £100,000 a year. The Welsh Baptists have more than 600 chapels; and the Welsh Wesleyans are a considerable body.

The number of worshippers, above ten years of age, adhering to these four bodies has been stated, on good authority, to be 686,220, of whom 656,000 worship in Welsh. Thus, out of 1,006,100 souls, who, according to Mr. Ravenstein, speak Welsh, 800,000 are attached more or less closely to the 3000 chapels. Statistical apologists will hint that these Nonconformists exist only on paper. Paper-adherents do not give money. The Welsh Nonconformists give far more than £300,000 a year.

Now Wales, with the Welsh parts of Monmouthshire, in 1871 had about 1,300,000 souls. Some 300,000 use English only, and of them a majority, probably, conform. Thus some 400,000 souls may profess more or less allegiance to the Church. But she has lost the mass of the Welsh-speaking population, of whom 500,000 must be virtually monoglots. There are many proofs that confirm this conclusion. Twelve weekly journals, eighteen magazines, and a large number of books are published in Welsh. Of this literature more than five-sixths are produced by Nonconformists for Nonconformists. Again, although the landlords of Wales are mainly Churchmen, at least two-thirds of the political power of Wales are Nonconformist.

Such is the present position of the Church in Wales. She has lost five-sixths of the Welsh-speaking people, and her strength survives among the English-speaking upper and upper middle classes. In 1715 she was confronted by thirty-five Nonconformist chapels, in 1879 by more than three thousand. Then the Welsh literature came almost entirely from the clergy; now it comes almost exclusively from Nonconformists.

These are facts which some would hide. The old Welsh principle, " Truth against the world," will prove to be the Welsh Church's best physician. To veil sores is not to heal them. To conceal ailments is not to cure but to perpetuate them. To unfold the worst symptoms is but to invite the remedies that will avail.

How has this exodus been provoked? Let the greatest Welsh pastor of the eighteenth century answer. " I must do justice to the Dissenters in Wales," said Gruffydd Jones, " that it was not any scruple of conscience about the principles or orders of the Established Church that gave occasion to scarce one in ten of the Dissenters in this country to separate from us at the first, whatever objections they may afterwards imbibe against conforming. No, Sir! they generally dissent at first for no other reason than for want of plain, practical, pressing, and zealous preaching, in a language and dialect they are able to understand ; and freedom of access to advise about their spiritual state."

That is true. None will deny it but those who,

being ignorant of the Welsh language, are unqualified to judge of Welsh life. Other causes, common to England, doubtless contributed. Some allege the poverty of Welsh endowments, forgetting that where the Church is poorest—as in Cardiganshire, where the tithes were small enough to be left to the natives—there among the Welsh she is strongest. The analogies between English and Welsh Dissent are partial. Dissent in England is sporadic, in Wales endemic; local in England, national in Wales; stronger than the Church in some English districts, in all Welsh.

In Ireland, Scotland, Wales—among every Celtic people—the Anglican Church lost her hold, because she became a Church *among* but not *of* the people. Was it from lack of endowments? No. In Ireland and in Wales unendowed rivals won the hearts which the clergy had lost. The Irish Sogarth and the Welsh Pregethwr, differing in faith, had this in common—natives of the soil, unfed by its wealth, they beat the stranger-clergy fattened by the chiefest of its offerings.

The tale of the Church's ruin in Wales is simple. Where did the malady begin? "As in human bodies," Pliny wrote, "so in states, the worst disease is that which is diffused from the head" ("Ut in corporibus, sic in imperiis, gravissimus est morbus qui a capite diffunditur").[1]

In the hundred and fifty years preceding 1700, when the Church had the Welsh people, Wales produced more than forty chief pastors; in the hundred and fifty years

[1] Epist. lib. iv. 22.

succeeding 1700, in which the Church lost the Welsh people, not one. For a hundred and fifty years the head of every diocese was an imported ecclesiastic, ignorant of the language, out of sympathy with the people. He came into Wales strong in his narrow national creed that all things un-English were unpardonable. To root out the sin of Welsh, he transplanted into all sunny places English brothers, cousins, connections, friends. Thus it gradually became the mark of the dignified clergy that they were dumb in the language of the people. To the Welsh the cathedral city became a fortress garrisoned by men who despised everything Welsh except Welsh endowments; the cathedral itself a consecrated ice-house, in which Welsh hearts were chilled to find strangers, wearing Welsh dignities in person, doing Welsh duties by deputy. This treatment was tried upon a people so proud of their race that, under their old laws, the descendants of a foreigner settled in Wales were not accounted Welsh, until after nine degrees of ascent by generations of intermarriage with natives of pure Welsh blood.

In Wales, as in India, natives were enlisted to fill the humbler posts. Who were they? The favourites were feeble, pliant, unpatriotic men, who cringed to climb; who told their patron not what was true, but what he wished to hear, viz. that all things Welsh were dying. Aping their masters, they affected contempt for the popular language. Ceasing to be Welsh, failing to be English, they became—Nobodies. Of Welsh enthusiasm, oratory, literature, poetry, patriotism, they were innocent. Obsequious to the squires, arrogant to the people, they had no influence. They had no Welsh culture, and very little English; for, like North American Indians, they learnt the vices sooner than the virtues of their conquerors.

Instinctively strong Welshmen, of eloquence, intellect, and influence, shunned the Church. Dissent was more attractive to them, because the chapels contained their countrymen, and the Church had lost them. They preferred flocks without tithes, to tithes without flocks.

The clergy, imported as apostles of English, retarded the progress of the English language, by associating it with ecclesiastical abuses, by throwing the people under the exclusive influence of monoglot Welsh teachers, by neglecting to promote higher education. During a hundred and fifty years these dignitaries—one of whom bestowed on his family more than half the revenues of a diocese—never endowed a single grammar school, and left Wales with barely a third of the school endowments existing in the average English districts of equal population. Chief pastors, devoid of Welsh sympathies and illiterate in the Welsh tongue, produced a clergy in their own image. Hence, for a hundred and fifty years, every teacher whose name lives in the hearts of the Welsh people has been almost without exception a Nonconformist. While the Bishops were laying hands upon unfit men, the natural Heaven-born teachers of Wales were influencing thousands in the Chapel and *Cymmanfa*. Of the clergy, those who were educated knew no Welsh, and those who knew Welsh were not educated; those who had something to say couldn't say it to the people, and those who could say it had nothing to say.

The Bishop, good easy man, went around to confirm Each pastor of empty pews filled his church for the day. How? Sight-seeing Nonconformists came to the Durbar of the great English official, and many knelt before him. Too often the candidates had received no instruction. Sometimes they were hired for the day, to make a show before the Bishop. They heard what was to them but a magical incantation, and gazed at a pompous mechanical rite without religious meaning to their minds. But the good Bishop, an overseer without insight, saw the crowd, and went away—delighted. No one told him that, if he had gone there on the following Sunday, he would have found the church empty, and the newly confirmed all in chapel! These Confirmations, themes of endless Welsh ridicule, confirmed the Bishop in happy ignorance of his diocese, and confirmed earnest Dissenters in their Dissent.

The Church has made material progress of late. Churches, parsonages, schools, have been built, and on the cathedrals, after great efforts, over many years, half as much money has been spent as is raised by Welsh Methodism in one year. But how many of the churches are empty? Five-sixths of the Welsh-speaking million are outside the Church. That is the present position. Is it satisfactory? I think not.

Well, how can it be altered? The Church must be treated as the Church of the Welsh people, and not as the Church of the English-speaking minority. As long as more than half the people of every diocese worship in Welsh, clergy occupying diocesan positions ought to speak and write both languages, not as schoolboys falter through a French exercise, but with power. But I shall be told by some worthy clergyman, whose sight is weakened by the strength of his will, who is blind to most Welsh facts, but has an eye to Welsh preferments, who tells his Bishop that all the Welsh in his parish are dead, because they are all gone to chapel, " Is not the Welsh language to die out?" My answer is, " It may die, but you'll die ages before it. You can't justify your present position by saying that you are waiting for the shoes of a dead language. You may serve the Church in Wales if you live till 2079. To-day you are a possible pastor for posterity, a light fitted to shine, only in the Church of the future."

But it is said, " There are no men of sufficient culture who know Welsh." Why? Because ignorance of Welsh has been treated not as a disqualification, but almost as a sign of fitness for high promotion in the Welsh Church. Let it be known that no man can minister in the chief places of a Welsh diocese unless he has power over both languages, and soon men so qualified will be forthcoming.

In every diocese, £2000 a year would be better spent in training devout, gifted Welshmen for the ministry, than in building churches doomed to be kept empty by ordained illiterates, and mouthers of marvellous Welsh. These men wisely chosen ought to be sent to the English Universities for general culture, and to be trained in the cathedral city for a few weeks of the long vacation in Welsh speaking, writing, and ministerial work. Such a system would dry the springs of Dissent. The flower of Welsh youth would give themselves to the Church, if she had a discerning spirit to choose, and charity to educate them. A clergy trained at the Universities, and masters of Welsh, losing narrowness and winning popular sympathy, will be at once eager and able to lead their countrymen in all paths of true social and religious progress.

As to the future of the Church in Wales, I have confidence in the religious instincts of my countrymen. Show them the Church in all her fairness, and they will see the meanness of sectarianism. Take away, if you will, the privileges of the Church; take away, if you must, her endowments; but give her back a living ministry that can win the heart of the Welsh people. That warm religious heart of Wales—chilled out of the Church—has built three thousand humble shrines, and gives £300,000 a year for God. Let the Church have a native ministry that can regain that Welsh heart, and she will be strong and rich; and when another Congress is held in Swansea by our children at the end of thirty years, some of us may then be living to hear them call her, not the Church *in* Wales, but the Church *of* Wales, strong in the love of the Welsh people; when their "nobles shall be of themselves, and their governor shall proceed from the midst of them."

APPENDIX.

THIS address was delivered at the Swansea Church Congress, on Thursday, October 9, 1879, in the discussion upon "The Past and Present Position of the Church in Wales." It attributes the decay of the Welsh Church to the anti-national policy by which prelates and clergy ignorant of the language were thrust upon the Welsh-speaking people. This policy, adopted in early times, relaxed, though not entirely suspended, from 1558 to 1700, was then revived and continued without a break till 1870. That policy is regarded in this address as the radical cause of the evils which have alienated five-sixths of the Welsh-speaking million from the Church.

The writer ventures to affirm that this opinion has never been seriously challenged by any living clergyman or layman who has a competent mastery of the Welsh language, and an intimate knowledge of the Welsh-speaking people. Its correctness has been questioned, but only by critics either ignorant of the Welsh language, or incapable of writing and speaking it effectively. Welsh Churchmen know how to estimate the value of such criticisms. But inasmuch as great ignorance prevails among English Churchmen as to the inner religious life of the Welsh people, the writer thinks it advisable to add in this Appendix some proofs that the view expressed is not a "pretty little theory" easily demolished, but a statement of historical truth.

The anti-national policy of appointing Bishops ignorant of Welsh to be the chief pastors of Welsh-speaking people prevailed down to 1558. Between that year and 1714, fifty Welshmen became Bishops. Of these, forty-three were born in Wales, and thirty presided over Welsh dioceses. From 1714 till 1870 no Welshman rose to the Episcopal Bench. To what cause is this long exclusion of Welshmen from the Episcopate to be attributed? Sir Thomas Phillips, in his well-known work upon Wales, published in 1849, traced it to the Jacobite sympathies of the Welsh clergy and squires. The Right Rev. the Lord Bishop of St. David's was therefore mistaken in suggesting at the Congress that this "little theory" was first formulated by Mr. Gladstone.

There are some interpreters of Welsh Church history, it seems, who regard the English appointments from 1714 to 1870 as a fortuitous succession, arising out of the apathy of the age, rather than as the deliberate expression of a political purpose.

The Rev. Canon Bevan was described by the Right Reverend President as having disposed of this "little theory." But inasmuch as his paper attributes these appointments to a cynical indifference to the true interests of the Church on the part of statesmen, who "prostituted the Episcopate into a reward for *political* services," Canon Bevan appears to be rather a supporter than a destroyer of Sir Thomas Phillips' theory.

But although Mr. Bevan acknowledges that a change of policy occurred at the beginning of the eighteenth century, he declines to agree with those who attribute to it the ruin of the Welsh Church, and he bases his conclusion upon the authority of Dr. Erasmus Saunders. "It is supposed," he says, "that the period of declension set in with the change of policy to which we have referred, and was mainly, if not wholly, due to that policy. I think the causes lie deeper and further back in the history of the Church. We have, fortunately, a most graphic description of the diocese of St. David's at this time from the pen of Dr. Erasmus Saunders. . . . Crushing *poverty* and disorganization consequent thereon *were,* in *Dr. Saunders' view, at the bottom of all the evils that then afflicted the Church in Wales.*"

If Canon Bevan has, in these words, correctly described the opinion of Dr. Saunders, the view of that graphic writer whose work was published in 1721 is opposed to the view set forth in this address. But let Dr. Saunders' view be given in his own language. In his work entitled "A View of the State of Religion in the Diocese of St. David's, about the beginning of the eighteenth century, with some account of the causes of its decay, together with considerations of the reasonableness of augmenting the revenues of impropriate churches," we find Section III. thus headed, "Wherein are considered the injuries occasioned to religion by pastors that neglect the use of our language, by non-residence," etc.

"*First*, then, if it were not an opinion that did not seem very well to comport and bear with the sense and practice of many learned and eminent men, I could not forbear thinking that the disposing of Welsh preferments, I mean those especially that are attended with cure of souls, to such as are wholly ignorant of that language, to be a practice that has contributed not a little to the decay and desolation of our religion; not that any gentlemen, and least of all neighbours, or natives, should be envied what benefits or preferments they can obtain in these parts, as being generally of so mean a value; but that it is humbly to be supposed that they should accept of them on no other view, but of being useful and doing the service of the Church, whose bread they eat, it being just and equitable that they should be qualified for the duty where they receive the profit; and I think it can't be well supposed that they are so, till they make themselves intelligible to the flock they are to guide and oversee. For as St. Paul observes, when the voice of him that speaketh is not understood, then both he that speaks and he that is spoken to are mutually barbarians to each other; and a greater yet infinitely than St. Paul hath told us, that it ought to go into the character of a good shepherd that his *sheep should know his voice*. . . .

"But if Revelation had been silent, and had not said so, the reason of the thing is so clear and unanswerable, as that it is in truth amazing that ambition itself, with all its fertile inventions, should think to find out arguments to justify the contrary; for of what use can one be (let his learning in other respects be ever so great) to instruct and teach those whom he can't speak to? And therefore what benefits are the people to expect, as to knowledge or information, from the ministry of such, who can neither preach nor pray so as to be understood by them? . . .

"Again, it was upon the same principle (as I am informed) that the present worthy and learned Bishop of Carlisle, though there were many motives to induce him to it, did yet decline accepting of a bishopric in Wales, namely, because he was a stranger to the language, and that he therefore conscientiously feared he should not be so useful to his diocese, nor so capable of edifying and instructing them, as he thought himself obliged to be. But all are not of his opinion; some have greater courage. . . .

"But to all this it will, I know, by some be answered with regard to Bishops, that their care devolves to the inferior pastors ; that their intercourse is little with the people, and their trust discharged by charges to the clergy. Admitting, then, it may be so, and that for this or other reasons *above the view perhaps of ordinary capacities*, it may be fit or lawful that my Lords, the Bishops, may be strangers to the Liturgy, strangers to the language of the people, and the people also strangers to or uncapable of understanding the offices they perform among them, or the benedictions they are pleased to give them ; yet I think it is allowed that this privilege should not be extended to the inferior orders, because it is alleged at least '*that it is a sufficient cause of refusal (when a clerk is presented to the cure of souls in Wales) if he does not understand that language;*' though, if the reason of this sanction be just, it is difficult to conceive *why it should not hold with regard to superiors as well as inferiors*, that hold themselves engaged to ministerial offices. . . .

"Absurdities of this kind are (God be thanked) pretty well understood now in most other places, where the Reformation is received, for there are but few that think themselves reformed, and continue still to have the service in a tongue unknown ; and were any of our more knowing neighbours, who (God be thanked) are not obliged to be in this respect as unhappy as we are, but treated in this manner, with what patience would they bear it ? Or how pleased would an English congregation be to have a Frenchman, a Dutchman, a Welshman, a German, or any man, officiate among them in a language they did not understand ? . . . The Church, our mother, does in this respect kindly give indulgence, even to the remotest and most savage infidels, by obliging all her missionaries first themselves to learn the language of those they are sent to address themselves unto ; and it is manifestly absurd to imagine they should be able to do anything to answer the design they are sent for until they do so ; nor can it therefore be supposed to be her design to be so unequal in her favours, as to deny so common and so just a privilege to her own children."

Dr. Saunders endeavours to illustrate to Englishmen the injustice which ruined the Welsh Church, by recalling the indignant protests addressed to the Popes against the introduction into *of the Church in Wales.* 351

English sees of Italian ecclesiastics. He quotes the following record of the remonstrance addressed by the Lords and Commons of England to Pope Innocent IV., at the Council of Lyons : " Proceres et populus Angliæ querelas per procuratorem suum, coram Innocentio quarto, in concilio Lugdunensi proposuerunt his verbis, scil. Jam ditantur in Angliâ Italici, nullam curam animarum gerentes, sed lupos rapacissimos gregem dispergere et oves rapere permittentes. Unde vere dicere possumus, quod non sunt boni pastores quoniam oves suas non cognoscunt, nec pastorum notitiam oves habent, hospitalitati, elcemosynarumque largitioni, sicut statutum est in Angliâ, non insistunt, sed fructus tantum percipiunt, the extra regna apportantes."

His appreciation of the spiritual efficiency in Wales of the non-Welsh-speaking Bishops and clergy, Dr. Saunders also illustrated by quoting, " Mutis conferuntur canibus qui latrare nesciunt, et malunt potius actores esse in Fabulâ pro exiguo, quam spectatores pro nihilo " (Annot. D. Powel in cap I. Giraldi Itin. Cambr.).

These extracts abundantly prove that Canon Bevan was not fortunate in the use of words when he stated that " crushing poverty and disorganization consequent thereon were, in Dr. Saunders' view, *at the bottom* of all the evils that then afflicted the Church in Wales."

Saunders distinctly describes the poverty and misery of the clergy as secondary evils, and states that, in dwelling upon the influence of Bishops and clergy ignorant of the language and people, he was proceeding " *to point out the causes that mostly seem to have contributed to the desolations I have been describing;*" and again he declares, " *disposing of Welsh preferments . . . to such as are wholly ignorant of that language, to be a practice that has contributed not a little to the decay and desolation of our religion.*"

No clearer or stronger testimony could be cited in support of the views enunciated in this paper than that of Dr. Erasmus Saunders. In 1879, as it was in 1721, the material poverty of the Church in Wales (if she can be pronounced to be poor) is due to the weakness of her spiritual hold over the people, not the weakness of her spiritual hold to her material poverty. The Welsh-speaking people, alienated by the influence of the imported ecclesiastics, contribute more than £300,000 a year to religious purposes in their

Nonconformity. If the Church had been blessed with chief pastors able to retain the religious allegiance of the Welsh-speaking million, the £300,000 now given in Nonconformity would have swelled the Church's treasury, and, when added to the income of her ancient endowments, would have made her richer in Wales, perhaps, than in any other district of the kingdom. Who can doubt also that the great landowners and employers in Wales would come forward to multiply the Church's resources, if they recognized in her the Church of the people? They can hardly be expected to give new endowments to the Churches, when they see the people on their estates worshipping in the chapels. To endow the Church is one thing, to endow a flockless alien clergy is quite another.

"Poverty," says Canon Bevan, "is still the besetting infirmity of the Church in Wales. Poverty is still the main cause of her existing inefficiency." This is a courageous statement when made in the presence of the obvious fact that ne native Nonconformist ministers, who have won the affections of the people whom the Church has lost, are hindered by far greater poverty, having no endowments whatever. The truth is that the poverty of the Church is due to her existing inefficiency, and her existing inefficiency due to the rule of chief pastors ignorant of the language and out of sympathy with the people.

The predominance of Dissent in every district of the country is peculiar to Wales, but the crushing poverty consequent upon spoliations in Tudor times was common to England and Wales. Dr. Saunders reminds his readers (p. 74) that, according to the account given by the Lower House of Convocation to Queen Elizabeth, there were then scarce sixty out of eight thousand eight hundred and odd benefices that were singly sufficient for the encouragement of learned men ; and again that Archbishop Whitgift had observed that there were in England four thousand five hundred benefices with cure, and not valued above ten pounds in the "Book of Firstfruits," and most of them under eight. He also quotes a saying of Archbishop Grindal, that for one Church in England able to support a learned minister, there were ten unable. Spoliation was common to the Church in England and Wales. Universal Dissent is peculiar to Wales. The Church in England has become strong and rich, because she is national and English in spirit. The

Church in Wales has languished, because she has been made anti-national and anti-Welsh, by Bishops and clergy who have reduced her into a little " Church of the lairds."

One noble speaker in the discussion attributed the past weakness of the Welsh Church to the immorality, and especially the intemperance, of the clergy in former years. The questions at once suggest themselves—Who were the Fathers in God appointed to produce the clergy? Who failed to draw into the Church the hundreds of devout gifted Welshmen willing to serve her, but alienated by neglect into Nonconformist pulpits? Who laid hands "suddenly" on unfit men without taking time or trouble to ascertain the moral stability of those whom they were about to ordain? Who utterly neglected to establish any effective system of clerical education for drawing into the ministry of the Church men truly capable of serving her? The faults of the clergy were secondary evils. The primary evil was the incapacity of the important Bishops, who had no insight into the spiritual forces latent in the population.

This introduction of Bishops and clergy ignorant of Welsh has been, as Haddan expressed it, "*that bane of the Welsh Church*," or to adopt Canon Bevan's phrase, while rejecting his opinion, "*the besetting infirmity*." This disease, suppressed for a time, and then recrudescent, has worked in her constitution ever since conquest gave to the Welsh-speaking masses of Wales an English-speaking upper class. The political influence of the squires and landowners, of whom the chief were English in blood, language, and sympathy, was always strong enough to overbear the will of the people. When Queen Elizabeth, with an unerring sagacity, saw that Welsh-speaking chief pastors were due to the Welsh-speaking people, the voice of that small anti-Welsh upper class was heard in the ears of Archbishop and Premier deprecating justice to Wales. When the secret correspondence of the nineteenth century is published, it is certain that there will come to light many similar protests, made by the non-Welsh-speaking clergy and gentry of these days, against those Welsh appointments that were demanded by the Welsh people, as soon as the extension of the suffrage in 1867 had transferred political power in Wales from the squires to the masses. It may be observed in passing that the national feeling of Welsh

Nonconformists upon this subject was, perhaps, never more vigorously expressed than by Dr. William Rees, well known as a poet, orator, and Nonconformist minister of the highest standing in Wales. In a political letter, addressed to Mr. Gladstone in 1868, he used these words: "We feel that, as a *nation*, we are insulted and degraded by the Government, in that it has always appointed aliens in blood and language to the Welsh bishoprics and the richest benefices in the Principality."

As the Bishop of St. David's alluded to one of these protests made in Elizabethan days, against the appointment of a Welshman to the see of Bangor, it may be interesting to recall the exact words in which it is recorded. It is found, apparently, in the following letter addressed by Archbishop Parker to Sir William Cecil, and dated 12th February, 1565–6:—

"I am about to make ready the instrument of Hugh Jones' *commendam*, to be at Llandaff,[1] *notwithstanding the last letters sent to your honour;* for I yet hear better of the party. Since which time I have conferred with some wise men *partly* of the same country, who in respect of good to be done there in that diocese, they wish no Welshman in Bangor. They band so much together in kindred, that the Bishop cannot do as he would for his alliance sake. I am desired by some well affected of that country to have a visitation, and to set order there, such as whosoever should come to the bishopric should be fain to prosecute it.[2] I hear that diocese to be much out of order, both having no preaching there, and pensionary concubinary openly continued, notwithstanding liberty of marriage granted. If I thought the Queen's Majesty would allow her own chaplain, Mr. Herle, to be placed there hereafter, I would join him with some other learned to go through the diocese; and I think Mr. Herle to be a grave priestly man, and should well furnish the

---

[1] In all the quotations made in this Appendix, the writer has italicized words to which he wished to call special attention.

[2] A venerable speaker at the Congress combated the views of this address by stating that disorders had existed in Llandaff, under Welsh Bishops, in the reign of Elizabeth and in 1644. The answer is obvious. Welsh Bishops could not undo in a generation the abuses of centuries; and the time of the Civil War was not a time in which Episcopal administration could be expected to be perfect.

office, with *commendam* of his livings, which he hath now, though he should give over Manchester, where he now can have little rest. If it would please your honour to send me some little signification of your mind in these causes, I would frame myself thereafter. I am now instantly sued unto, to have such a commissary there as can be proved to keep openly three concubines, as men of good reputation offer to prove."

It is not difficult for any one, who knows the inner life of Wales to-day, to interpret the significance of this letter. The antagonisms of 1879 throw light upon those of 1565. In Llandaff there had been no Welsh Bishop since the days of Nicholas ap Gwrgant in 1149, until Queen Elizabeth appointed this Hugh Jones in 1565. It is evident that the anti-Welsh heirs of a long usurpation protested secretly against the appointment of a Welshman, and to their protests the Archbishop probably alludes in the words, "*notwithstanding the last letters sent to your honour.*" In Bangor there had been no genuine Welshman for centuries, until Rowland Meyrick was appointed in 1559. It is, therefore, not difficult to decide who were the Bishops that had reduced the diocese into the horrible state described by the Archbishop, nor yet how little opportunity poor Welshmen had enjoyed of showing partiality for their kindred! It is not difficult to imagine who may have been "*the wise men partly of the same country*" who wished "*no Welshman in Bangor.*" They were doubtless the descendants of those superior English clergy, who for more than two centuries had enjoyed the endowments, and debased the religion of the Welsh diocese by their worldliness. It is an interesting inquiry, which may be commended to the attention of able antiquaries, whether these wise men, who "wished no Welshman in Bangor," were identical with those men who also instantly sued the Archbishop "to have such a commissary there as could be proved to keep openly three concubines."

The great Tudor Queen was able to appreciate the advice of these "wise men" at its true value. She must have declined to consent to the Archbishop's suggestion, that her English chaplain, Mr. Herle, should be appointed. Although the self-interested intriguers wished "no Welshman in Bangor," a Welshman, Nicholas Robinson, born in Carnarvonshire, and Archdeacon of Merioneth, was appointed, and was succeeded by a long line of Welshmen, unbroken for a hundred and fifty years, till the scandalous Episcopate of Benjamin Hoadley, in 1716. The two South Wales dioceses, although the majority of the people in both worshipped, then as now, in the Welsh language, seem to have had fewer native Bishops than Bangor and St. Asaph. This was probably due to the fact that the landowners and magnates of South Wales, whose influence controlled the appointments, were more generally of English origin than those in the North. - It is possible that in the diocese of St. David's the presence of the English colony in Pembrokeshire may have contributed to the result. How disastrous the influence of the English Episcopate and clergy had there proved, may be gathered from what Canon Bevan calls "a most graphic description of the diocese of St. David's . . . from the pen of Dr. Erasmus Saunders" (1721).

We are indebted to the Rev. D. W. Thomas, Vicar of St. Ann's, for the discovery of a letter in the Lambeth MSS., which proves that the English Episcopate in Llandaff was producing results equally injurious to the Church. That letter, found among the *Codices Gibsoniani* Catalogue, 930–933, was dated October 23, 1703, and addressed to the Archbishop of Canterbury by a Glamorganshire clergyman. Its opening sentences are as follows : " May it please your Grace to grant a country parson, who thinks himself the meanest of his own function, to petition your Grace, on behalf of others and himself, that you would recommend a Welshman always to a Welsh diocese,—for it is almost morally impossible for an Englishman to answer the expectations we, the clergy, have,— upon the next vacancies here in Wales. We have (more is the pity) great divisions amongst us, and, generally, our divisions are the wider where there is less of the English tongue understood ; . . . when we had Bishops that could preach in Welsh, and did take pains to instruct the people, the generality of the people did keep the unity of the Church, it may be, as well as any part of the nation. But now, of late, there has been another course taken, to make choice of perfect strangers to our country and language, who generally have large commendams in England, and seldom give up ; and besides, by their living from us, upon all vacancies of any dignity, strangers and Englishmen are the only persons that come in, *to the great decay of learning and virtue among us."*

Doubtless in all ages the imported Bishops have justified themselves in appointing strangers to the chief dignities in their dioceses, by saying that they could not find men of sufficient learning among the native clergy. So far from being a justification, such a statement is the severest condemnation which they could have pronounced upon their own Episcopate. That a Bishop, after many years of power, should have failed to produce in his diocese natives fitted by general culture and learning, as well as by special knowledge of the Welsh language and people, to do the higher work of the Welsh Church, is a sufficient proof that he was not equal to his position. If the English commander-in-chief were to complain that he had no officers in the English army fit for high command, and proposed to introduce foreign generals, unable to give orders in the English language, the world would know what to think of him. Surely the selection and training of clergy—and not merely the " sudden " incautious laying of hands upon unfit men—is one of the chief functions of a Bishop. Consequently, in condemning his clergy, he condemns his own work.

In dwelling upon "The Past and Present Position of the Church in Wales," it may not be undesirable to dissipate some popular fallacies that have been industriously propagated as to the religious condition of the Welsh people before the rise of Dissent in the eighteenth century. The Welsh people have been seriously misled by that collection of marvellous traditions and Puritanical reflections given to the world by Mr. John Hughes, as a history of Welsh Methodism. Those who have the patience to read and the credulity to believe such books, are led to the conclusion that the Welsh people, in pre-Methodist times, were a nation of barbarians without religious knowledge or feeling. The truth, probably, is that there was less sermon-hearing, nearly as much simple piety, and perhaps less of cant and hypocrisy, in 1721 than is found in 1879.

There is a popular delusion, not discouraged by some Dissenting ministers, that Welsh virtue has been coeval with Welsh Dissent, and that the Welsh people, when conforming to the Church, were little better than turbulent heathens. The law-abiding character of the people, the absence of crime, the "white-gloved" Assizes, and other favourable features, are attributed to Nonconformity. The great religious services rendered by Nonconformists ought not to be depreciated. But neither is it right that modern Welsh Nonconformists should glorify themselves by underrating their ancestors. The leading virtues that are peculiar to the Welsh people are older than Nonconformity. Dr. Saunders has described those virtues as exhibited in 1721. There is still earlier evidence. In a letter addressed to Sir Francis Walsingham, on March 1, 1583, Sir Henry Sidney, then Lord President of Wales, described his presidency as his "great and high office in Wales, a happy place of government; for a better people to govern, or better subjects, Europe holdeth not."

It is painful to be under the necessity of feeling ashamed of our ancestors. Our Nonconformist friends will be relieved to find that Welshmen labour under no such necessity. In the days in which Welshmen loved the Church, they also loved righteousness and hated iniquity.

It has been necessary, in these pages, to declare some truths which the writer would have been glad to omit. He well knows how true are Dr. Saunders' words, "*This is a part very disagreeable, and what I wish my subject would permit me to overlook and pass by; and so prevent the angry resentments which (I am sensible) the telling of unacceptable truths must expect to meet with.*" But being convinced that the telling of these truths, though very unacceptable to some few, will tend to promote the revival of the Welsh Church and the welfare of the Welsh people, the writer has not shrunk from publishing them "without regard to any other view or interest but that of truth."

The oft-repeated protest, made by Dr. Saunders in 1721, and renewed by Welsh Churchmen to-day, against the intrusion of ecclesiastics ignorant of the Welsh language, has been unfairly and disingenuously described as a Home Rule cry of "Wales for the Welsh!" Those who so describe it choose to ignore solid facts. It can hardly be denied that in each of the four Welsh dioceses *a majority of the Welsh people worship in the Welsh language.* If ecclesiastical endowments exist for the good of the people, and not for the comfort of clergymen, no candid man will deny that *the*

Welsh-speaking people have a right to a Welsh-speaking ministry. The denial of that right has been "the bane of the Welsh Church." The ruin wrought in a hundred and fifty years cannot be repaired entirely in a generation. But if justice is done to the Welsh people, the Welsh Church will revive.

Injustice, assuming the form of superior light, has darkened the inmost life of Wales. It has desolated her sanctuary. It has poisoned her wellsprings. Bitterness and sourness have been infused into the social life of her genial, gentle race. Unity of action for national purposes, such as higher education, has been made impossible. Her men of talent, uneducated, have had the gates of light shut against them by strangers who held the keys. Her endowments, the patrimony of the many, have been treated as the prey of the few. Her voluntary offerings, lavishly given, have been wasted because not dedicated at the shrine of that unity which is strength (Deut. xii. 11-13), and her sacrifices, though many, have been made vain by the rending of her altars. Let justice give to Wales her ecclesiastical and educational rights. Her people will advance in unity of spirit, if not in uniformity of worship, according to their gifts received from God. To their seriousness and peacefulness and industry they will add sweetness and light.

THE CALLING AND EDUCATION OF THE CLERGY FOR THE CHURCH IN WALES.[1]

THE calling and education of clergy is at all times one of the most important subjects that can engage the counsels and energies of those who have it in their power to shape and direct the progress of the Church. But in Wales, at the present time, there exist, I am profoundly convinced, in the religious state of the people, in the changes induced by the extension of political privileges, and in the influences of railway communication and a cheap press, manifold forces that contribute to invest the subject with more than ordinary importance. The times are, I believe, at hand which are destined to witness either to a very great revival or a very rapid deadening of religious life among the Cymric people. During the last sixty years, since the schism of the Calvinistic Methodists was finally consummated in 1811, the religious instruction and pastorate of a large number of the people have been assumed by

[1] A paper read on Thursday, August 4, 1870, at a Church Conference held at Bangor.

unauthorized teachers. The violation of the central law of Church unity, in the defiant ignoring of Apostolical Orders, has produced its necessary consequence. Religious creeds and systems have been indefinitely multiplied, until the Welsh people has been divided against itself into nine or ten religious societies. This religious anarchy has been accompanied by its inseparable result, viz. unhealthy religious excitement followed in due course by a proportionate deadening of religious vitality. The people are gradually growing weary of endless divisions, strife, and excitement in religious systems, the leaders of which are not seldom wanting in the deep earnestness that characterized the unworldly spirit of the early Methodists.

It must be acknowledged that the aspirations of the founders of Methodism in Wales were true and noble, and that they proved their earnestness by the great personal sacrifices which they made in seeking their realization. The action of the Methodist clergy in the last century, led by Howell Harris and Daniel Rowlands, was a sincere protest against the selfish worldliness which disgraced too many of the clergy, and the ignorant unspiritual formalism which was too often substituted for the power of godliness in that age. They never intended to protest against the doctrines and Sacraments of the Church; nor yet against the inalienable authority of Apostolical Orders. But in 1811 that system, which in its early spirit might well have been called "Bethel," became in its schismatical development "Bethaven;" the Methodism which was originally a revival within, became a disorderly movement without, the Church.

Gradually, by a slow but sure process, the masses are beginning to understand that the evils against which the original Methodists protested, were not evils inherent in the Divine constitution of the Church, existing in its doctrines, Sacraments, and orders, but arising from the human infirmities and shortcomings of those to whom was committed the administration of its system. They are learning, day by day, that it is not possible to ensure the life of the religious spirit by destroying the beauty of religious forms intended to embody it; and that the Divinely appointed subordination of ministerial offices is essential to the permanent life of the Church. They are also beginning to master the great truth that religious feeling and reverence can no more exist without expressing themselves in forms, than thought can exist without its instrumental signs. Furthermore, while it has been proved by experience that there are worldly peasants no less than worldly gentlemen who occasionally assume the office of religious teachers for the sake of "the piece of bread," it has dawned upon intelligent minds not a few, that the formalism of vulgar irreverence and conceited mannerism, unredeemed by the pristine earnestness of Methodism, has too often succeeded to the formalism of the authorized rites and ceremonies of the Church. Hence perhaps has arisen that yearning among Dissenters, as witnessed in their imitation of Church architecture, and their adoption of Church music, for a return to that elaborate comeliness in the external habit of worship enjoined by the Apostle in the significant word εὐσχημόνως. On the other hand, the attempt made to create a more educated and settled ministry, which has excited the opposition of the traditional Methodists represented by "Thesbiad," proves that the largest Nonconformist Society of Wales are unconsciously being led to recognize the necessity of that Divinely constituted subordination in the ministry of the Church, the principle of which is suggested by the same passage of the Apostle in the expression κατὰ τάξιν.

A people so profoundly religious in their national tendencies as the Welsh are, cannot fail to discover that negative protests against the shortcomings of men, and the subjective excitements created by impassioned preaching, and vociferously intoned extempore prayers, are not sufficient to satisfy the soul. These religious resources of the Dissenting systems are gradually giving place to another style of teaching, attractive in its novelty, like the popular airs of American minstrelsy, but soon losing its power, which is but a feeble echo of the Germanizing speculation that would fain stir up religious feeling and sentiment, without any strong development of historical and objective truth. So great is the doctrinal vagueness of religious teaching, and so completely have even the preachers of Welsh Dissent lost sight of some of the eternal obligations flowing from the revelation of the attributes of the Divine life in Jesus Christ, that a believer in the primitive creeds of Christendom is constrained to say of them what the

Saviour said (notwithstanding the lovingkindness shown by ône, and the gratitude by another) of the Dissenting Samaritans, "Ye worship ye know not what."

This doctrinal vagueness of the religious systems, destitute of objective authority, cannot feed the soul of man in green and fresh pastures; cannot give him rest by leading him forth to satisfy the aspirations of his being beside the waters of comfort that spring in inexhaustible abundance for those that truly believe in the great mystery of the Incarnation of Godhead. Hence the religious watchwords and religious exercises, divorced from objective truth and order, are gradually becoming worn out, and are perceptibly losing their hold upon the minds and consciences of the people. What, consequently, is the cry that is everywhere heard among earnestly religious Dissenters? "Y mae crefyddwyr yn farwaidd iawn."

The state of the masses in Wales at the present time is, I honestly believe, that state of religious relaxation and practical indifference due to the want of an efficient pastorate of souls which called forth the Divine compassion of the Lord. "When He saw the multitudes He was moved with compassion on them, because they fainted, and were scattered abroad, as sheep having no shepherd." What is the significance of that wonderful expression, ἐκλελυμένοι? It describes with Divine accuracy the state of men whose souls are unbraced by religious uncertainty, when the old forms and watchwords which swayed the soul have lost their power of obligation, and cease to govern the will and the conscience. It describes the state of the sheep who straggle hither and thither, without the binding, directing, bracing power of definite guidance. It describes the state of shepherdless sheep, who spend their time not in feeding, but in speculating whether there are any fields of pasture to be found.

The second word of Divine wisdom, ἐῤῥιμμένοι, describes the effects of this religious uncertainty. The sheep at last become weary of straggling in diverse directions, broken in spirit, apathetic, indifferent. In this mood they cease to graze the exhausted surface which they have trampled down in their narrow wanderings. This state is very vividly described by that Welsh word "marweidd-dra," so frequently heard in our days. To what is that state due? To the want of a more efficient and powerful pastorate. "As sheep having no shepherd." That Church, which is the Body of Christ, "in Whom are hid all the treasures of wisdom and knowledge," has in her doctrines, Sacraments, and ordinances inexhaustible food for souls—green pastures and living fountains, fenced by her creeds and Divinely commissioned ministry from the desolating, befouling tread of infidelity. But for the support of the sheep it is not only necessary that there should be pastures and fountains, but there must also be shepherds who can lead to them. For the salvation of souls it is necessary, not only that there should be Divine truth, but also teachers capable of leading to the knowledge of it.

Now, those who are in living sympathy with the

mind and heart of Wales at the present time, know that the relaxation of old religious ties and the apathy exhibiting itself in growing indifference to religious ministrations, which I have described, is in many forms perceptible in the state of the Welsh people. Not many weeks ago a man of sagacious insight, keen in intelligence and vigorous in expression, whose writings weekly influence thousands of Welsh minds, gave utterance in my hearing to the following opinion: "The time is come for some new movement in Wales; the people are tired of the old systems and watchwords. They no longer charm." What is the interpretation of that language? If the people are in expectation, musing in their hearts concerning some new system, why is it? It is because they have no shepherds. Their shepherdless souls are hungering, unguided through an efficient authorized ministry, by the full preaching of God's true and lively Word; and unsupported in the inward cravings of their deepest religious aspirations, by the heavenly manna of the Blessed Sacrament of the Body and Blood of Christ. The enlightenment and the sustenance afforded by the fulness of the Church's Divine system alone can satisfy these cravings. It is, therefore, the part of the Church's seers, in looking abroad upon the restless, weary, craving multitude, to be moved with compassion on them, because they faint. They cannot fail, in surveying the state of Wales at the present moment, to be convinced that the harvest is plenteous, and that the fields are already white for the harvest.

There are forces, as I have attempted to describe,

working in the social, political, and religious state of Wales, that would lead back vast numbers of the wandering sheep to feed within the folds of the Church, if the true policy of conciliation were wisely and courageously conceived, and carried into vigorous and immediate operation.

What do I mean by the policy of conciliation? Do I mean that we should approach Dissenters, and attempt to conciliate them, in that false, untrue, compromising attitude so often tried, and always tried in vain, by assuring them that there is no important difference between the Church and the Nonconforming societies? Are we to tell them that there is no difference between the Church which owes its existence to the Divine mission of its Apostolical founders, and those societies which had their origin in the well-meaning but disorderly impulses of men whose action has been fatal to religious unity in this land, and productive of a defiant violation of one of the fundamental laws of the kingdom of Heaven? Are we to tell them that there is no difference between a ministry deriving its authority from above, in the objective order of unbroken succession from Christ, preaching the Word and administering the Sacraments according to the authoritative creeds of the primitive Church; and a ministry chosen from below by the people to reproduce popular ideas, and recite, instead of the unchanging creeds of Christendom, popular, variable, and ignorant interpretations of Holy Writ? Are we to tell them that there is no difference between Sacraments administered in loyalty to Divinely appointed authority, and rival rites celebrated in defiant violation of that authority? The inalienable authority of Holy Orders is not a personal prerogative, which a clergyman can lay aside at his will in order to please the multitude, but the Divinely ordained power, which is the bond of union, that can alone preserve harmony in the Church, and enable humanity to reflect the image of the Eternal Unity. To attempt to conciliate Dissenters by sacrificing these everlasting realities is a vain and fatal policy. The clergyman who, for the sake of popularity, adopts language which leads men to suppose that the difference between the principles of the Church and of the Nonconforming societies is slight and unimportant, is guilty of very grave inaccuracy, lends his aid to weaken the obligations of religious unity, and incurs a very solemn responsibility. Such language, in a land which is torn by endless divisions, is especially mischievous, and utterly indefensible upon any plea but that of well-meaning ignorance.

For clergymen living in the midst of a Dissenting population, the pardonable desire of popularity creates a great temptation to forget the authority of their mission. To lower the authority of mission has always been popular. " I am come in My Father's Name, and ye receive Me not; if another shall come in his own name, *him ye will receive.*" But if we betray the solemn authority of our ministerial office (however personally unworthy we, as earthen vessels, may be of that office) by resting our claims to attention, not upon the truth committed to us, but upon our personal gifts; by saying, as the world would have us say, that we come in our own name, and not in the Name of Christ—the King of the Church, and the Fountain of orders—we are not loyal to the kingdom of Heaven. To win the ear of the crowd, and make our ministry popular by such language, is not to feed the sheep, but to lay waste the pasture.

The policy of conciliation, which alone can restore the wandering souls of the deeply religious people of Wales into the fold .of that Church which received original mission to this land, which has a sacred ministry authoritative in the unbroken succession of Holy Orders, which teaches the full truth of the One Catholic and Apostolic Church, which rightly and duly administers the holy Sacraments, which is equally removed in its glorious constitutional freedom and order from the spiritual anarchy of an innovating Dissent, and from the spiritual despotism of an innovating Papacy—must be a policy not of destruction, but of creation. It will not avail, in the hope of conciliating Dissenters, to mutilate the doctrines and Sacraments, nor even the rites and ceremonies, of the Church. But it is essentially necessary that, in the practical administration of the Church, her rulers should open fields of energy and religious usefulness for the men endowed by God with ministerial gifts who are now tempted into disorderly activity, because the practical machinery of the Church, as hitherto administered, has offered them no place in its ministerial system.

It is my profound conviction that thousands of the

Welsh Dissenters are ready in their hearts, as far as acceptance of essential doctrines go, to return to feed upon the pastures of the Church. The harvest is plenteous; why cannot it be reaped? The sheep are scattered abroad; why cannot they be led back? While the harvest is ripe, the really effective labourers are few. The multitudes are ready to return, but they are "as sheep having no shepherd."

The primary function of the Church, from which it takes the name ἐκκλησία, is to call. In the preaching of her ministry, ever summoning men to rise out of the lower corruptible life of the flesh and the world into the most high unchanging life in Christ, is heard the Voice of God. "By Whom ye were called into the fellowship of His Son Jesus Christ." By whom is that Divine call to be sounded? "He ordained twelve . . . that He might send them forth (κηρύσσειν) to preach;" in other words, to summon men into that ἐκκλησία which is "the Church of the Firstborn." The function of preaching, committed in that ordination by Christ to the twelve, is vested in their lineal successors, to whom alone it authoritatively appertains by their own lips, and by the lips of those whom they ordain, to preach the Gospel, and to summon men into the ἐκκλησία of the kingdom of Heaven. Πῶς δὲ κηρύξουσιν, ἐὰν μὴ ἀποσταλῶσι; "How shall they preach, except they be sent? as it is written, How beautiful are the feet of them that preach the Gospel of peace!" They who preach without having been authoritatively *sent* by the commission of Apostolical Orders, assert that they preach the Gospel. But can it be said that it is the Gospel of *peace?* Can the rival preaching organizations among the mountains of Wales, that divide every hamlet against itself into bitterly jealous sections, be said to preach the Gospel of *peace?* No. The systems that exist, in open violation of the Divinely constituted order of the ministry, perpetuate in the land strife, divisions, heart-burnings, and bitter jealousies.

But if the preaching of the κηρύξ must be authoritative by virtue of his commission, it must also be effective in its practical power. To undervalue the power of preaching is to paralyze one of the most important functions in the Church's organization. To undervalue the Sacraments and ordinances of the sanctuary is to sweep away the feast from the table of the Church, or to lay waste her pastures.

The powerful preaching that does not teach definite doctrine, that calls not to the blessed Sacraments, and to the ordinances of confession, prayer, praise, and thanksgiving, is but the ill-directed labour of the shepherd, who excites his sheep, but leads them only along bare lanes, to lie down with hunger and thirst unappeased, and the strength and hope of the soul unrevived.

On the other hand, the frequent administration of the Sacraments and the other ordinances of grace, when unaccompanied by the call of powerful preaching, is to prepare the table, but to neglect the hearty invitation of guests.

At the present time the Church in Wales is inefficient in both these respects. Here and there she has eloquent κηρύκες who proclaim, with fervid earnestness, uncertain sounds which lead to no objective channels of grace. She has also many well-instructed, devout clergy, who are diligent in the administration of the Sacraments and other holy ordinances, but who are unable to command attention, and are deficient in teaching power. Hence in some parishes the Church is as a banquet-hall furnished with a feast, but without guests. In other parishes the guests are summoned by stirring appeals, but no objective ordinances of grace are prepared in sufficient abundance to feed their souls. How are these deficiencies to be remedied? The calling and education of the clergy will give this question its answer.

In considering this important problem, it is necessary to bear in mind the characteristics of the country in which the work of the Church lies—that it is the work of the Church in Wales.

The Apostolic rule, which I may call the rule of ministerial accommodation to circumstances, must be observed by the Church in Wales, as in every other land. "I made myself servant unto all, that I might gain the more. . . . Unto the Jews I became as a Jew, that I might gain the Jews ; . . . to the weak became I as weak, that I might gain the weak : I am made all things to all men, that I might by all means save some." The Church, in her Apostolic mission and ministry, must accommodate herself to the national peculiarities of the peoples whom she would save—must, in a certain sense, be made "all things to all men." Thus, in her ministry to the Welsh people, she must become as Welsh; not treating them with arrogant superiority, but making herself subservient to their peculiarities for their good; not coming among them to be ministered unto, but to minister; describing the attitude she would assume in the words of the Apostle, πᾶσιν ἐμαυτὸν ἐδούλωσα, " I made myself servant unto all."

In considering the problem which I have called " The Calling and Education of Clergy for the Church in Wales," it is necessary to its solution to bear in mind—

I. The social condition of the people.

II. The national peculiarities of language and temperament.

I shall briefly dwell upon some points in the social condition of Wales. In a country comparatively poor, a country of hills and valleys, the highest class is comparatively small. The upper middle class is also, I imagine, less numerous in proportion than in England. The great mass of the people of Wales belong to the classes known as the lower middle and working classes, composed of the small farmers, small shopkeepers, artisans, quarrymen, colliers, miners, shepherds, and labourers. These two classes, closely united in views and sympathies, are socially and politically powerful enough to outvote all other classes in Wales. To these classes, as forming the main body of the population, the Church is bound to devote her main exertions. The clergy in Wales must learn, what they ought to have learnt long ago, that it is their duty to be the priests of the people. It is the glory of the Church, when her system is developed in healthy life, to have a clergy comprehensive of the sympathies of all classes, and reflecting, in their collective character, all that is best in every class of society. By the learning and refinement of the clergy, the Church enters the palace, to purify, to enlighten, and to extend the sympathies of its tenants. By the self-devotion and pastoral labour of her clergy, she enters the cottage, to brighten the clouds of poverty, and to make the burden of toil in humble life easier to bear. Thus she combines in herself all that is noble in aristocracy with the grand, broad, popular, human sympathy that gives all its truth to the democratic spirit. And thus only can her ministry represent Him, Who was at once loftiest in human social rank, "born of the house and lineage of David," and also at home amid the humbler scenes of human life in the cottage of the carpenter at Nazareth.

The clergy are rarely in danger of being tempted to neglect the rich; but we may sometimes forget to understand the mind and to sympathize with the heart of the poor. The true ministry of the Church, however, must be a popular ministry. Popularity was one mark of the Divine-human ministry of the Head of the Church—"The common people heard Him gladly." Great is the glory of a clergy who are popular, but have not purchased that popularity by the sacrifice of truth. It is well that we should do all that we can to gain for the Church's organization the support of "the wise men after the flesh, the mighty, and the noble," whenever, unlike the Corinthian aristocracy, they answer the calls of the Church. But in doing so we must beware of minding high things, and forgetting to follow the Apostle in condescending to men of low estate. If, like the Pharisees, we sneer at the devotion of the unlearned classes, and talk with scorn of "this common people that knoweth not the Law," while measuring the value of every movement by the approval of the wealthy, and ever asking, " Have any of the rulers believed " in it? we shall never gain among the masses that influence which can enable us to guide and benefit them.

The social characteristics of Wales render it not only unnecessary, but, even if it were possible, absolutely undesirable, that the majority of its clergy should come from what are called the higher classes. But if it is undesirable that the clergy of Wales should *be* exclusively of those classes, need I add that it is still more undesirable that (in their attitude towards the people) they should affect to be so when they really are not? I do not think that any one can, with truthfulness, accuse us as a body of being too aristocratic, or too far removed from the people in our origin. But there are many who in times past were disposed to accuse us of being too aristocratic in our notions, and of socially forgetting the classes from which, at no very remote period, we are sprung. Now, if this temper existed among us, it would be most injurious to the influence of the Church. The clergy cannot be too gentlemanly in manners, cannot be too refined in tastes, cannot be too elevated in sentiment. But the thin veneering of social pretentiousness, that serves to irritate the observer, but fails to cover the originally moderate social rank of the pretender, is greatly calculated to lessen the influence of the class who assume it. As the clergy of the Church of Christ, we are placed in a position that ought to raise us in heart and mind above the socially necessary, but spiritually unimportant, distinctions of rank. Certain it is that nothing more surely tends to make the clergy uninfluential than the feeble self-forgetfulness which marks the type of Welshmen represented by the name of " Dic Shôn Dafydd."

As I have already indicated, it is necessarily certain that a large proportion of the clergy in Wales will always be drawn from the lower middle and working classes. It is most conducive to the influence of the Church that it should be so. A clergy so derived, by virtue of older associations and more living sympathy, will influence the masses of the people more powerfully than a clergy who have only a professional acquaintance with their social atmosphere. At the present time a large proportion of the clergy derive their origin from the classes which I have named. But it is my conviction that the young men from those classes who now seek Holy Orders, are not always the men who are marked by the proper natural gifts for the sacred ministry, and that they are often very insufficiently educated. At the same time, the education, scanty as it is, which now suffices to secure Holy Orders, is unfortunately up to the present time so far costly as to be beyond the reach of very many young men who, with respect to their natural endowments, are admirably fitted for the ministry. It often happens that the naturally clever and eloquent son of a small farmer, artisan, or collier, who is most anxious to receive a fitting education for Holy Orders, is unable to do so, because his friends have absolutely no command of money. At the same time, perhaps, the dull ungifted son of a neighbour who happens to have scraped together some £200 or £300, is sent for the shortest available time to some college, where he acquires that amount of classical lore and theological science (that I shall not attempt to describe) which suffices, inasmuch as better men are not forthcoming to fill the vacancies, to command the *forced* leniency of the Bishops' chaplains. Into what channel does that other youth throw his energies? Supported at some Dissenting college by the contributions of Dissenting congregations, he is in due time enabled to devote his energies, with an embittered spirit, to the irregular ministry of the Nonconformist pulpit, and to do much to weaken the influence of that Church which has practically denied him any sphere of usefulness.

I must, in dealing with this question, say a few words concerning the peculiar conditions created by the distinct language and national temperament of the Welsh people. As to the future extinction or non-extinction of the ancient language of Wales, I will venture no prophecy. We are none of us blind to the great advantages—commercial, social, and literary—that are only to be gained by the knowledge of English. Doubtless that knowledge will, in the next twenty or thirty years, become almost universal among Welshmen. But whether the ancient language of the people will also die, as the language of their hearths and altars, admits of some doubt. Its extinction has often been foretold. It has often been "doomed to death," but whether we can also add, "fated ne'er to die," I cannot attempt to determine. But I will venture to assert that the youngest child living will not live to witness its extinction. For many long years (possibly for ever) it must continue to be, as it is now, the religious language of hundreds of thousands. It follows, then, that as long as it exists, and is the intellectual instrument by which nearly a million of souls express their highest thoughts and deepest feelings, it ought to be cultivated to the highest degree by the clergy who assume to be in charge of those souls. While our missionaries abroad have been striving to master the dialects of every insignificant tribe of barbarians for the love of Christ, and inspired by the Divine Spirit of Pentecost, it is simply monstrous that the clergy of the Welsh people have neglected to obtain, in speaking and writing, a mastery of the noble Welsh language. I say it fearlessly, that the clergy, as a body, have not that command of the native language which they ought to have. Our Welsh, whether spoken or written, is too often stiff, unidiomatic, and powerless. I will also remark that literary power exhibited in the native language has not been recognized among the Welsh clergy in the degree which the importance of its possible services to the Church deserves. If the clergy are content to be, not the ministers of Christ to the people, but to the thin upper strata of society in Wales, they can afford to despise the cultivation of the Welsh language; but not otherwise.

There are also peculiarities in the national temperament of the Welsh people that affect this question. One only of those peculiarities can I now notice. The Welsh are lovers of impassioned stirring oratory. I think, also, that we Welshmen may assert, without untruthfulness, that a large number of our countrymen are gifted with those natural powers which, when duly cultivated, render them eloquent speakers and writers in their own language. These gifts, as existing in the working classes of Wales, and aided by very scanty means of cultivation, maintain the influence of the Dissenting press. The men whom God has endowed with these gifts are the natural teachers of the people. If the Church does not enlist and train them in her schools of the prophets, they will go to a hostile state, and some day return to attack the influence of the city which has neglected them. By her past neglect of these gifts, the Church has in a great measure lost the powerful forces of Welsh oratory and of Welsh popular literature. Second only in value to a hearty acquaintance with the definite Scriptural and Catholic theology of the Prayer-book, is the possession by the clergy of the power to teach that theology with power both of writing and speaking in the language of the people. In a word, the Church in Wales wants a clergy at once popular and educated. In order to be influential the clergy must be popular, understanding the sympathies of the masses, connected with them by manifold interwoven bands of live-long associations.

They should also be popular by virtue of possessing cultivated gifts of native eloquence and literature. I would not assert that the clergy, who are to recover the Welsh people to the Church, must be less refined or more exclusively drawn from the humbler social strata than the clergy of Wales in the past. It is desirable that they should come from the same classes which supply them now. But it is, I think, more than possible that they should receive a training that will render them more refined, more highly educated, than the clergy of the last five or six generations. No wise objection can be found to the social classes that now mainly supply the clergy of Wales. But I think it desirable that those who rise out of those classes into the sacred ministry should do so by virtue of other gifts than those which now oftenest secure their Ordination. What are the gifts that now enable the sons of small tradesmen, small farmers, and artisans to seek Holy Orders? The possession by their friends of £200 or £300 required for that most abbreviated course of education that unhappily suffices. I well remember the case of an avowed atheist (a character happily rare in Wales) who spent his savings in educating his son to become a clergyman. When asked why he did so, holding his peculiar views, he replied that he had simply regarded the matter as an investment.

Now, I should be sorry to condemn the son (in this case, I think, he became a very useful man) for the father's unbelief. Nor do I think it possible to guard against instances of the kind. If an infidel has money, and chooses to spend it in that way, and his son is morally blameless, however much we may regret that a clergyman should come out of the atmosphere of such a home, no obstacle can be raised. But I think that the Church should so organize her nurseries of clergy, if possible, as to give the least possible encouragement to young men whose parents are actuated by sordid motives, and should prove that she measures ministerial aptitudes by a different gauge from that of money. The gifts that ought to command admission into the sacred ministry for youths of humble parentage, are religious character, a reverential disposition, natural intelligence, and eloquence.

How can the Church obtain a clergy endowed with these gifts? She must encourage them by lowering the pecuniary standard, and by raising the religious and intellectual standard that regulates enrolment in her clerical ranks. The attitude of the Church in Wales, in the nurture of clergy, is at present too passive. She must take a more active part in the calling and education of those whom she sends forth to teach. She must go forth as her Divine Head went forth among the avocations of human life, and choose and call those who are marked by their natural gifts, by the courage of St. Peter, the enthusiasm of St. John, or the thoughtfulness of St. Thomas, for the great work of her Divine commission. She must exercise a wise discernment in choosing servants in the Name of her Master, and take them when they are marked by fitness that reveals itself to the eye of her seers, even from the sheepfolds, and bring them to feed Jacob His people, and Israel His inheritance. In the past she has not gone forth to make this choice. The old grammar schools, originally intended for the education of poor scholars, have been diverted to other purposes. The Church has need of clergy, but takes no sufficient measures to secure duly qualified men. Instead of going forth to choose and call, she remains passive, until unfit, ungifted, uneducated men come to offer themselves. In her need she is compelled to lay hands suddenly upon them, because better men have not been prepared for her ministry. It will be her wisdom to depart from this attitude of passive expectation, and to go forth for the choice and calling of fit men.

To this end I would suggest that a fund be raised in each diocese, to be called "The Diocesan Clergy Education Fund," and to be dispensed in exhibitions of the value of £20 or £25 per annum, to poor scholars from the humbler ranks of life. For the awarding of these exhibitions a Diocesan Board of Examiners should be appointed in each diocese, to examine and test not only the knowledge and intelligence, but also the other necessary ministerial aptitudes of youths desirous of being prepared for the ministry. Youths of fifteen years recommended by the clergy of their district as having evinced the gifts and graces most required, might get exhibitions that would enable them to obtain for four years a good preliminary education in the classical department of such a school as the commissioners propose to establish at Bangor, and in three other districts of Wales, probably conterminous with the three other dioceses. At the close of that period they would be enabled to spend four years more at St. David's College, Lampeter, or at some other approved college, to obtain the special education required for Holy Orders. At present it is, I fear, true that the youths who go to St. David's, and to similar colleges, are so scantily prepared beforehand, that the tutors are obliged to do the work which ought to have been done by others, and to spend in rudimentary classical instruction the time that they would gladly devote to the higher training in theology and the cognate branches of study. A preliminary preparation during four years at a good classical school would fit youths of ability to avail themselves effectually of the teaching of the professors at Lampeter and other colleges.

Now, when we consider that the wealth of Wales is mainly in the hands of Churchmen, who are, I believe, ready to contribute liberally when it can be shown that there is a prospect of real and fruitful work being effected, there ought to be no difficulty about raising in each of the Welsh dioceses a fund of £1000 per annum. That annual income would afford a sufficient number of exhibitions to maintain at school and college forty students. Thus, eight years being the average term of preparation, five talented and well-instructed candidates for Holy Orders would present themselves every year in each diocese. At the same time, the duly gifted men from the higher classes, able to obtain the advantages of a University education, would continue to be forthcoming in the same numbers as at present. But the constant supply of candidates educated by the Clergy Education Fund would place the Bishops and their examining chaplains in a position to reject candidates not duly qualified. Thus the standard of clerical education and efficiency would be gradually, but certainly, raised far above its present height. It cannot be doubted that the "Diocesan Clergy Education Board of Examiners" in each diocese would be in a position to command great influence in the counsels of the professors at Lampeter and other colleges, and would be able to make with effect, from time to time, such practical suggestions as would offer themselves more readily to men employed in actual work among the masses, than to those engaged in the lecture-rooms of colleges. We should probably find, as a consequence, that such exercises as the practice of elocution and sermon composition (to say nothing of rudimentary theology) would no longer be as they are now, too often overlooked in those nurseries of our clergy.

Such an organization as that which I have thus sketched in bare outline would ensure a constant, equable supply of twenty able and well-prepared candidates for Holy Orders in the Church of Wales in every year. These men, drawn from the most numerous, and in some sense most powerful, class in Wales, would conciliate to the Church, by the workings of a popular ministry, the sympathy of the masses, and make her truly, what in many parishes she now is only in name, the Church of the people. Such an organization, for promoting the education of young men of talent from the humbler classes, supported by the liberality of the landowners and wealthy members of the community, would tend to conciliate towards them also the kindly feeling of the masses, whom the exertions of those same young men of talent, now employed in other directions, largely alienate from them. Thus a healthier social feeling would be created, and in all Wales, to use the phrase of an eloquent popular statesman, "the breath of society would be sweetened."

Some such plan as that which I have now indicated would, I believe, be feasible, conservative, and effective. It would not be above the resources at the command of the Church in each diocese. It would not weaken, but strengthen, all the existing educational agencies.

If the Church in Wales is destined to regain the masses, and to be raised from her low estate, some such organization must be boldly adopted, and must be vigorously worked. We have to rejoice in the frequent repair and multiplication of churches. But we must beware of putting all our trust in wood and stone. If the ecclesiastical buildings of Wales were taken from the Church to-morrow, provided only that she could retain the earnestness, the talent, and the eloquence of the men whom Providence has marked as the teachers of the people, she would rise again. But without the

2 C

living agency of hearts and minds filled with the love of God, and His Son Jesus Christ, and without lips prepared, by the live coal of religious earnestness and the burning desire for the salvation of souls, to give fervid expression to the everlasting truths, the Church cannot feed the sheep or reap the harvest. Such an organization as that which I have suggested, would unfailingly draw into the sacred ministry of the Church a very large proportion of those naturally gifted and religiously earnest men who now often seek irregular employment for their energies in the Dissenting pulpits. A devoted, popular, well-instructed ministry, thoroughly trained in the Scriptural and primitive theology of the Church, would regain the lost heart of Wales, would preach among her mountains good tidings, and reunite her divided sections by the blessed power of the "Gospel of peace." Such a body of clergy, "replenished with the truth of her doctrine, and endued with innocency of life," is the great want of our Church. Never was it more truly the solemn duty of those who love Wales, and who love the Church of God in Wales, earnestly to pray the Lord of the harvest of souls in her own beautiful words: "Almighty God, our Heavenly Father, Who hast purchased to Thyself an universal Church by the precious Blood of Thy dear Son; mercifully look upon the same, and at this time so guide and govern the minds of Thy servants, the Bishops and Pastors of thy flock, that they may lay hands *suddenly* on no man, but faithfully and wisely *make choice* of fit persons to serve in the sacred ministry of Thy Church."

HOME REUNION.[1]

DURING the few minutes allotted to me I will speak of three things—union, disunion, reunion.

The law of union is laid upon mankind. It draws its sanctions from the unity in the Godhead. We men exist to reflect the image of God. Therefore the family of God on earth must be one, as He is one. There is "one God and Father of all" in Heaven. Therefore there is to be "one body" on earth. In the infancy of life mankind lived in union. "The Lord said, Behold, the people is one, and they have all one language." Union, like other powers, may be abused to evil ends. When the spirit of a united body becomes evil, God decrees that forces no longer directed by love shall no longer be strong by unity. At Babel God revealed the law under which forces corrupted by false aims are made harmless by their own confusion. The spirit of Babel destroyed unity. The Spirit of Pentecost renews it.

When mankind were brought together into one household, as a family of God, the Divine unity reappeared in human life. He Who said, "Ye shall be

[1] A paper read at the Bangor Diocesan Conference, August, 1880.

holy: for I the Lord your God am holy," also said, "That they all may be one, . . . even as We are one." In the patriarchal Church the one patriarch was the centre of unity. In the Mosaic period, the Divinely called ministry of the house of Aaron, guarding the ark upon which God's glory rested, was the centre from which no Israelite could separate himself. "Ye shall not do . . . every man whatsoever is right in his own eyes. . . . There shall be a place which the Lord your God shall choose to cause His Name to dwell there." "Three times a year shall all thy male appear before the Lord thy God in the place which He shall choose."

In the Incarnation the unity existing eternally in the Godhead was declared by Christ, when He said, "I and My Father are one." As men in Christ are to be renewed into the life of God, the declaration of the unity that is in God is followed by the declaration of the unity that is to be among men: "There shall be one fold, and one Shepherd." Thus the Christian faith is, " I believe one Catholic and Apostolic Church."

It is true that unity of life is not perfect in the Church. Neither is holiness perfect. But holiness is her aim; and when she ceases to pursue it, she dies. No less is unity, *as an aim*, an eternal obligation. There can be no unity in a society without a centre of authority. In the Jewish Church the centre was a sanctuary, a priesthood, and a Divine Presence. In the Christian Church the centre of unity is not local. It is described in the words, " They continued steadfastly in the Apostles' doctrine and fellowship, and in breaking of bread, and in prayers." The Apostolical ministry, teaching and administering, is still the centre of the Church's unity.

We know that the political unity of our country is centralized in the one throne, out of which authority goes forth to the humblest official who can act or speak in the name of national order. Likewise in republics, the chair of the President is the centre of the national unity. Every diocese is a kingdom, and the throne of the Bishop is the centre out of which Holy Orders go forth. In his ministry all the members of the Church meet as brethren in the presence of a father—the earthly type of the one eternal Father.

In the parish the one parish priest, authorized by Apostolical Orders, ministering in the congregation, is the father of the spiritual household. Thus the Holy Communion, administered by the Apostolical ministry, and bearing the light of the Shechinah into all lands, is the Divine bond that unites souls on earth. "We being many are one bread, and one body." As of old, so in our own Israel to-day, every soul is invited to adhere to this Divine unity. "Every parishioner shall communicate at the least three times in the year." Thus union, which is the outcome of love, is centred in the showing forth of that Divine death which expressed infinite love.

What, then, is disunion? It is the work of our human self-will marring the harmony of the Divine life. It appeared on the plain of Shinar, when man raised from the clay of earth a structure by which he professed to scale heaven. Human pride was the force that then broke human unity. In the patriarchal household the impatience of his brethren, provoked by the apparent favouritism of Jacob in the promotion of Joseph, raised the cry of equality and shattered the family in disunion. In the wilderness the disunion in the camp owed its origin to selfish ambition playing upon popular ignorance and passion. A movement born of earthly motives was doomed to sink into the earth that gave it being. Disunion threatened to rise when Reuben, Gad, and half Manasseh built an altar by Jordan. Israel fiercely resented what looked like a breach of Divine unity, saying, "What trespass is this that ye have committed against the God of Israel . . . in that ye have builded you an altar?" But the builders proved that they had raised an altar to perpetuate unity, not to destroy it.

When Rehoboam, the small son of a great father, oppressed his realm, there came political disunion. But the politically separated tribes would have continued religiously united, had not Jeroboam, for his own selfish interests, made Israel to sin by leaving the centre of intercommunion, at which they were bound to assemble before the Shechinah three times a year.

In the body of the disciples, when the God-Man was the centre of their unity, ambition disturbed harmony. "There was a strife among them which should be accounted the greatest." But ambition did not break up the society, or bring the hour of darkness upon the Divine life. The power that broke up unity and scattered each to his own was the greed of him who bore the Church's money-bags, and sold the Divine Love for pieces of silver.

In the early Church there was strife. But there was no final disunion until the papal system built its high structure of earthly, miry polity, and affected to reach heaven on steps of clay. The evils of a union that built with slime-bound bricks of earthly mould, are greater than the evils of honest disunion. Thus papal tyranny has everywhere been, if not the parent, the grandparent of divisions. In the lands where its yoke has not been broken, it has created worse divisions than here. There it has dug a deep black chasm across which the fanatics of superstition are glaring at the fanatics of atheism. Here no chasm exists that cannot be easily bridged. Here Christians not united in communion are not far apart in faith. Those who stand aloof from the Apostolical fellowship hold what they conceive to be Apostolical doctrine. The Roman Church is separated from her dissenters by a bridgeless ocean; the Church of England from many of hers by only a rill.

But here the waters of that rill are sometimes bitter, and sometimes swell into an angry torrent. Our religious divisions break the unity of social sympathy in every city, town, village. Whence have they arisen? As in every place, so here, selfishness has been the disuniting spirit. The Rehoboams, the Jeroboams,'the Judases, men exalted by interest, men living on the merits of the dead, the men of ambition, the men of greed, have broken up the Church's unity. What are the fruits of disunion? The Divine Spirit is quenched, spiritual motives are weakened, education is heathenized, missions are paralyzed, atheism is encouraged, social life is poisoned, social sympathy is narrowed, countrymen and neighbours are estranged, energy, time, and money are wasted, jealousies are fed fat, evil spirits of envy, hatred, malice, uncharitableness intrude into the holy places, call themselves angels of light, and masquerade in the garb of love. This fiend of disunion threatens to bring upon religion anew the powers of darkness, to expose it to the mockery of foes, to fix its Divine Life upon the Cross of shame, and to hide its sleeping Form in the tomb of a rocky materialism.

Earnest men, working in disunited bands, are crying out, as they feel the chilly twilight of doubt around them darkening into the cold, starless night of atheism, "We want a revival." In all love I will say to them, "Christianity, the religion of unity, will not revive in you as long as you bow to your idols of disunion. The movements you call revivals may stimulate, but cannot feed, the decaying life in systems stricken to death in vital organs by consumption bred from the old taint of the poison of disunion."

What, then, shall we say of reunion? Whether men will hear or will forbear, we must in love teach the truth of Divine unity. Whatever men may say, disunion in itself is not good, but evil; not the child of God's Spirit, but the offspring of subtle, secret human self-will; not from above, but of the earth, earthy. We believe that the centre of unity in the Church's organization is the one Apostolical ministry, inheriting in its highest order the twelve thrones to judge the tribes of the Israel of faith, and deputed by the one King invisible to preach

Home Reunion. 393

His Word and administer His Sacrament. Men, however learned and eloquent, can no more validly administer the chief function in the Church without the sanction of Apostolical Orders, than a citizen, however gifted and virtuous, can administer formal justice in the Queen's name without her commission. The popular theory of a subjectively authorized ministry seems to me to imply a subjectively originated Christianity, to involve the denial of Christ's having come in the flesh, and to destroy the foundations. The temple of the Church is "built upon the foundation of the apostles and prophets, Jesus Christ Himself being the chief Corner-stone."

What are the prospects of reunion? "If the foundations be destroyed, what shall the righteous do? The Lord is in His holy temple."

Reunion is not near, but it will come. Outside and inside the Church it has foes, but it has also friends. Outside it has foes in ignorance, in bigotry, and in the selfish interests of the "men of renown" in the congregations, who love to be great leaders in small circles, who love to carve out demagogic careers for themselves by widening the wounds of the Church. But it has friends in the thoughtfulness and social sympathy and increasing culture of the young men in the sects. The narrow-minded believer in the all-sufficiency of his sect is generally a man over fifty. The younger, more educated men are not, perhaps, attracted to the Church; but they are not satisfied in their narrow religious birthplace, and are longing for a nobler atmosphere.

Inside, reunion has foes in the self-seeking that seeks

ministerial positions for personal ends; that uses ministerial authority as Turkish pashas use political; in the sloth of priests who do not sacrifice time or toil, and go not into the Holy of Holies of communion with God; in the baseness that makes the freehold of a benefice a stronghold of worthlessness; in the well-meaning rigidity of traditionists who mistake the cramping fetters of iron uniformity for the cords of love, the elastic bands of unity; and, again, in the unsympathetic narrowness of Churchmen who will not do mental justice to those outside, by trying to look at things from their point of view. Let us bear in mind that the forerunner of reunion is the grace that turns the hearts of the *fathers* to the children, so that when the fathers have the wisdom to be just, the *children* may cease to be disobedient. That grace will teach us the attitude we ought to take towards Nonconformists. I would define it in a word. *More social sympathy and less religious compromise.* Not to realize by sympathy the position of an adversary is to march blindly to defeat. Every cause draws its strength not from the evil but from the good in it. The strength of Dissent is in its protest for liberty; its anarchy and disorder are its weakness. The Church will reunite souls, not by abusing the vices of Dissent, but by absorbing its virtues. Before unity can return there must be more liberty—a liberty under which diversities of gifts, differences of administrations, and diversities of operations can find full play within one Church, animated by one Spirit, bowing to one Lord. "Where the Spirit of the Lord is, there is liberty."

May we not hope that, when the fear of a common foe awakes in Christians a common love, a *concordat* may be framed under which all who believe in the Triune God defined in the Nicene Creed, while worshipping in various meeting-houses, some with simpler, some with more elaborate rites, shall come at least three times a year before the Lord of unity as one body to partake of one bread? Let us remember that each of us has his work to do for reunion. If in us and in our parishes the Church is dead, it is vain to talk of reunion. It is only when the Church lives that she reunites souls. When the brethren found that Joseph alone could feed them, they came to live near him, and there was home reunion in the house of Jacob. When souls find that the Church opens for them the granaries of grace, they will come to her.

Let us do our part. Let us not try to work out God's righteousness by our wrath. Let us not be narrow, unsympathetic, self-righteous, and, above all, let us not be patronizing. Let us remember that the sins of Churchmen no less than the sins of separatists form that dark pit of evil out of which the fiends of disunion wing their flight to poison life. While never ceasing to assert the Divine unity of the Church of God, and the authority of the ministry, "called of God as was Aaron," to be the centre at which the Shechinah of that unity promises to shine, let us be just to those who have not yet come to see what we see. Let us say to them, "We admit your virtues, eloquence, zeal, learning, earnestness; we admit, if you wish, that many of you may be superior in personal gifts to many of us; but we believe that your systems are contrary to God's Word, *so far as they encourage disunion*—that they are not in harmony with the general sense of Holy Scripture, but built upon half-truths and the misconstruction of isolated texts. We should like to join you in spiritual work, and to hear your eloquent voices in our pulpits; but our conscience forbids us to partake of the altars of disunion, and to admit that there can be concord between unity and systems born in disunion."

American patriots who fought for the union of their country would have said, "We do not deny that the soldiers of Secession have virtues, but we deny that they have the right as their cause. Robert Lee and Stonewall Jackson are gallant warriors, equal to our best; but they fight under the Secessionist flag, that floats in the name of a false independence, that severs brethren, rivets human chains, breaks up national greatness, and causes foreign foes to rejoice. We admire their valour, but mourn to see it misdirected. We cannot let them go from us. We mean to regain them, and by the aid of the Divine Spirit that broods over the troubled waves of life, and gives victory to truth in the end, we shall regain them." So we, believers in the Church's unity, will say, "You, our brethren, who justify corporate disunion, who fondly cherish faith in such a figment as a fragmentary Christianity, and after a hundred "splits" dream that in disunited bodies unity of spirit can dwell,—we believe that you are fighting under a flag that represents a false cause. You may reject our advances, shut your ears against our arguments, forget the Scriptures that rebuke, and read only the texts that encourage, you; you may call our firm convictions bigotry, and you may ignore the evils of disunion that force themselves upon unprejudiced minds every day and hour; but we dare not give up what we believe to be a Divine truth. We dare not sacrifice true liberty for the sake of false order at the bidding of Rome, nor yet true order for the sake of a spurious liberty at the bidding of Geneva. The house of God in which the Shechinah will shine in its full brightness is one. "God is not the author of confusion, but of peace." Reunion will come. The tendency to aggregation among peoples, the spirit of combination and co-operation among men, is abroad in the material sphere, and will soon come into the spiritual.

Unity will not come back in its old form. The unity of a people educated to think for themselves will not be the old unity of a people glad to follow their leaders. The old unity was that of acquiescence; the new unity will be the nobler unity of tried conviction. Reunion may not come for centuries, but come it will. Who shall live to see it? We only know that divisions must cease, when the hour comes in response to that Almighty prayer, "Sanctify them through Thy truth . . . that they may be made perfect in One; and that the world may know that Thou hast sent Me, and hast loved them, as Thou hast loved Me."

"STRIKE FOR THE KING!" [1]

THE great question which we are met to discuss—how to promote temperance among our countrymen—is not a new one. It has been treated so frequently of late years that any novelty or charm about it is absolutely impossible. I can say nothing new. It is no doubt known to you that 140 millions sterling, more or less, have been the sum annually spent by the people in this country in the purchase of strong drink, which high medical authorities pronounce to be not only unnecessary, but in many cases absolutely injurious to human life. It has been proved again and again that this tyrant vice brings crime, pauperism, lunacy, disease, and death in its train. The policeman, the gaoler, the magistrate, the judge, the executioner, the coroner, are the most effective orators upon this subject, because they can tell us that two-thirds of their most sad work are due to the ravages of drink. Doctors, economists, statesmen, and moralists tell us that physical decay, the

---

[1] An address delivered in Hope Hall, Liverpool, at the annual meeting of the diocesan branch of the Church of England Temperance Society, the Right Rev. the Lord Bishop of Liverpool in the chair.

ruin of the intellect, the deadening of the moral sense, the brutalization of man, domestic misery, social discord, national embarrassment, and the darkness of despairing death are the fruits of this wide-spreading deadly tree. These are truisms. None know these ravages better than the unhappy victims of the curse. I am not this evening going to denounce the evils of intemperance without trying to analyze the motives that lead men into its bondage. Denunciation had its work to do, in the moral order, but to my mind denunciation is always more effective when tempered with sympathy. It is possible to denounce an evil in such a tone as to provoke a reaction in its favour, and to suggest the idea that even the chief of the spirits of darkness may not be quite as black as he is painted.

Let us try to realize the motives that led men to their ruin. Every sin proceeds from some tendency in human nature that is in itself good. The meaning of the word "sin" in the New Testament is "a false aim, a missing of the mark;" to have life, and have it more abundantly, is the aim of all men. Now, intemperance is simply a false way of trying to secure a fuller life. Strong drink, as we all know, does for the moment appear to give a fuller life. It stimulates the energies, enlarges the horizon, it lifts the clouds, elevates the depressed spirits, it stirs the sluggish stream of feeling, it quickens all the emotions, it makes thought vivid, gives a glow to the imagination, fills the despairing with fictitious hope, and penetrates the heavy leaden atmosphere of dull, commonplace, vulgar existence with fitful gleams of a short-lived and delirious glory. But we all know that this enlivening power of strong drink is a lie. It stimulates only to paralyze; it lifts up only to cast down into deeper and darker depths; it stimulates the feelings only to deaden them; it warms the imaginations and stirs the intellect only to debase and destroy both; it kindles hope only to leave behind the cinders and ashes of despair; it sheds upon existence some wild flashes of boastful, feverish glory only to light up the dark, downward passage that leads men headlong into the dungeon of outer darkness.

Drink is like a dealer in spurious coin, who takes from his dupe all that he had worth having, and, after fooling him with his fill of fancied wealth, leaves him to awake in moral nakedness and famine—an outcast, a bankrupt, and a slave. But the secret that helps strong drink to do its trade is that it promises to pay at once. Its coin is spurious, but it is ready cash. The joys it gives are base, but they are immediate. Therefore, when men are short of life they take to drink. All that impedes, cramps, lowers, weakens, darkens, disturbs life is an ally of intemperance. Too little work, too much work, the stagnation of solitude, the rivalries and jealousies of society, the hunger of failure, the satiety of success—all the worries, trials, collisions, the chills and the heats, the clouds and the sunlights of life—all tempt the shallow, unprincipled man to drink. When existence is dull and slow, when the body is depressed, when the nerves are relaxed and the brain weary, when the affections have lost their object, and, above all, when men have no aim in life that excites hope and unfolds a prospect, they will seek in sensual indulgence sedatives for their pains and stimulants for their languors. All men have this desire to be filled with life. Gautama Buddha, more than two thousand five hundred years ago, told his fellow-men that all human evils come from the Trishna—the thirst for external things that impels them into vain, restless efforts. That thirst is the spring of all that is evil in man, but it is also the spring of all that is good in him. The steam that hurls to ruin the train that has left the rails is the same force that would have taken it, rightly directed, to the terminus where the traveller would be. And so the desire for life, the thirst for fuller existence—what we call "go"—is in the well-regulated character the energy that bears him on to joy and rest; and in the "fast man," the blind, unguided impulsiveness that leaves him a broken wreck on the wayside of life.

We cannot expel this thirst from human nature, but we can teach men how to quench it at the springs that God has given. The world is full of poisoned wells, but it is also full of the springs of purest joy, from which men can draw rich draughts of living water for every stage in the journey of life. In the first stage of life, the toys, the games, the little treasures of childhood, gave a keen joy, to which we all look back and wish we could still enjoy as we then enjoyed. In adult years, work, business, the profession drawing out the energies of body, mind, and spirit, give to the well-regulated man a lifelong pleasure in his pursuit. The daily intercourse of social life, in all the common scenes of existence, gives a stream of gladness which, like common water, is never fully valued until it is lost. The home, love, union of hearts, the care and nurture of children,—in these a virtuous man finds a bright, cool, covered spring that keeps his life green, and refreshes the lips parched in the less sheltered stages of his journey.

The improvement of the physical and social conditions of life is one of the great means to which we must look for the cure of intemperance. Workshops and dwellings in which men can breathe the air and drink the water that God has given unpoisoned; the light of education, social recreations, deliverance from the excessive burdens that brutalize, must be afforded to all before we can hope to reclaim that moral wilderness in which the beast grows more and more, and the man grows less and less. Schools, colleges, museums, art-galleries, libraries, open parks, public gardens for the people,—all these are agencies that help to brighten and cheer the common life, and to check the craving for sensual excitement. A great American thinker and orator, while denouncing the degradation of the stage, the monkey-like indecencies of ballet-dancing, the dissipation of all-night balls, gave it as his opinion that a purified drama, a general cultivation of music, and the adoption of dancing, under healthy and virtuous conditions, as an everyday recreation in social and family life, satisfying the human craving for beauty by the gracefulness of form and the harmony of movement, would open up a new spring of natural joy and brightness for the people. I offer no opinion upon the subject, which has its difficulties. But this I will say—when England has become more virtuous, she is sure to become more merry. Gloomy, narrow views of God and life darken, depress, and stunt the nature of man. Puritanism is not always purity, and rank weeds grow in the shade as well as in the sunshine. But when education, culture, the beauties of art, the lights of science, material progress, and social recreation have all done their utmost, man will still desire a life that these cannot give. He may drink and drain them all, but he will thirst again. Let him work and win, let him love and build up a home, let him succeed ever so well in the world, yet after all the thirst will return. Work has its worries, health decays, the home has its bereavements, society has its jealousies and disappointments; wealth, position, fame, although dazzling in the distance, cease to enchant when you become accustomed to them—they "crumble into dust," and leave man "thirsting in a land of sand and thorns." All things become vulgar, commonplace, and unsatisfying in the order of the lower life. Man craves a satisfaction external things cannot give.

Where is the well that shall slake human thirst? Some dream that it is to be found in the miry bog of atheism. It is not there. Tell man that he has nothing to expect, deprive him of every prospect, and you at once destroy the charts, the compass, and the rudder of life, leaving him to drift like a log at the wild will of the winds and waves of lust and passion. Tell man that he is only a brute of the earth, earthy, only a superior animal, dreaming for a few brief years his fitful, feverish dream of life, and then passing away into nothingness, and he will cast away the restraints of human self-respect, and will rush into a frenzy of bestial excitement, singing as he goes that old song of the human brute, " Let us eat and drink; for to-morrow we die." Deprive man of eternal hope; seduce him to receive the lie of the Sadducee, that there is no hereafter; take down from his firmament the sun and the stars of faith;—what will follow? You will have left him nothing but the mists and vapours of this cold, dark earth. He will not be satisfied to sit down in the chill and gloom. He will seek warmth and light from below, if he is not to have it from above. The flames of sensual passion, set on fire of hell, will be his refuge when you have deprived him of all the lights of heaven. Where, then, is the well out of which man can draw fulness of life? The power of religion is the only source out of which an unfailing stream comes forth. It reveals to man his nobler self. It unfolds within him the mystery of a moral and spiritual being, which, by God's grace, he can develop so as to rise into the consciousness of an inward rank and an inward wealth, compared with which the highest position of the worldling is degradation, and his hoards of gold but dross and destitution. In the daily, hourly, momentary culture of that life he finds a well of water springing up to give unfailing satisfaction to his being. Thus the Church of Christ is the great Temperance Society. To those who take and keep her pledges she gives peace and joy in the present by revealing within them the true life, and kindles the fire of an inextinguishable hope by quickening within them the consciousness of immortality. They who have found the experience of true life here, and the prospect of deathless promotion hereafter, will not drown their present dignity or forfeit their future heritage by sinking into the slimy pit of sensuality. The rock of eternal truth follows them, and, when parched in the wilderness, in sickness and in health, in failure and in success, they drink freely of the waters of life.

I have spoken of social progress and religion as the two influences that are to destroy intemperance. They are but different aspects of one force. All true social progress is the outcome of that love which is the central principle of religion. These two influences are to be exerted by two classes of men—the social leaders and the ministers of religion; the princes on one hand, and the priests and prophets on the other, whom Jeremiah held responsible for the woes of Israel. Let me speak first of the princes of the people. The stream of fashion flows down from the men of high position to the masses on the level in every community. Therefore a vast responsibility rests upon the men of position and wealth. If selfish luxury, idolatry of money, trust in uncertain riches—that is, riches the use of which they do not clearly discern—prevail among the upper classes, the same spirit, in coarser forms, will appear among their humbler brethren. If social leaders think more of privilege than of duty; if they regard themselves as chosen vessels of porcelain to be set apart on the high shelf of social exclusiveness, and the masses of men as ware of commoner clay only fit to be filled "with the scornful reproof of the wealthy, and the despitefulness of the proud;" if the men of wealth fly away from the hives of industry in which they have made their fortunes, taking all the honey with them, doing nothing to sweeten life for the toiling myriads in the grimy quarters of the town deserted by fashion, but crowded with souls; if they spend their thousands upon pleasure, upon the moor in Scotland, the stable and kennel in England, and the yacht in the Channel, while they patronizingly send their paltry pittance to the Church, the school, and the philanthropic institution,—then they are not doing the work of social leadership, and will not long retain the position. A selfish, luxurious, unintellectual, money-worshipping upper class, putting their trust in ceiled houses, in horses and chariots, in purple and fine linen, and in the sumptuous faring every day, while they drop their contemptuous crumbs to the human brother who is lying at their door covered with sores, will by their malign influence create a drunken, dissolute, discontented, unhappy community; and some day those toiling myriads, grinding in the mill, and now about to be brought forth, enfranchised, to grasp the pillars of the constitution, will, like Samson, in their blind misery pull down the house to overwhelm the lords of the Philistines. I congratulate you in Liverpool that you have among you some leaders of heart and mind who know how to use nobly the wealth that God has given them. Your educational institutions, your new University College, your noble library, your art-gallery, your Episcopal throne, founded on the munificence of your sons (and ere long, I doubt not, your august and stately cathedral), prove that you have citizens who wish to broaden, deepen, elevate, and glorify human life in this great city. Depend upon it, the power of a nobler spirit, pervading the leading classes, and going down from them to the skirts of society, is one of the most potent influences for bringing moral and physical weal to the body of the nation.

The clergy have also their share in the work of moral emancipation. The Church's message must be delivered with power. Her truths are old and unchangeable, but the forms of thought and language in which they are taught must be new in every age. The scribe well instructed must bring out of his treasure things new and old—new in form, old in essential truth. If we would save the men of to-day, we must translate the truths of eternity into the language of to-day. The well-worn, hackneyed phrases, the traditions of the elders, the fossils of petrified platitudes, which were once alive but are now dead as Egyptian mummies, will not save souls from drunkenness or any other sin. The hard blows of loveless controversy, the hollow roll of the sounding brass, and the empty din of the tinkling cymbal, will not satisfy souls or slake their inward thirst. We must not pose as the monopolists of wisdom, forgetting that truth has many aspects, and that our little narrow view is not the only one in the universe. The dust and the heat of warring sections are enough to make a whole nation take to drink. If we would save society we must preach the living God, and not our narrow dead party watchwords. We must preach the Cross of Christ, which means infinite love, and not dark, cruel, blind bigotry.

What, then, is the special mission of this Church of England Temperance Society? It is to awaken the sleeping consciences of all who are directly or indirectly responsible for multiplying the temptations of their fellow-men. First, we must press upon the national conscience the question whether the millions of revenue now drawn from the Excise duties are not a source of rottenness and decay. Here and in India finance and righteousness, we are told, are opposed to each other. For my own part, I dread the opium traffic as the chief peril of our Indian empire. I dread it because I am afraid that God cannot go forth with the armies of a Power that equips its soldiers with weapons bought with the profits of human degradation. I dread it more even than the stealthy advance of that crafty, cruel empire which exports all its chivalry and benevolence for gain, so that it has neither justice nor mercy left at home for the sons and daughters of the foremost of the races —the race of Abraham and David and Isaiah, "and of whom as concerning the flesh Christ came, Who is over all, God blessed for ever." For the same reasons I regard the millions of money flowing from the vices and lusts of the people at home as a source of weakness and a chief cause for national alarm. It is the

Church's duty to teach that "righteousness exalteth a nation."

It is also our duty to teach the conscience of the individual. There are limits within which the manufacture and sale of alcoholic drinks are as legitimate as any other trade. But when the drink traffic is unduly pushed, and men seek to become rich by the manufacture of vice and misery, it is time to lift up our voices, and say that after the fortune is made comes death, and after death the judgment. For my own part, I do not envy the man who has risen high upon the ruin of myriads. Let such a man try to summon up before the eyes of his mind all the scenes that he has darkened on this earth—the homes that he has debased, the husbands and fathers that he has turned into brutes, the wives and mothers, once innocent young girls, whose cheek knew no darker colour than the blush of modesty, whom drink has made broken-hearted women, furrowing their faces with frequent tears, or, still worse, has transformed into swinish viragoes with bloated countenance and bloodshot eyes, with hearts full of lust and fury, and mouths full of filth and blasphemy. Let him call to mind the children whom his trade has blighted in their earliest bloom—the criminals, the paupers, the raving lunatics, who are the accompaniments of his fortune,—let all these pass in long procession before the sight of his soul, and I will venture to say, that if he has one ray of right reason and one spark of true human feeling unquenched within him, he will feel that no palatial residence, no liveried luxury of outward life, can compensate for the agony of that review, the thoughts of which crawl in the chamber of the soul like worms that will not die, and the self-reproach glares like a fire that will not soon be quenched. It is for the Church to teach men to look upon themselves as they will be looked upon in the searching light of the great white throne of judgment. Then every man's life-deeds, and all their remotest consequences; in long procession will pass before him, and he will be judged according to their nature.

One function of this society has been to raise the temperance cause out of the atmosphere of declamatory vulgarity into which feeble, well-meaning friends were taking it, and in which its enemies would have been glad to keep it. By making the temperance spirit at home in many of the palaces, this society has made it more powerful in the cottages of the land. English deference to fashion and gentility, in its excess, may be a weakness. But as long as fashion and gentility are an undoubted power, the society that enlists them under the banner of virtue does good and effective service. It has also done much to conciliate, by the moderation and tolerant reasonableness of its platform, those sober-minded and weak-kneed people who are alienated by the excesses of unadulterated teetotal enthusiasm. It seeks to promote counter-attractions of all kinds, and, by making the people more comfortable, to make them less vicious. It seeks to reduce the number of drinking-houses, those open pitfalls of temptation, that yawn with open doors at every step in our towns and villages to engulf unhappy men in the ever-ready ruin. It seeks to advance the physical, moral, and spiritual elevation of the publicans and their servants by securing for them the priceless blessing of the Divinely ordained day of rest. In Wales we have won that boon. We have as yet but partially enjoyed its advantages. But before the year is out, the Welsh publican will be saved from himself, and raised, as far as spiritual opportunities on one day in the week can raise him, to the moral level of his countrymen.

We are sometimes told by the argumentative parrots, caged in their prejudices and repeating to every comer the few phrases of reasoning they have learnt, that you cannot make men sober by Act of Parliament, and that it is very wrong to interfere with the liberty of the subject. Liberty of the subject! The subjects with whom we wish to deal are not at liberty. The enslaving poison has long since crept into all their veins and riveted his chains around heart and brain. They are not masters of themselves. Reason has lost her throne, and a foreign unclean spirit reigns in her place. The strait-waistcoat is made for madmen. The law is for the lawless. So compulsory restriction of the drink traffic is for the emancipation of those drunkards and drunkard-makers whose name is legion. In the deliverance of the demoniac in the synagogue at Capernaum our Master has given a typical revelation of the process of moral emancipation. Then, as now, the frenzied slave hugged his degradation and protested against deliverance. "Let us alone; . . . art Thou come to destroy us?" What were the stages in the work of liberation? First, "Jesus rebuked him." Rebuke, exposure, denunciation, breaking the self-confidence of evil, is a Divinely ordained agency for good. Secondly, the word of restraint was spoken with power—$\phi\iota\mu\dot{\omega}\theta\eta\tau\iota$, "hold thy peace;" literally, "be thou gagged," or, "muzzled." Lastly was given the word of final expulsion, "Come out of him." These are the three stages in the process by which the demon of intemperance is to be expelled out of our national life. The word of Christ, spoken in the Christian consciousness of the country, denounces the evil spirit in argument and remonstrance. Then it seeks to restrain its power by the word of legislative restriction—$\phi\iota\mu\dot{\omega}\theta\eta\tau\iota$. But its perfect work will not be done until the evil spirit has been driven out of heart and mind by the free spirit of reason and self-control. To-day we are rebuking this unclean spirit in the Name of our Master. Soon we hope to apply the forcible gag of legal restriction. Finally, we hope to see the nation emancipated by the One mightier than the evil—the Divine Spirit of life. "*Strike for the King!*"

This war, fought for the freedom of souls and the expulsion of a great foreign tyrant force out of our national life, is a struggle in which we all have an interest. In fighting under the banner of temperance, we are fighting—*pro aris et focis*—for hearths, homes, and altars. If the destroying power is to go on poisoning the atmosphere of life around us, slaying his thousands and tens of thousands, our nearest and dearest may some day be in danger. He may invade our homes. Our children may be his victims, if he is allowed to march on with forces unbroken and progress unchecked. Let us, then, take our places, shoulder to shoulder, in the ranks of the grand army of temperance. Let us hasten to the battle and fight for the King of souls, our "Fair Father, Christ." Let us war a knightly warfare that the beast may be driven from the land, and the true King reign over human life. Our cause has already passed through the winter of cold discouragement. The ice is broken and gone. Temperance is now in its month of May, full of hope and promise. Let us, then, rise, " Strike for the King and live!" Let us summon all men of knightly souls to the field to fight for our King.

> "Blow trumpet! He will lift us from the dust.
> Blow trumpet! Live the strength and die the lust.
> Clang battle-axe and clash brand! Let the King reign.
>
> "Blow! for our Sun is mighty in His May.
> Blow! for our Sun is mightier day by day!
> Clang battle-axe and clash brand! Let the King reign."

www.ingramcontent.com/pod-product-compliance
Lightning Source LLC
Chambersburg PA
CBHW030558300426
44111CB00009B/1027